JABALI

A KANSAS CITY LEGEND

7/9/19

To Doug Elgin –
With my
very best wishes –
David Thomas

JABALI

A Kansas City Legend

An Extraordinary Athlete's Place in History

David Thomas, PhD

Fifty-Six Street Press • Omaha/Kansas City

ISBN: 978-0-578-48235-4

Distributed by IngramSpark and Fifty-Six Street Press

Cover photo: D. Thomas

Cover design: D. Thomas/Frances Nefsky

Printed in the United States of America

"If he would have played in the NBA for any length of time he would have been among the 50 greatest players of all time. No question. You can take that to the bank."

—Fatty Taylor
LaSalle University
Washington Capitols (ABA)
1969–70

"What we must never do is willingly hand over our own bodies or the bodies of our friends. That was the wisdom: We knew we did not lay down the direction of the street, but despite that we could—and must—*fashion the way of our walk.*"

—Ta-Nehisi Coates
Between the World and Me

Table of Contents

Acknowledgments

There are a number of people without whom this book would not have been written. I want to begin by thanking Warren's wife, Mary Beasley. Mary was the love of Warren's life and was wonderfully supportive throughout this project. I particularly want to thank her for granting permission to include Warren's two essays in this book.

Warren's family of origin, the Armstrongs, have been wonderfully supportive as well. Beginning with Warren's mother, who lent me her scrapbook of Warren's playing days, to Sheree, Warren's sister, to Greg and Reggie, two of his brothers, all have been very helpful.

Warren's closest friend was Len Trower-Mfuasi. He has become my friend as well. I thank him for his support and for the many ways in which he contributed to this book.

Early in the development of my friendship with Warren, when we were talking only occasionally on the phone, Warren suggested that I meet his long-time friend Alex Ellison. Without the friendship I have with Alex and without his guidance and assistance, substantial portions of this book could not have been written.

Part II of this book is entitled "Naming and Necessity: Calling a Thing by Its Proper Name." It details the effort to name the Interscholastic Field House Court in Warren's honor. There are a number of people to thank. Before thanking them, however, I want to acknowledge that I am aware that there is a classic book in the field of philosophy entitled *Naming and Necessity.* I borrow the title here because it captures the feeling I had when I entered the field house after having been away for forty years: *The field house is not called by its proper name!* Thankfully, due to the efforts of many individuals, the field house court is now the Warren Armstrong Court. Special thanks to Alex Ellison, Kennie Denmon, and Murvelle McMurry, the core team that saw the initiative through from beginning to end. I also want to acknowledge and express thanks to Roger Pendleton, Willie "Sparkles" Stewart, the Rev. Nelson "Fuzzy" Thompson, Coach Jack Bush, Vicki Shelton, and Paul "Too Tall" Alexander for their participation in the video tribute to Warren. I would also like to thank Ed Corporal, Ray Wilson, Kenny Wesley, David Smith, and the Kansas City School Board (chaired at the time by Marilyn Simmons) for supporting, and in some cases, championing the cause of the initiative with the school board and others. Finally, special thanks go to Larry Rankin, Sports Information Director at Wichita State University, Kevin M. Gray, President of the Kansas City Sports Commission and Foundation, and former ABA players Al Smith, Eugene "Goo" Kennedy, Chuck Williams, and Ira Harge for their letters in support of the initiative.

Part IV, "The Odyssey of Black Men in America: A Kansas City Perspective," would not exist without the assistance and participation of a number of individuals. Principal among these was, of course, Warren. But many others played pivotal roles. My thanks to Bill Tuttle, Carl Boyd, Leon Dixon, and Alex Ellison for helping to envision the event and by their participation, making it the rich experience that it was. Thanks also to Bill Robinson, Rev. Willie Baker, Archie Williams, D'Morris Smith, Maurice Copeland, Chester Owens, Michael Walker, Eb Effrant, Joe Lewis Mattox, Mike Thiessen, Norman Pendleton, Elvis "Sonny" Gibson, Will McCarther, Leonard Jones, Sr., Ron McMillan, Ronald Harland, Sr., Marod Kareem, Monte Owens, and Mr. Tolbert for their willingness to participate and for their insightful contributions.

Part V, "Kickin' It," was solely Warren's idea. *I want to kick it with old friends,* he said. And for two days that is what he did, as I tagged along. My thanks to the following individuals: Will McCarther, Coach Jack Bush, Leonard Jones, Sr., Ralph Brown, Alex Ellison, Michael Walker, Jerome Holmes, Rudolph "Snake" Riley, Willie Moe, Bill Robinson, and (as Warren referred to him) the great Ernie Moore. In addition, there were a number of individuals with whom it was not possible to meet at that time. I have contacted a few of these individuals, and in some cases have met with them. Their memories and reflections are included in Part VI, "The Sumner Connection." In this regard, I want to thank Monte Owens, Dr. Herman Watson, J.B. Hill, John Battles, and the Rev. Nelson "Fuzzy" Thompson.

There are several other individuals who have not been mentioned above but who contributed to this book (or to the events described within it). My thanks to Reggie Marshall for granting permission to include his essay on Warren; Steve Marantz for recognizing the importance of Warren's story; Cincinnatus "Cincy" Powell, Eugene "Goo" Kennedy, Les Hunter, Bob Netolicky, Mike Storen, Rick Barry, Artis Gilmore, Fatty Taylor, and Coach Al Bianchi for making time to discuss Warren's ABA career; Melvin Reed, Kenny Lee, Joan Minor, Mansa Moussa Abdul Allahmin, Bob Lutz, Lanny Van Eman, Mohamed Sharif, and Ron Mendell for sharing their Wichita State recollections of Warren (and Ron Mendell again for granting permission to include his article on Warren); Leon Harden and Al Smith for their ongoing support (Al was mentioned above, but not sufficiently); Stan Slaughter for permission to include his

Kansas City Star piece written following Warren's death; Mike Thiessen for sharing his write-up of the tribute to Warren implicit in Pem Day's 1964 yearbook; Bryan Holmgren for his assistance with WSU's athletic archives; and Arthur Hundhausen for providing pictures from Warren's ABA career (and, in general, for RemembertheABA.com). I also want to thank Michael Herzmark and Don Mayberger for giving their time and energy to video record both the court-naming celebration and the "Odyssey," and I want to thank Janet Tilden of Executive Rewrites and Frances Nefsky of FN Design for their editing and design services.

Last, I want to express my sincere gratitude to my best friend and life partner, Paula Ziegman, who provided the ongoing dialogue and thoughtful suggestions that improved many areas of this book.

David Thomas
June 2019

Preface

This book began in 1962. It was then that I first saw Warren Armstrong Jabali play basketball. Observing him was a revelation. If I could have played like anyone, I would have played like him. As my friend, Reggie Marshall, put it: *Warren was the perfect blend of power and grace.*

What I did not know in 1962 is that Warren and I would become friends; that he would open his life to me (his circle of friends included); that we would talk at length about his life and career; and that I would be among those who spoke at his funeral. It was an honor to know him. This book is an attempt to keep alive his memory in the Kansas City area and beyond.

—

I once read that great athletic gifts rarely occur without the potential for a comparable degree of psychic integration. Warren was enormously gifted athletically, but he possessed other gifts as well. He was extremely intelligent. Alex Hannum called him the smartest player he had ever coached. And Warren may have been among the "toughest" players to ever play the game. Both Hannum and another coach, Al Bianchi, agree on that point. But "psychic integration" implies something more.

The gifts that allow you to excel at basketball show up early in life and then fade away. Psychic integration, on the other hand, is a lifetime pursuit. It shows up later in life, if at all, and requires that you come to terms with yourself (unruly though you may be) and with your circumstances (whatever they are). It is the hero's journey à la Joseph Campbell and it results in a person who, among other things, is at home with himself. Psychic integration implies personal integration, wholeness and balance. It is an important achievement, perhaps even a moral achievement.

This book is about Warren's prowess as a basketball player, but it would not have been written were it about that alone. It is, as well, about Warren Jabali himself: the person he became, what he cared about, his effect on others. And, to a degree, it is about race in America, though only to a degree. I do not consider myself qualified to speak on that topic. I do believe, however, that insight into that topic is gained through an understanding of Warren's life.

—

Many people are involved in telling the story told in this book. Warren tells his own story in his essays and in his comments and exchanges with others. Numerous individuals offer their reflections on Warren and on the time during which he (and they) lived. The events described in the book, including the court-naming initiative, the odyssey of black men in America, and so on, form the backbone of the book. These events were collaborative efforts, meaning that many voices and varying views are expressed. I'm grateful to all contributors. The book does not tell the complete story of Warren's life, but a more complete story is told as a result of the many voices represented in these pages.

—

Finally, I found it necessary and I hope helpful to tell some of my own story in this book. To a degree, this book is about the relationship that developed between Warren and me. I do not know how many white friends Warren had, but I am grateful to have been one of them.

Perhaps some measure of insight into our relationship can be gained from the fact that when I sat down to write this book, two movies came to mind.

The first was *'Round Midnight,* an American-French film from 1986. This film, set in Paris, is about two men and the brief time they spent together. One is a Frenchman, an "everyman" who loves American jazz. The other is a great American jazz saxophonist near the end of his career. The two men meet, become friends, and affect one another's lives.

The other film was *Chocolat,* a 1988 film set in 1940s French Colonial Africa. It is a film about the fading of the colonial period in West Africa. The young African man at the center of the film is named Protee. In Roger Ebert's review of the film, he writes that Protee "embodies such dignity and intelligence that he confers status upon himself in a society that will allow him none."

Whenever I reflect on my relationship with Warren Jabali and on why I so appreciated him as a person, I think of these two films.

Part I

Athletic Greatness in America:
A Tribute to a Time, a Game, and a
Most Remarkable Player

"It is a rare privilege to see true greatness in its infancy and on behalf of all those who have been so privileged, I want to publicly thank (Warren) Armstrong and to urge him for the sake of his race, his city, his now lifelong fans, and most importantly for himself, to devote real dedication to the development of his gift."

—Clifton O. Lash II
Kansas City Star, April 3, 1964

Lash served as honorary coach of Central High School in the Missouri State Tournament of 1963. Reprinted in an article by Mike DeArmond, *Kansas City Star,* March 13, 1974

Warren Armstrong Jabali grew up in Kansas City, Kansas, the oldest of eleven children. By his sophomore year in high school (1961–62) his family had moved to Kansas City, Missouri, where he attended Central High School. Within a year, his name was known throughout the city. In the words of his close friend, the Reverend Nelson "Fuzzy" Thompson: "It was at Central that Warren became one of the greatest high school athletes of all time."

I first saw Warren play in the fall of 1962, the year Clifton O. Lash II saw "true greatness in its infancy."

The Interscholastic League Field House had just opened. A remarkable facility for the time, the field house remains to this day the site of inner-city high school basketball in Kansas City, Missouri.

—

I attended Southeast High School and, as a sophomore, had made the varsity squad. We were co-champs that year of the Interscholastic League (1962). Jim Laffoon and Ken Christopher were All-Star guards who could compete with any in the league, and Russell Washington, our center, was a mountain of a man. At 6'6" and 250 pounds, he would go on to a stellar career at tackle for the San Diego Chargers. We were a good team with good players in a league with many good players. But when I saw Warren play, I became aware of a standard and a gift that no one in the league could match.

Warren graduated from Central High School in 1964. He accepted a scholarship to Wichita State University where, over the course of his collegiate career, he established himself among Wichita State's all-time leaders in points, rebounds, and assists. He then entered the American Basketball Association, the upstart league that would eventually merge with the NBA.

—

I consider myself fortunate to have attended an integrated inner-city high school. My friends were black as well as white. I'm sure it was basketball that made this possible. I was accepted by black players and I spent time playing in the inner city. Sometimes I was the only white player on the court, and sometimes my girlfriend and I were the only white couple at parties.

—

Every summer, my good friend Bill Boykin, who is African American, and I would enter a three-man team in one of the City's summer leagues. It is a treasured memory. Bill was a beautiful player. The first time I saw him play, I marveled. The older fellow standing next to me remarked that Bill had "it." I had not heard that expression before, but watching Bill play gave me an inkling of what it meant.

—

After graduating from college I signed up for VISTA (Volunteers In Service To America). In my application to VISTA I asked for an urban placement on the East Coast. Instead, I was sent to Pueblo, Colorado.

Pueblo was thirty percent Mexican-American at the time. My VISTA assignment was to serve as the coordinator of an all-Chicano organization, the Mexican-American Service Agency (MASA). At MASA, I met Wilford Martinez, the best community organizer I have ever known; Dan Luna, Sr., the first Chicano elected official in the history of Pueblo and, in the mid-1950s, the Big Seven Men's Tennis Champion; and Tony Romero, a fireman. Smart, educated by the streets, Tony was as tough as they come. Although I was the coordinator of MASA, it would be more accurate to say that I served as an assistant to these remarkable men. I learned from them, followed their directions, and found myself immersed in what could only be described as a graduate internship in community development.

—

I had been in Pueblo less than two months when the *Pueblo Chieftain* announced that an ABA exhibition game between the Washington Capitals and the Denver Rockets would be played in a local high school gymnasium. That gym was within walking distance from where I lived.

Though I had lost touch with Warren's career while he was in college, I had never stopped thinking of him or of how privileged I was to have seen him play. By the time I got to Pueblo, however, I was again following his career.

I knew, for example, that Warren had been drafted by the Oakland Oaks, that the Oaks had won the ABA championship during his rookie year, and that Warren had been named Rookie of the Year in the league and Most Valuable Player in the championship series. I also knew that the Oaks had folded or perhaps had been moved, and were now the Washington Capitals.

While sitting in those high school bleachers, I struck up a conversation with the fellow sitting next to me. He had no idea who Warren was. When introduced, Warren trotted to center court in his distinctive style. "So that's the guy?" "Yep," I replied, "that's the guy."

—

This was 1970, Spencer Haywood's rookie season as a pro. At 6'8", Haywood was a dominating player who later that year would win Rookie of the Year honors. Heads turned, however, when Warren, at 6'2", nearly blocked Haywood's shot. And later, on a breakaway layup, heads turned again when Warren made a beautiful left-handed layup high off the backboard despite a hard foul delivered by Lonnie Wright. (Wright was an exceptional athlete who also played professional football for the Denver Broncos.)

I was still new to Pueblo at that time. The friendships and working relationships alluded to above had yet to form. I missed Kansas City. But as I walked home from the exhibition game, my homesickness was gone. I've always felt a boost from the fact that Warren came from Kansas City.

—

At the end of '71 I moved to Denver. Warren was then playing for the Floridians. I went to the Denver Rockets games whenever the two teams played. It was at one of those games that Warren was introduced as Warren Jabali. I remember thinking that the announcer was obviously an idiot if he couldn't even get Warren's name right.

Later, I learned that Warren had changed his last name. *Jabali,* in Swahili, means rock—a large, conspicuous rock. Still later, I learned that by changing his last name rather than his entire name, as Kareem Abdul Jabbar would later do, Warren was making a cultural and not a religious statement.

—

Warren was traded to the Indiana Pacers in 1970, the year they won their first ABA title. I watched the championship game on television and saw plays that remain vivid in my memory, including a behind-the-back-pass on a fast break for a teammate's open layup. Not just any behind-the-back pass, however. Warren was moving across the key (free throw lane), his back to the teammate who would make the layup. Warren bounced the ball higher than I had ever seen with such a pass, but his timing was perfect. The ball came down just as his teammate arrived.

I was thrilled two years later when Warren was traded to the Rockets. I lived near Colfax Street, one of the main drags leading into downtown Denver, and for two years I caught the bus to McNichols Arena to watch Warren and the Rockets play.

During that time I saw the Rockets play an exhibition game against the Milwaukee Bucks with Lew Alcindor (Kareem Abdul Jabbar) and Oscar Robertson. The event was standing room only.

Alcindor, in his athletic prime, was an amazing force. His height, length, and jumping ability surpassed anything the Rockets could match or anything I had ever seen. And Robertson went anywhere on the court he wanted to go, a comment that Julius Erving (Dr. J) would later make about Warren (2015 radio interview).

Despite his success in the league, Warren was released by the Rockets following his second year with them, and was not picked up until mid-season of the following year by the San Diego Conquistadors. That year proved to be his final year in the league. Twelve years after he graduated from Central High School, seven years after graduating from Wichita State, his playing days were over.

CATALYST / GALLERY INSTALLATION

After two and half years in Denver, I entered graduate school. This took me back to the Kansas City area and in particular, to Lawrence, Kansas. Following the receipt of my degree, I took a job in Omaha, Nebraska.

Within a year of my arrival in Omaha, I published a small book entitled *the catalyst*. It was largely a book of quotations pulled from books I had read in recent years, but it also contained profiles of individuals I admired. All of the profiles were of friends, except for my profile of Warren. I did not know Warren at the time but I felt I owed him something. The way he played as well as the way he carried himself since the first time I saw him play had impressed me deeply ("His manner embodied dignity and intelligence," to use Ebert's words).

At the end of each profile, I provided a quote that in my view fit the person (at least that slice of the person detailed in my brief profile). I found Warren's address and sent him his profile. He returned it having crossed out the quote I had included and replaced it with (all caps): THE SECRET TO LIFE IS TO HAVE NO FEAR.

I had a hundred copies of *the catalyst* printed, and over the course of weeks and months I distributed them to friends and acquaintances.

—

That was that, until a few years later when it was suggested to me that I should turn *the catalyst* into a gallery installation. That project came together rather quickly. I knew the Dean of the Fine Arts Department at the University of Nebraska at Omaha, and I knew the director of UNO's Art Gallery. Both individuals gave me the go-ahead.

Each profile from *the catalyst* became an exhibit. I gathered pictures from the individuals in question, mounted them on foam core boards, and had the text of the profiles laser printed in large, readable type—twenty-one exhibits in all. For five weeks in the late summer of '86, the installation was displayed at the UNO Art Gallery.

In preparation for the gallery show, I phoned Warren with the hope of getting some pictures of his ABA days. I told him that I had played at Southeast High School and had graduated one year after he graduated from Central. I mentioned some plays I saw him make as a Denver Rocket, spectacular plays: an incredible dunk, a drive to the basket, a block in which he seemed to come out of nowhere. I mentioned his dominance of a particular player or of a particular game. He said that, for whatever reason, he didn't remember very many specific plays, a few, perhaps, but that he did not recall the plays or games to which I was referring. I said: *Even if what I am recalling didn't happen, it's the truth.* He laughed and said he would send me some pictures.

I also contacted Mrs. Armstrong, Warren's mother. She was very welcoming. I spent well over an hour in her living room discussing

Warren's life, explaining the gallery installation project, and asking for any pictures she would feel comfortable loaning me. Among the things she told me was that she used to visit on the phone with Lucius Allen's mother discussing "these men in suits who walk up the sidewalk to talk about our son's futures."

Toward the end of my visit, Mrs. Armstrong left the room and returned with a large box containing her scrapbook and several 8×10 photographs of Warren's playing days. It was a treasure. I don't recall her asking me to return it. She simply put it in my hands. I made copies of everything and got it back to her or to Warren as soon as the gallery installation was over. Today, thanks to Mary Beasley, Warren's wife, many of these items are in the archives of the Black History Museum in Kansas City, Missouri.

—

When the gallery installation was in place, I called Ron Boone. Ron lived in Omaha at the time. He was a rookie in the ABA the same year that Warren joined the league, and he, too, was an All-Star, with stints in both the ABA and NBA. Because of his durability, Ron was known as the iron man of professional basketball.

I told Ron about the installation and, in particular, about the Jabali exhibit, and asked if he would be willing to come by and discuss his experience playing against Warren. I audiotaped the interview with Ron and sent it to Warren. Looking at the pictures of Warren's ABA playing days, Ron remarked: "I would have to put Jabali among the top ten guards I ever played against (or with) in either league."

—

Some years later, on a flight to Denver, I came across a brief news item in the sports section of the newspaper. The American Basketball Association had prepared a list of its thirty all-time greatest players. None were named in the article, and I remember thinking that if Warren's name was not on the list, then the list was a farce. I thought his name might have been omitted given the controversy surrounding his career.

Warren was on the list alongside some of basketball's greatest players: Julius Erving, George McGinnis, Artis Gilmore, George Gervin, Rick Barry, Marvin Barnes, Zelmo Beaty, Ron Boone, David Thompson, Moses Malone, Roger Brown, Billy Cunningham, Louie Dampier, Mel

Daniels, Connie Hawkins, Spencer Haywood, Dan Issel, Maurice Lucas, Doug Moe, Bob Netolicky, James Silas, and Willie Wise.

In the process of researching the list, I discovered the "Remember the ABA" website created by Arthur Hundhausen (remembertheaba.com). This website is a remarkable accomplishment. It offers a comprehensive history of ABA teams and players, including performance statistics by team, player, and year. It also invites fans to submit their recollections of players, games, and the extraordinary league that was the ABA.

—

The essay that follows is an expanded version of the profile I wrote for *the catalyst* and expanded further for the gallery installation. It was posted on the "Remember the ABA" website. Following the essay is a letter Warren wrote to the *Kansas City Star* newspaper along with reactions from readers to both my profile and Warren's letter. I should add that both the essay and Warren's letter appear in *Thanks to You: Memories of Warren Edward Armstrong Jabali*, the book that Warren's wife, Mary Beasley, wrote following Warren's death.

For Warren Jabali: A Tribute to a Great Player

I played against Warren Jabali (formerly Warren Armstrong) in high school. He was the greatest high school basketball player any of us had ever seen. This was Kansas City, Missouri, in 1963 and '64, and some of the best high school basketball in the country was being played there. Lucius Allen was across the river in Kansas City, Kansas. Jo Jo White came up from St. Louis for the state tournament. Other remarkable players went on to have solid college careers, even pro careers, but the best—and everyone knew it—was Warren Jabali.

Here are excerpts from the *Kansas City Star*'s coverage of the 1963 Missouri State Basketball Tournament:

> Armstrong, opening with a flash of brilliance, turned friend and foe alike goggle-eyed as he rebounded, blocked shots and funneled in 26 points on his own.

> Then Armstrong scored on a tip-in, stole the ball and stuffed in a 2-hand dunk shot that almost pulled the basket off the backboard.

> Armstrong now has pumped in 87 points in his last three games, and it was his 17 points in the first half that got the Eagles off and flying.

> With apologies to the ones I didn't see, the best all-around players I saw were Warren Armstrong of Kansas City Central in Class L, ...only a junior, Armstrong faces a great future if he consistently exercises all his tremendous talents.

It's important to remember that Jabali was only 6'2". Important also to remember that he could fly, really fly, a fact not known by those who came late to the ABA. I once saw him graze his forehead along the rim. It occurred in that same state tournament following a very slick steal and in the middle of a slam-dunk that brought everyone to their feet. It was an electrifying time. Legendary. In Kansas City, to this day, among men of a certain age—black and white—there is a bond because of it.

Jabali went on to set rebounding and assist records at Wichita State and was, at the time, their fourth all-time scorer. During his senior year, Wichita State was considered to have the most difficult schedule of any college team in the country. Still, it was Wichita State. Had Jabali gone to Kansas or UCLA, he would not have been—or be today—so little known.

Following his senior year, Jabali signed with the Oakland Oaks in the ABA for what was even then a modest amount. The first thing he did with his signing bonus, his mother told me, was to free his father from one of the two jobs he had held for years.

During his first season in the ABA, Jabali won Rookie of the Year honors. Rick Barry, his teammate, described him as follows:

> He's unbelievable. As a guard, he's in a class by
> himself. I've never seen a player his size with so much
> strength. As great as Oscar Robertson is, well, he
> couldn't come close to matching Armstrong in jumping
> and rebounding. Nobody can. He can out-jump and out-
> score the Warriors' Al Attles. He's stronger than I am,
> stronger than Robertson. He's so powerful that even at
> 6'2", he can come in and rebound with 6'7" forwards.
> And you should see him drive into the basket. No doubt
> he's one of the best guards I've ever played with or
> against. Just wait till he gets more experience—nobody
> will be able to stop him.

It was an injury to his back and another to his knee that stopped Jabali, or at least slowed and lowered his highwire act. Even so, he exerted a commanding presence. During his fifth year in the league he was voted "Most Valuable Player" in the All-Star Game held in Salt Lake City, a game that included Julius Erving, George McGinnis, and Artis Gilmore. That same year he was First Team All-ABA Guard and later, Alex Hannum called him "the smartest player I ever coached."

I lived in Denver when Jabali played for the Rockets and went to nearly every game. It was a great pleasure for me to watch Jabali do what I felt he had always done: control and direct the game. He knew where to stand and what to do. The game flowed from him and through him as he interacted creatively with it (much as Larry Bird later would do), and for that reason alone he remained for me the most fascinating player by far to watch.

Once, in a very close game against my high school team, Jabali made a beautiful 30-foot jump shot, giving his team a lead they held to the end. When he made the shot I heard my coach refer to Jabali as a freak. Jabali was anything but a freak. He was the star of the show. When the Denver Rockets had "Halter-Top Night"—*yes, that's right, Halter-*

Top Night!—the two winners ("Best Halter-Top Outfit" and "Best-Looking Girl in a Halter Top") were asked to name their favorite Rocket. Both said, "Warren Jabali."

And yet, despite all of this, there was apparently another side. I do not know the details surrounding the Jim Jarvis incident nor have I ever seen the tape. I did see Jabali's temper on two occasions, once in high school in response to a series of intentional fouls, and once with the Rockets in response to a hard elbow to the lower back. On both occasions, he stopped short of doing anything that would have removed him from the game.

He was tough, no question about that, and strong, and proud; and he had a remarkable presence. In high school we sometimes remarked on how everyone in the league—or so it seemed—walked like Warren Armstrong. But even there—despite ourselves—we were on to something, *walking:* one of the four "dignities of man." And Jabali did have dignity. He may have lost it on occasion. The Jim Jarvis incident may be something he deeply regrets. I do not know. But for him to be remembered as a thug seems way off to me. I never saw a single incident in his two years as a Rocket that would have justified such a label. Indeed, I saw quite the opposite.

Nevertheless, after his most effective year as a pro—his last season with the Rockets—he was released and not a single team picked him up. He was an unemployed All-Star guard. Of course, he also had been the players' representative and had led the black players in a boycott of a recent All-Star Game. He did have a reputation as a militant and he no doubt did champion views that were unpopular with some number of ABA players and observers. It's also the case that the Denver franchise was in trouble and even Larry Brown was quoted in one newspaper report as saying that Jabali had been made the scapegoat. I do not know the whole story. I do believe, however, that whatever the story, the truth itself was served by another of Brown's comments (from the same report): "Warren has...never been hesitant about expressing himself," said Brown. "But he's a person of high ideals, and an unselfish, dedicated basketball player."

Nine months after his release from Denver, Jabali was picked up by the San Diego Conquistadors, with whom he played out the final season of the ABA. Shortly after his arrival, Alex Groza, the San Diego coach, said, "One guy has made a difference in this team. Warren is a very smart basketball player. He never gets excited, keeps his cool and helps out the other guys." Said backcourt partner Bo Lamar: "This is a different team. Warren has made a big difference... every team has a leader. But before we got Jabali, I don't think this team had one... I think he inspires the rest of us and gives us confidence."

From very early on, Jabali played with intelligence and for keeps, often inspiring others with spectacular play. For many of us in the Kansas City area, he represented the first time we had seen such a gift. It was genius, foreshadowing what we later would see in a host of players who now are the new standard. Had it not been for injuries to his back and knee, had it not been for the politics of the time, had it not been for the specific requirements of his own development as a person—whatever they were—many more people would have had the pleasure of watching a truly gifted and remarkable player. As it was, many did see him play and many of these, myself included, were enriched by it.

I believe that if you are given a talent, then you must use it. There may be exceptions to this rule, but on the whole I believe this is so even though you may never know the good that comes from it. A great talent, like the one Jabali was given, may excite and entertain, but it also does more. Invariably, it leads to reflection and self-review. "What is *my* gift?" asks the person who is conscious of what he is seeing, "and how can I bring it out?" We were all better off in Kansas City for having witnessed the great early—and then later—years of Jabali's career; his brilliance made better players of us all, though the "games" we chose to play have varied considerably. I do not know whether Jabali ever realized the extent to which his great play, the expression of his remarkable gift, also raised and expanded our standards and aspirations. Many of us, I am sure, were never consciously aware of it. But I deeply believe it is so.

In 1975, the *Kansas City Star* carried an article reviewing Jabali's career. Jabali had been invited to speak in a newly built community center to the kids playing in the league that carried his name. The article quoted Jabali's remarks:

> "Some of you probably saw the movie Super Fly," Jabali
> began, then fixed the attention of a few giggling boys in
> the corner of the gym. "I know you guys are gonna be
> hustlers and pimps. Black people have always been
> hustlers and pimps. But get out of there as soon as you
> can. You'll get hurt, you'll get killed. Take advantage of
> this building. I know everybody says, 'When I was
> comin' up,' but when I was comin' up we didn't have
> this. Use it; get some books in here and read. It's going
> to be hard. It's hard now. You can't go down to Ford or

General Motors and work, they're laying off now. It's
hard on your parents and it's gonna be hard on you."

The writer of this article, who may never have seen Jabali play,
closed the article by saying that there was more to Warren Jabali than "a
ball and an iron ring." He felt "the man had a gift."

It is now twenty-five years since that article was written, and
twenty-five years, or nearly so, since the ABA disbanded. I do not know
what Jabali is doing today. The last I heard he was teaching in an
elementary school in Miami. If he is teaching, I wonder if the children
with whom he now works, or his fellow teachers, or his own children for
that matter, have any idea of the regard with which he is held in certain
circles. In Kansas City, there is an entire cohort that speaks of him with
enormous respect. The mere mention of his name conjures a time that
shines far more brightly because of his presence in it.

This brief tribute is a way of remembering, a way of saying
thanks. Whatever Jabali is doing today, I hope it is something that allows
his spirit to soar. He was something special. For many of us growing up
in the Kansas City area, his play gave us a vision without which, I
believe, we would have settled for less in ourselves. I thank him for that.
He was a player's player, and by his play would-be players like myself
were inspired out of our limits.

Postscript I-A: Greatest High School Athlete

In March of '98, the *Kansas City Star* ran an article examining an issue of considerable importance (judging by the reactions it generated) to area basketball fans: namely, *who was the greatest player ever to come out of the Kansas City area?* The major contenders were Jabali (Warren Armstrong), Lucius Allen, Anthony Peeler, and a young player graduating from high school that year (and hence the reason for the article), JaRon Rush.

Here are a few quotes from the article:

Many of the people who saw all four wouldn't necessarily admit it, but they sounded as if they'd give a slight edge to Armstrong, a dominant force at Central in the early 1960s.

"I played against Elvin Hayes and Don Chaney in college, but Warren was better than them," said Mike Thiessen, a first-team All-Metro selection…in 1965. "He did things in high school that Michael Jordan does now."

Thiessen continued: "Warren and Lucius Allen played the best competition. JaRon hasn't been challenged like that. I haven't seen JaRon play this year, but I don't think he's in the same league as (Armstrong). Warren had a court sense that was scary. He had a soft touch and could jump over the backboard. As good as JaRon is, he isn't in the same league as far as being a complete basketball player. He doesn't play defense like Armstrong and Allen did."

"He (Armstrong) was a man among boys," (Charles) Weems (a former official) said. "You knew what he was going to do, but you couldn't stop him. I always felt like he was two steps ahead of everybody."

"He (Peeler) had eyes in the back of his head," said Central coach Jack Bush, "…Peeler could pass… He could thread a needle from 50 yards. But Warren Armstrong had wings. He'd jump up and dunk off a missed rebound from the second block."

"Armstrong was like Julius Erving," said former
Rockhurst High coach Graig Cummings. "There wasn't
a term yet for some of his dunks. But JaRon might be the
most complete player of them all. He handles the ball,
shoots and, when he wants, plays outstanding defense.
But Warren just could do things beyond anybody else.
He might have been the best."

In late May, two months after the article appeared, Warren sent
me a copy of a letter that he had sent several weeks earlier to the *Kansas
City Star*. I found the letter powerful and moving and certainly deserving
of a far wider audience than it had received to date. For whatever reason,
the *Kansas City Star* never printed it.

Greatest High School Athlete: A Reprise
Warren Jabali

In 1964, the year in which I graduated from Central High School, an article ran in the *Kansas City Star* that I have kept until this day. The article was written by a man whom I had never met, nor had any subsequent contact with. The article was stirring but I was for the most part oblivious to its deeper meaning. I knew intrinsically that it was important but I could not accurately interpret its message at the time. I eventually came to realize the depth of admiration, respect and hope that encompassed his words—and the onus.

Life, as it unceasingly does, has come full circle. I now have the opportunity, privilege and duty to speak about a young man with great potential who has been given the designation of "greatest high school basketball player" in the Kansas City area. The author of the 1964 article who assumed me that position, pointed out that with the passage of time we see an improvement in the quality of players. I therefore have no doubt that JaRon Rush has superior basketball skills than Lucius Allen and myself. However, skills alone do not result in ultimate success. If the concession is made that I was more skilled than Lucius, how then should that concession be impacted by the facts that Lucius enrolled and graduated from a better university, made the college All America team and played in the dominant league. Meanwhile, I with the "superior skills" never matched his accomplishments.

I would submit that great skill, if it is to be actualized, must be combined with maturity of intellect, social development and morality. Therein lies the problem. The average 17-year-old person has not yet developed sufficient measures of intelligence, morality and social skills and is therefore compelled to make decisions impulsively. The 17-year-old super athlete, while usually ordinary in intellectual and spiritual maturity, is confronted with extraordinary options which must be acted upon. These options, once decided upon, translate into extraordinary responsibilities. As a consequence of bearing such responsibilities, young people frequently find themselves "bent out of shape."

In any of the world's scriptures we can find the advice to seek wisdom. This is especially important for young people who have such responsibilities. Since it is foolishness that abounds in the hearts of the young, it is prudent for them to seek counsel. The decision as to who is to provide counsel is crucial. Parents are generally best qualified to operate in this role. It is no accident that Kobe Bryant is having a successful career so far. He clearly accepts the guidance of his parents.

His parents, however, are completely qualified for the role since his father is a former longtime professional basketball player himself and his mother a college-trained professional There are occasions when parents may not have the exposure themselves to assist in the decision-making process. My parents could not aid me in making my decisions because I was involved in issues that were beyond their areas of expertise. Parents must be careful not to over extend themselves. Players themselves must feel that their choice of college and any subsequent contracts are in their best interest or they will be unable to sustain the proper attitude with which to attain their full potential.

The key to greatness, in my opinion, is the ability to freely express one's gift. One's talent must flow as a direct and uninhibited stream that seeks and finds its own level. Things that inhibit the free flow of talent are not being coachable, not maintaining optimum conditioning, a lack of leadership skills and selfishness. The item selfishness may seem out of place; however, a review of all truly great players will reveal that they always made everyone around them better. Kareem Abdul Jabbar did not win an NBA championship until Oscar Robertson (the man who averaged triple doubles for a whole year) joined him in Milwaukee, and he did not win another until Magic Johnson joined with him in Los Angeles. These players brought out the best in each other. Greatness requires commitment, dedication and teamwork.

The writer of the 1964 article that challenged me to strive for athletic greatness also "urged" me to be an example for my race. I have no way to know how he would view my accomplishments on these two fronts. I sincerely hope that he would be pleased. My own opinion on the subject is that I became a good player and not a great player. Factors for not being better were injuries to my knee and back. Another factor was that I never considered sport as a higher priority than the struggle of African American people to gain standing in the human community.

That struggle remains a focus of my energies today. It is paradoxical that in spite of the spectacular achievements of African Americans, the race as a whole is actually worse off than it was 34 years ago when I left Kansas City. For example, in 1964, a significant percentage of the African American population lived below the poverty line, were unemployed, under-educated and segregated. In 1998, there are still significant percentages of impoverished, unemployed, under-educated and segregated African Americans. 1998 is worse than 1964 because in 1964 we had more stable neighborhoods, we had a movement and we had hope. We had an agreed-upon enemy, which we identified as racism, and we had clear purpose in mind. In 1998 we have an expanding underclass, drug- and crime-infested neighborhoods, mounting numbers of out-of-wedlock children being born to teenagers, an appalling lack of interest in education in light of the monumental struggles and disillusionment in the ranks of upwardly mobile African Americans. In 1964, the music, always an accurate reflection of culture, promoted unity and struggle. Curtis Mayfield sang "Keep On Pushing" and "We're a Winner." James Brown sang "I'm Black and I'm Proud." In 1998, Ice Cube represents by singing, "Today Was a Good Day, I Didn't Even Have to Use My AK."

The "Talented Tenth" (the most well-to-do African Americans) that W.E.B. DuBois theorized would lead and uplift the race has in fact detached and abandoned the race. It may be that Gil Scott Heron, who also sang in the '60s, was prophetic with his lyrics: "It's winter in America... All of the healers have been killed, sent away and betrayed... And ain't nobody fighting, cause nobody knows what to save."

As a result of all this, I am not at all certain whether the "race" baton, which was passed to me, can be now passed to JaRon. But someone else sang a long time ago, and they sang that "The Darkest Hour Is Just Before Dawn," and therefore I choose to be optimistic. I choose to believe that African Americans will eventually develop as a people and address our own problems. I choose to believe that young men like JaRon, who most likely will soon join a growing fraternity of African American multi-millionaires, will figure out some way to serve and profit from development in their own communities. I have hope that Florida A&M University (FAMU), a predominantly Black institution which has a business school which ranks in the top 2 percent in the country (this is a ranking of all schools, not just Black schools), will recognize its potential. FAMU currently trains its business students for "employment" in the corporate world as opposed to training in the creation of corporations. Perhaps one day the athletes will sit down with the business majors to create the ways and means for African American participation in the economic mainstream. Such is the nature of my faith.

At this moment, none of this should be the focus for JaRon. He should be preparing to embark upon a great adventure. The most important thing for him is to enjoy and appreciate the blessings that will result from his gift. Involvement in social affairs may result from this appreciation. JaRon himself will determine how he is to pay his dues to the creator for giving him the potential to have such a wonderful life.

Warren Jabali (a.k.a. Warren Armstrong)
Miami, Florida
1998

Postscript I-B: Responses from Readers

The Jabali tribute and Jabali's response to the *Kansas City Star* article were posted on the "Remember the ABA" website. Here is a sampling of responses I received from visitors to the website:

> You may find this silly, but I'm currently playing on an online fantasy basketball league, which is, actually, a tribute to the ABA. It's named the Old School Basketball League, and I'm the recently appointed Denver Rockets' "general manager."
>
> I'm Portuguese, born and raised in this country, so I had never before heard much about the ABA or its players. It also has to do with the fact that I'm only 24 and an ocean away from the North American culture. Even so, I developed a love of the basketball game, which was spawned in my youth by watching a couple of Magic Johnson's games in Portuguese on late night television in the mid '80s. From then on, I was hooked on basketball and the NBA.
>
> I had heard about the ABA before, but only through a few televised clips from NBA's shows. I knew that Dr. J played in that league, that it had the three-colored ball, that the 3 pointer emerged there... and not much more than that.
>
> Luck has these kinda things. I bumped into a computerized simulation of basketball called "Fast Break Basketball," immediately ordered it and, due to a post in the computer game's forum, I became acquainted with the commissioner of that Old School Basketball League I mentioned previously. He then invited me to his league, and I took the Rockets' former GM place.
>
> Being a journalist in formation, I had the curiosity of researching a little bit about the Denver Rockets. John, the commish, sent me a link to the "Remember the ABA" site. That's where I had the chance to read your tribute to Warren Jabali... and that's where I had the chance to read his letter to the *Kansas City Star*.
>
> First of all, this message has the point of thanking you for the enlightening and vivid tribute. It brought me an unusual sense of pride for playing in a fantasy league, and that is indeed a strange sensation.
>
> Secondly, I am also proud that I had the opportunity to read about such a special man. The way he writes is a true

inspiration, and his words are everything but deeply void of meaning. His is the voice of a people I used to disregard due to all the cultural displays I unfortunately have to cope with nowadays (of a people I kept thinking had lost their own pride and self-respect), bad music being one such sample. Now I see how unfair I was, how ethnocentric of me.

If you ever have the chance to speak to Jabali, please tell him he has a Portuguese fan.

Thank you very much,
R. S.

I just read your piece on Warren Jabali on the "Remember the ABA" website (though I know it has been posted there for a long time.) As a young Air Force pilot stationed in Denver during Warren's Denver Rockets days, I was thrilled to watch him perform. I was always struck by his fierce competitive nature, his determination and his apparent immunity to pressure.

It was a great time to enjoy the game and to enjoy watching Ralph Simpson, the slow, white guys Byron Beck and Dave Robisch (with whose limited talents I could most identify), the other Rockets and the visiting stars like Dr. J, Artis, and Darnell Hillman, and even that pain-in-the-tail Keller from Indiana. But, Jabali was our favorite. I was moved by his letter to the *Kansas City Star* and happy to know that whatever he is doing now, Warren Jabali is a successful man. As a product of an inner city, row home origin myself, I appreciate his words of advice and wisdom. Thanks for bringing them to my attention.

Regards,
J.M.

I was around nine or ten years old when I became a *huge* ABA fan. I can remember Warren ("The Rock") Jabali and how he would shoot over and out-rebound players 5–6 inches taller than him. I can only remember him as a Miami Floridian though.
An old ABAer -- M.N.

I came across the "Remember the ABA" web page tonight and saw your article on Warren Jabali. I grew up in Boulder, Colorado and was a Denver Rockets fan. I also should mention that I was a black kid growing up in Boulder, which was usually a great experience, but sometimes a kind of lonely experience.

I listened to the Rockets on KOA radio and my favorite Rocket was Warren Jabali. I liked the way he played. But more than that. he stood for something. When he won the ABA all-star game MVP, I remember how excited his wife was when he got the trophy. If I recall correctly, the prize was a trip. He announced that they were going to Africa, which I thought was very cool.

Thank you for a nice article on someone who I always knew had a lot of substance.

Sincerely,
C.N.

From the "Remember the ABA" discussion group:
(I have) the program from the first pro basketball game I ever attended—Kentucky at Pacers 11-9-70. My ticket stub is attached. I sat in the South Parquet Box 112, Row E, Seat 1 of the Indiana State Fairgrounds Coliseum. Pacers, 130–Colonels, 112. Perfect condition. Warren Armstrong made the most incredible defensive play in that game I have ever seen.

M.

When I requested details, M sent the following reply:
I assume you want to know about the play. I can't be sure about the details—I only saw it once, a long time ago. What I do remember is that the Pacers got the ball and moved toward their goal, which was to my right. All the Pacers except Armstrong, who just stood on the far side of the court at about the centerline. I remember being unhappy about his lack of effort to join the

offense. Kentucky got the ball and it was passed to one of the Colonels who were streaking down court on the near side of the floor. This player, I don't know who it was, had passed the free throw line and left the floor to dunk the ball before Armstrong moved. Amazingly, Armstrong got to the basket at the same time as the Kentucky player and knocked the ball away. I just couldn't believe he had traveled so far from a standing start and beaten a player who was so far ahead and had so much momentum.

M.

———————————

Hi — I was so glad to see your info on Warren... I lived in Berkeley California back in the day and I saw Warren play in the ABA... He was awesome.... there has never been a man his size like him and really no one quite like him period... we used to watch the guyz work out...he would pin Rick Barry's shit to the backboard...he would extend his arm you could not do anything with him....nobody could. There would be famous guyz working out during the summer...Slick Watts...Robert Parrish...Jamal Wilkes... Nate Thurmond and many I have forgotten. They liked to hang out in the bay area in the summer... This guy is really so great there should be a statement about him in the Hall of Fame.... I am surprised that since he played in the S.F. Bay Area that more has not been said about him but I suppose it is just the times—no one cared about the ABA... I use to have free tickets all the time...interesting, a lot guyz had flash and moves out of this world but they could not play defense... Warren was a defensive phenom...he did things nobody had ever seen and have not seen since...

Thankx for the memory.
Peace
E.

———————————

I am a 56-year-old American who has lived in Germany for nearly 30 years but still a devoted US sports fan.

I can't say how much I enjoyed and appreciated your article about Warren Jabali (Armstrong).

Although a Bostonian and therefore, a Celtics fan, I well recall the old ABA and recall hearing about Warren Armstrong's feats and potential. The sense seemed to be that the potential was largely unrealized despite the world of talent that he had. Your article has done much to put this in perspective and I found it fascinating. In particular I am most impressed by what a fine man Mr. Jabali has become. A very gratifying story.

He had the misfortune along with a number of other great black basketball players to reach their peak at a time before American society was ready to accept them as men rather than just performers and woe betide any black player who at that time stepped "out of line."

The other great tragic case was Connie Hawkins, arguably one of the greatest talents ever to play the game. As good as he was playing for the Phoenix Suns at the twilight of his career, the pity is that so few fans got the chance to see and appreciate his talents when they were at their zenith, back when he played for Pittsburgh, first in the ABL and then the ABA.

The one question about Warren that I have, which your article does not comment on, is what made him sign on with the Oaks and the ABA rather than the NBA after his graduation from Wichita State. Had he gone to the NBA who knows what his future might have been?

Once again thanks for the service you have done to the memory of a fine, largely ignored basketball player and human being. I hope that I am one of the many on whom your piece has made quite an impression.

Sincerely,
N.F.

I saw the videotape of the Jim Jarvis incident (1968 I think). It was pretty vicious as I recall. Jarvis had several teeth knocked out. However, I do remember Jabali as being a very good player. It's a shame guys like him and James Silas didn't get to play in the NBA in their prime or injury free. George Gervin was my favorite player. I really enjoyed the ABA and was glad a lot of the players got to showcase their talents later in the NBA.

Regards,
R.B.

Excellent article. I'm R. "Da Guru" H. I submitted the ABA's All Time Team article but yours had much more depth because you actually saw and played against Warren. When I was in high school, I had the privilege of experiencing the same thing when I saw a then unknown player single-handedly lift his less talented teammates to victory over the eventual state champions. That player has had to sacrifice his talents for the good of his current teammates but, in high school, Ron Harper was something to see. Anyone that was at that game against Keith Byars and Roth High School still talks about it.

Well, enough of my nostalgia, the article was great.
Take Care
R. "Da Guru" H.

Just read your extremely fine article on the ABA website. …All I have to add is that despite his reputation for meanness, at the ABA reunion Saturday in Indianapolis I found him among the most cordial of the dozen or so ex-players from whom I obtained autographs. And when I went through the line a 2nd time to get another autograph for a friend, he graciously asked the friend's name so that he could personalize the signature. In retrospect, of course, I regret not asking what he's doing now…

I enjoyed reading your tribute to Warren Jabali. My first pro basketball game I watched Dr. J play at the Hampton (Va.) Coliseum in his last season with the Squires. (My next game came at the Richmond Coliseum when the Squires, at this point led by Tricky Burden and Fatty Taylor, were in the midst of what I think was about a nine-win season).

I'm a reporter at the Roanoke (Va.) Times and a free-lance writer on the side. I have been writing articles of late about sports and race. Did Jabali have to deal with racial tension—taunts, etc.—during the era when he was in high school; Missouri being a border state at a time when schools in the South still hadn't integrated? I'd appreciate any info you might have on this, or on other athletes who may have had to fight prejudice at some point in their careers.
Thanks.

———————————

Wow!!!! That is a great article! Over the years when talking to people about the interscholastic league Warren's name always comes up and yes he was also my favorite all-time player. Besides Warren, I have one story you might get a kick from. In '61, we played against Bill Bradley (Crystal City) in the state tournament in St Louis. When they introduced the players, they read off their stats…Bill Bradley, 47 pt average, over 3000 pts in career, 109 pts in one game. Well, after that we looked at each other and knew we were in trouble!! Of course, we lost the game 74–49. I got to play the last 3 minutes (Russ and I got to make the trip). I scored 3 pts, fouled Bradley (he hit both shots). In the locker room we felt we had done a good job at stopping him ...he scored 39 and set out much of the fourth quarter—"ha". Some of our players were getting his autograph after the game.

Old school --
J.L.

Postscript I-C: Comparing Backcourts

In July of 1973, *Rocky's Report,* the official publication of the Denver Rockets Basketball Club, published the following article comparing the Denver Rockets backcourt with the backcourts in the rest of professional basketball. (Vol. 3, No. 1)

Best Backcourt in the Game?
You betcha!!! According to the stats

The Denver Rockets have the best backcourt group in professional basketball. A far-fetched statement? Not when you consider contribution to the team with respect to points scored, assists and rebounds.

A statistical survey conducted recently involved comparing the combined output of the top three guards from each team in the above three categories.

The results showed that the Rockets' trio of Warren Jabali, Ralph Simpson and Al Smith ranked first in total output. Following were the Los Angeles Lakers (Jerry West, Gail Goodrich and Keith Erickson), the Atlanta Hawks (Pete Maravich, Herm Gilliam and Steve Bracey); the San Diego Q's (Chuck Williams, Larry Miller and Ollie Taylor); Phoenix Suns (Charlie Scott, Dick Van Arsdale and Clem Haskins); Houston Rockets (Jim Walker, Mike Newlin and Calvin Murphy) Utah Stars (James Jones, Ron Boone and Glen Combs); Milwaukee Bucks (Oscar Robertson, Lucius Allen and Jon McGlocklin): Kansas City–Omaha (Nate Archibald, Nate William and Mat Guokas); and tenth were the Memphis Tams (George Thompson, Johnny Neumann and George Lehmann).

The Rocket trio placed third in scoring with a combined 51.4 point average; were second in assists with a total of 1,238 behind KC–Omaha; and were fourth in total rebounds with 1,009. The Lakers topped the scoring with a 55.7 average followed by Phoenix at 54.2 points. Chicago led in rebounds with a total of 1,061 followed by Boston, 1045, and the New York Knicks, 1044.

Archibald of Kansas City topped all scorers among guards as he led the NBA in scoring with a 34.0 averages. Denver's Simpson placed fifth in the ABA with a 23.1 average, but was top-ranked among backcourt men. Simpson's average placed him sixth among the top scoring guards in basketball with Archibald, Pete Maravich, Charlie Scott, Geoff Petrie and Gail Goodrich rated higher.

Jabali's 17.0 average ranked him sixth in the ABA while Smith finished with an 11.1 mark.

Archibald also led both leagues in assists with 910 for an 11.4 average. Bill Melchionni of New York's Nets topped the ABA with a 7.5 average on 453 assists. San Diego's Chuck Williams actually had the most total assists but played more games. Jabali finished with 539 for a 6.6 average and Smith totaled 477 and averaged 5.7.

In rebounding, Walt Frazier of the Knicks led all backcourt men with 570 and was followed by Fred Carter of Philadelphia with Jerry Sloan of Chicago third; Don Chaney of Boston, fourth; Norm Van Lier of Chicago, fifth; Ron Boone of Utah, sixth; and Jabali, seventh. The Rocket guard totaled 425, one shy of ABA guard leader Boone. Simpson had 371 to rank eleventh.

Rocket coach Alex Hannum feels that his backcourt corps should do even better this coming season. With Jabali appearing to be on a complete road to recovery after undergoing a back operation in the off-season; Simpson maturing rapidly after three pro seasons; and Smith gaining more playing time last season as a second-year man; the Rocket backcourt could continue to dominate the game. Claude Terry, the fourth man in Denver's playmaking group, had an outstanding rookie season, according to Hannum.

Seeing limited play until late February, the former Stanford sharpshooter averaged close to 10 minutes a game for the season and finished with a 4.8 scoring output. Terry was the only rookie in the ABA to hit 10 three-pointers last season, gaining that many in 24 attempts.

Jabali and Simpson also ranked high in the league in steals with Warren placing fourth with 175 and Simpson, eighth, with 127. Both were named to the ABA All-Star and All-League teams last season. Jabali also added the All-Star's Most Valuable Player award to his list of honors.

Postscript I-D: Jabali's ABA Career—An Appreciation

Reginald Marshall is President of MarsJazz, a booking agency for jazz musicians. Thanks to the "Remember the ABA" website, I discovered that Reggie felt as I did about Jabali's great talent. His comments, which appear on the "Remember the ABA" website, are reprinted here.

I should add that Reggie and I became friends as a result of our mutual appreciation of Warren. Reggie's knowledge and love of jazz is considerable, but so, too, his knowledge and love of basketball. Though we live in different parts of the country, we have managed to get together on occasion. For example, Reggie was able to come to Kansas City to visit the "Warren Armstrong Court," a location/experience he had placed on his "bucket list."

The 1969–70 season, when I was 20 years old, was the year I got hooked on pro basketball. I lived in Washington, where the Caps played, and took a special bus from downtown DC to Baltimore to watch the Bullets. That year there were 25 pro teams in the two leagues, and I saw them all, in person. While I was a big Bullets fan, on the whole I preferred the more wide-open ABA style of play. My favorite players were Gus Johnson (later a member of the Pacers' '73 championship team) and Earl Monroe of the Bullets, and Warren Armstrong of the Caps.

I have an indelible memory of literally the first minute I ever saw Armstrong play. The Denver Rockets (with rookie Spencer Haywood) controlled the opening tap in one of the first games of the season, and their point guard Lonnie Wright (who was also a defensive back for the Denver Broncos) was guarded by Warren. Wright attempted what he thought would be an uncontested pass into the high post, but cat-quick Warren got a hand on it and the ball shot a good twenty feet straight up in the air. Lonnie was directly under it but Warren got behind him, jumped, reached back and snatched the ball with one hand, then glided down court and threw down one of the wickedest slam dunks I'd ever seen (left-handed, of course—even though he was right-handed he always dunked left-handed). Twenty seconds later, with the teams back down at the other end, I looked back and the backboard was still quivering. I was awestruck.

Warren went on to have a great game and for the next couple of months every game I saw him play was more impressive than the previous one. When healthy he truly was one of the great all-around players of all time—a great shooter, great passer, great rebounder (that year he was a unanimous selection to the all-star team as a 6'2" forward!), great defender—with a style that was a perfect blend of grace and power. Alas, he hurt his knee and a week after he scored a career high 46 points he went under the knife and his season was over. Of course the Caps moved the next season, and I moved to a non-ABA city, and I thought I might never see him play again, although I followed his career closely in the newspapers, through several teams and a name change.

In 1973 he was 1st-team all-ABA for the Denver Rockets, as well as MVP of the All-Star game. The next season he was also a Western Conference starter in the All-Star game, and then something happened which to my knowledge has never happened before or since in the history of professional sports: the day after the All-Star game Jabali was placed on waivers, and no team picked him up. I was aware of his reputation as a black militant and a troublemaker but this was incredible. I remember reading that he'd done something during All-Star weekend that embarrassed and enraged the (white) owners, and they'd obviously blacklisted him. Shortly after that I read that he'd moved to Africa, and it seemed his career was over.

Then, in the fall of 1974, I moved to Los Angeles. Around that time, the San Diego Conquistadors were desperate for a point guard. They tracked Warren down in Tanzania and signed him. I drove down and saw him play several times that season. In the five years since I'd seen him in DC he'd put on weight, and knee and back problems had robbed him of his leaping ability, but he had his moments and was still a great floor-general. I went down for a Nets game in February, looking forward to seeing Dr. J for the first time since his rookie year with the Squires. Going in, the "Q's" had a seven-game losing streak and the Nets had an eight-game winning streak. The only memorable thing about this game's regulation play was that Dr. J scored 45 on a dazzling assortment of moves and shots. In spite of this about half the crowd filed out with several minutes to play and the Nets comfortably ahead. Then the Conquistadors came to life. Travis Grant and Dwight "Bo" Lamar started filling it up from outside, and Jabali started taking it to the hole. I'd long since resigned myself to never again seeing Warren dunk like he used to, but to my amazement, with about 30 seconds left and the Q's down five he drove the lane, took the ball in his left hand, lifted off like a great bird of prey, and threw down a thunderous dunk, getting fouled in the process. That cut the lead to two and a Grant jumper from the corner at the buzzer sent the game into OT.

Dr. J scored 12 more in the 1st OT period, giving him 57, but the Q's hung in there and another buzzer-beater sent it into OT #2. With two minutes left in that period, Doc had 61 and climbing. At this point Warren was in the groove and they decided to switch him onto Erving. The 2nd overtime period ended with another last-second shot to tie, as did the 3rd. In the 4th OT the Q's finally pulled away. The final score was 176–166, at that time the highest-scoring game in the history of pro basketball. But Dr. J finished with "only" (a career high) 63. In the last 12 minutes of the game, with Jabali guarding him, he managed only a meaningless dunk shot in the final seconds with the game out of reach. Warren scored 19 of his 23 points at the end of regulation and in overtime.

That was Warren's last season. My final memory of him, from the last game I saw him play, is him walking off the court, his tiny son next to him holding his hand. He didn't look like the angry young man anymore. He looked more mature, more at peace with himself and the world. After his career ended I had no idea what happened to him, and I was glad to see that he is alive and was able to come to the ABA Reunion in Indianapolis. I wish I could have been there. Certainly he deserves the honor of being named one of the top 30 players in the league. I'm still an avid NBA fan, but I'm not as impressionable as I was then. Yeah, I know Michael is the greatest player who ever lived, but Hakeem is the only player to crack my all-time favorite five in the last quarter-century. The rest of the team consists of the idols of my youth—Honeycomb, The Pearl, Doc, and The Rock— Warren Jabali.

Reginald Marshall
Charlottesville, Virginia
1998

Postscript I-E: Interview with Coach Al Bianchi

Al Bianchi is a former professional basketball player and coach. The Oakland Oaks were moved to Washington, DC, in 1969 and became the Washington Caps. Bianchi was hired as their coach. This was Warren's second year in the league.

Here are excerpts from an interview I conducted with Al Bianchi in April of 2013:

> For the 1969–70 season, the Oakland Oaks were moved to Washington and became the Washington Caps. That was the year I coached Warren. Everyone knew who he was. The year before he was Rookie of the Year and also had won the Most Valuable Player award in the championship series.
>
> In those days, you never knew what you would get with and from Warren. Everyone knew—players and coaches alike—that he would dance to his own music. You could go in the locker room and he would be cordial or you could be met with a hard stare. You never knew. George Gervin said to me not long ago that he "always wondered when things would explode between us." It was uncomfortable at times. But that was off the court.
>
> On the court, you always knew what you would get. He was one of the toughest, most competitive players I ever coached. Here's an example of how tough he was: Toward the end of his year in Washington, Warren tore up his knee. When the doctor examined his knee, he (the doctor) said he had never seen anything like it. It's a testament to how tough Warren was that he came back and played five more years in the league. Very few players would have been able to do that.
>
> It was then, after his knee injury that his game changed. There was less explosiveness in it. He relied more on his basketball savvy. He was a smart player.
>
> He was well up there among the thirty greatest players in ABA history. He would have made his mark in the NBA had it not been for his knee. One thing though: he had little patience with players who didn't play well. That's not surprising. All great players are that way. That's why they seldom make good coaches. They think the game should come as easily to others as it comes to them.

The last time I saw Warren was at one of the ABA/NBA player reunions. I told him, "You are one of the toughest SOB's I ever coached." I think he appreciated that. He laughed and all our issues, if there were any, were behind us.

I remember in one game—I don't remember the team or the player involved, but there was a breakaway, a steal and a breakaway for an easy layup. Warren caught up with the player, left his feet and blocked the layup with two hands. There was no foul but the player collapsed like he had hit a ceiling. I haven't seen a play like that since.

Postscript I-F: The End of a Career

At the time of the interview excerpted below, Warren taught physical education in an elementary school in Dade County, Florida. For several years he also directed the Miami Midnight Basketball Program.

In August 1999 he was invited to return to Kansas City as a special guest of the Annual Midnight Urban Symposium & Tournament, a midnight basketball tournament sponsored by the Kansas City Midnight Basketball Program.

While Warren was in Kansas City, he was asked to reflect upon his career.

"I went to New York and sat down in Madison Square Garden to talk with Red Holzman," said Jabali, whose NBA rights were owned by the New York Knicks after the demise of the American Basketball Association. "His first question to me was: 'Do you have a problem with authority?'

"That was the only question. I was looked on as someone who had a problem with authority.

"During the civil rights struggle everybody was focused, everybody believed in the same thing," said Jabali, a former Central High School star. "It wasn't anything like today. Everybody believed in civil rights. You have not had that level of cohesiveness in the black community since then.

"The athletes were emboldened and strengthened. Without the civil rights movement, it would be very unlikely they would have stepped out that far. The civil rights struggle gave us sustenance.

"At the time, I really thought that there would be no price to pay," Jabali said. "I really thought we would accomplish what our struggle intended, which was black self-determination, black political power, black economic power. I really believed we would accomplish those things. So I was not afraid.

"I still believe it was the correct thing to do. My answer to Red Holzman was 'No, I don't have a problem with authority. I have a problem with authority that is unjust.' I don't remember him saying anything after that."

Kansas City Star
August 1999

Part II

Naming and Necessity:
Calling a Thing by Its Proper Name

In Kansas City today, Troost Street is considered the dividing line between black and white. West of Troost is white; east of Troost is black. Further east of Troost is Paseo, then Prospect, then Swope Parkway. I grew up at 56th & Swope Parkway. It was, at the time, an all-white, working-class neighborhood.

The house I grew up in has long since been torn down and so, too, the elementary school I attended (Mark Twain Elementary). The neighborhood, the school, the church at the corner, the Boy Scout troop to which I belonged; all were white experiences. It wasn't until I went to Southeast High School that I encountered black students.

———

Southeast High School is located at the corner of Swope Parkway and Meyer Boulevard. At the time (1950s and '60s), it served working-class neighborhoods primarily. Southwest High School, on the other hand, located west of Troost served middle- and upper-middle-class neighborhoods.

I entered Southeast in the fall of 1961 when the school was just beginning to integrate. By my count, there were only 19 African American students (freshmen to senior) in the school. By the time I graduated in 1965, there were 170 African American students. Still, that number represented only 11.3 percent of the student body.

In the middle of my freshman year, my family moved into the Southwest school district. By the time of our move, however, I was already involved with basketball at Southeast. I was on the freshman team and was increasingly involved with my friends and with the athlete culture at the school.

When my mother went to the School Board to request my transfer back to Southeast, the person with whom she registered the request was shocked: *"No one transfers back. The transfer requests we receive all go the other direction. But if this is what you want…"*

———

In a certain sense, I never made the move with my parents. I continued to live my everyday life in the neighborhoods and with the experiences provided by the Southeast community.

Had I gone to Southwest, I would have been introduced to an upper-middle-class milieu and perhaps met students with aspirations different from my own (I don't remember having any aspirations at the time). I also would have been introduced, at least to some degree, to the

Jewish community with its strong commitment to education and to the intellectual life in general. I know I would have been enriched by these factors, but I never would have experienced what I experienced by remaining at Southeast. (This is not to say that high aspirations and intellectual pursuits were not on the minds of others at Southeast and elsewhere—black and white—only that in my case, such concerns were not front and center.)

Because of my involvement in basketball, my black classmates at Southeast and their counterparts at other schools opened themselves to me, as I did to them. We became friends, spending time together both at school and after school. I traveled with them to courts in the inner city where I learned a way of playing—a way of being together, perhaps—that I don't believe I would have had the opportunity to learn (or enjoy) at a later point in my life.

—

As for basketball, I was not a particularly good player. I did, however, show a modest degree of promise and so (as indicated earlier) I was placed on the varsity, the only sophomore on the squad. Our team had some very good players and early in the season we were ranked number one in the City. This was the year the Interscholastic League Field House opened (1962) and it was the year I first saw Warren play.

—

In the early fall of my junior year, Steve Schwartz, Claude Hannahs, Maurice Herdon, and I went out after a game. Steve and Maurice played football. Claude, the only senior among the four of us, and I played basketball. Steve was my locker mate. He was quarterback of the football team and president of "the round table" (essentially, president of the student body). Claude was philosophical and also an artist, and Maurice was smart, quick to laugh, and very popular.

We decided to go to the King Louie Bowl, a bowling alley and pool hall located at 87th and Troost. It was a high school hangout. We parked behind the building and walked to a long ramp that led to the main door. A large crowd had gathered at the door, and when we were just about to walk up the ramp, someone yelled out, "Look at those two white guys with those n____s." We turned around and walked back to the car. We did not run, and we were not pursued.

As we drove away, I remember Claude shaking his head, not surprised but looking as though he had been through similar situations before. Maurice was angry and asked if any of us knew who had yelled at us.

—

On Monday, Leon Harden came up to Steve and me and asked if we had heard about Maurice. He told us that Maurice had gone up to the fellow who he thought had yelled at us and asked, "Are you the guy who called me a n____?" The fellow responded, "I'm the guy!"

Maurice hit him hard then and there. The fight went to the floor, and finally, after the two were separated, they were taken to the principal's office. Both were suspended for ten days.

When Maurice returned from his suspension, he told us that the principal had asked: "Is this over?" The fellow in question had older brothers, well-known tough guys, but he responded, "Me and my brothers have talked it over, and as far as we're concerned, it's over." Maurice said, "Fine," and that was the end of it.

—

After graduation, I lost touch with Claude after a year or so. I saw Maurice once or twice after we graduated. He went off to a small college to play football and later, sadly, died before turning thirty. Steve graduated from college and went off to Vietnam where he served as a helicopter pilot. After he returned, we spent time together but were unable to remain in touch. Steve lived out of town and I knew from the time we did spend together that his mobility was beginning to be severely limited due to the effects of the war.

—

Other than the event at the bowling alley, I don't remember racial problems at Southeast. The fights I remember were between whites, and the bullying that took place was among whites. As I remember it, the ongoing "integration" was peaceful.

This lack of conflict may have been due, at least partially, to the presence of Russell Washington and his older brother Preston. Preston was among the first to integrate Southeast. Both were towering figures, very well liked and key to the success of our teams. They were leaders from the moment they arrived, and perhaps they set the tone. Or maybe the peacefulness that I believe characterized the integration of Southeast was due, simply, to how gradually it occurred. Or maybe my impression is entirely incorrect. It's possible that I was unaware of the discomfort and alienation that many black students felt.

—

Looking back some fifty years, it's hard to describe the experience of high school—not what happened but the way it felt. High school is such an intensely self-centered and self-conscious experience. I don't know that it can be otherwise. For some students, by dint of luck, high school offers them the time of their lives. For others, the "fit" between themselves and their school is not at all right. It's not fair. You're just beginning to know who you are, just beginning to be sensitive to the concerns of others. The struggle with competing loyalties and values, so crucial to forming who you will become as an adult is, for most of us, just getting underway. The following story is perhaps illustrative in that regard.

—

During my junior year I met the girl who would become my high school girlfriend. We started dating and I was crazy about her. In my eyes she was beautiful, and I felt lucky to be with her.

Every year, the seniors on the varsity basketball team would nominate girls for basketball queen, and the nominees would then be voted upon by the student body. When our time came, I nominated my girlfriend.

During eighth grade and my freshman year at Southeast, I had idolized a player four years ahead of me named Larry Norris. He was the star of the team and his girlfriend had been elected basketball queen. I wanted that for my girlfriend and me.

However, two of my close friends on the team, John Walton and Lonnie Simmons, nominated a black girl for queen. Both John and Lonnie are black. When it was time for the players to narrow the field of candidates, I did not vote for their candidate. I remember John looking at me quizzically but not saying anything. I also remember thinking that I needed the black vote for my girlfriend to win. I was quite deliberate in my vote.

—

Later that week, a black girl with whom I was friends came up to me and said, "Dave, we heard that you let us down behind closed doors." As it turns out, a black girl had never been nominated for basketball queen at Southeast. I knew immediately what she was referring to, and I suddenly sensed the way in which I had fallen short.

I told her the truth—namely, that I didn't think my girlfriend would win without the black vote and that I thought I could carry the black vote. I shudder at the arrogance of it now, but that is essentially what I believed and what I said.

Later that week, the same girl came up to me and said, "I told everyone what you said, Dave, and everybody understood why you did what you did. It's all okay."

—

As it turns out, my girlfriend did win. I remember how happy she was. After she had been told she had won but also told not to tell anyone, she came up to me in the hallway and whispered the news. She was crying and laughing and very happy.

Nevertheless, I believe we should have seen whether she could have won with a black candidate on the ballot. I don't think I ever told my girlfriend what I had done, and though the topic never came up (I saw John and Lonnie often over the years), I have often thought about how my selfishness and unconsciousness blocked the way. (I was conscious, certainly, of what I wanted and voted accordingly, but I was not sufficiently conscious of the good that could have come had I voted differently.)

—

As for the academic side of things, I never applied myself in high school. I passed my courses easily enough and looked forward to spending time with my friends (my girlfriend, in particular) and to playing basketball.

As mentioned, I played varsity basketball for three years, the first three years that the Interscholastic League Field House was open. It all came together at the field house. We had our friendships, our academic requirements, our everyday dramas at our respective schools, but it was at the field house each weekend that the community gathered to watch us play. There we saw some of the best high school basketball in the country and the star of the show, unquestionably, was Warren.

—

What follows is the story of the effort to name the field house court in Warren's honor. I should add that by the time of the court-naming initiative (2008), Warren and I had become friends. Our correspondence began following the publication of *the catalyst* and the creation of the gallery installation and picked up considerably with the posting of my tribute to him on the "Remember the ABA" website. We met in person when Warren was invited to participate on the panel commemorating Kansas City's Midnight Basketball Program (Warren had directed Miami's Midnight Basketball Program), and thereafter, we would get together when Warren came to Kansas City. I sat with Warren and his wife, Mary, for example, when he was inducted into the Kansas City Sports Commission Hall of Champions (2004). It was that evening, following his induction, that Warren and I began to talk seriously about some kind of project—a book, perhaps—that we might do together.

In 2006, I was invited to Warren's sixtieth birthday celebration in Miami. It was a remarkable event. In attendance were friends from different periods of Warren's life and from around the country. Friday evening was the party with dinner and tributes, followed the next day by a bus tour of Miami and the surrounding area. (I videotaped the tributes and later returned to Warren an edited DVD.)

The tributes were heartfelt, hilarious, and thoughtful. Al Smith, one of Warren's teammates with the Denver Rockets, offered the following comment: *A lot of people don't know this, but I played with Warren and I played against him. I also played against him in college. He was baaad! He was one of the top five players (in the ABA): I'm talking Artis Gilmore, Moses Malone, Dr. J., George "the Iceman" Gervin, and Warren Jabali. And if you never saw him play, you missed it! I really hate it that a lot of people didn't see him play, a lot of the reporters, a lot of the sports writers... the old guys know.*

When I spoke to the group, I mentioned that I felt Kansas City owed Warren a great deal... that it is an important moment in a person's life when he or she sees "true greatness", as Clifton O. Lash II had put it. That, I suggested, is what Warren gave an entire cohort of young men and women in the Kansas City area the opportunity to see. I added, however, that I doubted that Kansas City would ever find a way to acknowledge Warren's contribution. I did not know that within a year many of us would be involved in the effort to name the Interscholastic Field House Court in his honor.

Naming and Necessity:
Calling a Thing by Its Proper Name

On Wednesday, September 19, 2007, I drove to Kansas City to interview seven individuals who had played with or against Warren Jabali in high school, and in one instance, an individual who had coached against him.

I wanted to gather material for a second DVD to accompany the one created at Warren's sixtieth birthday celebration. Thanks to Alex Ellison, Warren's long-time friend, I was able to interview the following individuals: Coach Jack Bush, Rev. Nelson "Fuzzy" Thompson, Paul "Too Tall" Alexander, Kennie Denmon, Roger Pendleton, Murvell McMurry, and Willie Stewart.

The final two interviews—with Willie Stewart and Murvell McMurry—were conducted at the Interscholastic League Field House, the scene of Interscholastic League play from the 1960s to the present. Even to this day the Field House is an exceptional arena for high school basketball, seating well over three thousand. Fittingly, the first game played there (November 1963) was between Central High School (Warren's high school) and Lincoln High School, both basketball powerhouses.

Shortly after arriving in Kansas City, I was told by Raymond Thompson, Athletic Director of the Interscholastic League, that plans were underway to redo the Field House court and other aspects of the building's interior; and further, that trophies and artifacts were being sought for a trophy case that would tell the history of the building. I suggested that, if at all possible, a plaque or installation of some sort commemorating Warren's playing days should be exhibited. Mr. Thompson was very helpful and made arrangements for me to call Kenny Wesley, the person in charge of the building, to arrange access for the interviews.

Currently (2008), the Kansas City School District is in terrible disarray. It is not like it was when Warren played; twelve schools, each serving its part of the city, each using the talent within its district to form its team. Today, according to Coach Bush, the best players transfer to schools where they can play together and usually to schools outside the city (and thus outside the Interscholastic League). There is not the balance or the frequent battles between rival schools that there once was, nor the quality of play. And that's only the basketball side. The academic side is worse.

In 1999, the Kansas City School District lost its accreditation. The experiments it has run in an effort to regain its accreditation and status have not—so far as I know—been successful. It's a source of considerable concern to local residents.

—

I offer the preceding passage as background. When I walked into the Field House, no one was there. The floor seemed in perfect condition, the stands as they had been for forty years. It did not look to me like it needed a makeover (though I hardly examined it carefully), but since it was scheduled for one, I found myself struck by an idea that seemed utterly right: *The Interscholastic League Field House is not called by its proper name—it should be renamed the Warren Jabali Field House.* Why not? Such a step would be good for the school district and good for the city, as well. The best of our history—at least in one area—would be brought forward to benefit the present. That is the way it is supposed to work. The greatness that a community produces, if it is remembered and held in mind, acts like a magnet on the development of others, raising consciousness and drawing up the standard of play. Why not use that principle here in this very specific way for whatever difference it might make?

What follows is the story of how that idea-turned-initiative (to rename the Interscholastic League Field House in honor of Kansas City's greatest basketball player) did—or did not—happen.

THE PROPOSAL

I immediately began to share the idea with everyone I thought might know something about Warren's high school career, particularly the individuals I interviewed. All seemed to be in support of it. In the course of this sharing, Alex Ellison, a former school board member as well as Warren's friend, suggested that while every effort should be made to have the building named after Warren, a backup (and perhaps more realistic) goal might be to have the court named in Warren's honor.

With that advice in mind, I examined the policies of the KC School Board and found the following:

Naming of District Schools and Facilities

    3. When selecting a name, preference will be given to names of local persons. A person's name will not be used until that person is deceased for at least ten (10) years.

With this information, the focus changed. Rather than renaming the Field House in Warren's honor, the focus now—as Alex had suggested—was on naming the court in his honor.

Even so, there were other potential complications. The School District's policy statement also seemed to suggest that not only buildings but also "parts of buildings" could not be named after living persons, and further, that proposals to rename buildings (or parts of buildings?) should be submitted in writing to the Superintendent of the District who then would refer the proposal to a committee. That committee, charged with the task of researching the proposal, would present its findings to the Board for its consideration and ruling.

> 1. All requests for naming or renaming a school
>   or portions of a building should be submitted
>   in writing to the superintendent who will
>   present them to the policy committee for
>   preliminary review, approval and submission
>   to the Board. The Board will decide if the
>   building or portion of the building should be
>   named or renamed.

However, by this time I was already pursuing another strategy. In part because the Superintendent's job appeared to be in peril (articles appeared in the *Kansas City Star* daily—or so it seemed—detailing a growing tension between Board and Superintendent; and given that there had been six Superintendents in almost as many years, there was little reason to think this situation would end differently) and in part because Roger Pendleton, another of the interviewees and someone strongly in support of the proposal, had suggested that I might want to contact the president of the School Board directly. David Smith, Board President, had been a basketball player, had graduated from Central High School, would be familiar with Warren's high school career, and thus might prove to be an important ally in our effort.

With this in mind, and given that I would be traveling to Kansas City shortly after the New Year, I decided (somewhat on the spur of the moment) to stop by Mr. Smith's office in the hope of obtaining his view of the proposal's potential. Unfortunately, he was unavailable.

As a follow-up, some three weeks later I sent Mr. Smith a letter in which I introduced myself, discussed the proposal, and then, leading with a quote from the Wichita State University "Shocker's Alumni" Magazine, concluded with the following:

*"Among the too-oft overlooked superstars of WSU
basketball is Warren Jabali (who played under the
name Warren Armstrong...). Though only 6'2", Jabali
was the unsung architect of the slam-dunk; he
possessed such incredible jumping skill that he once
bashed his forehead into the rim during a game. He
played professionally in the ill-fated ABA (American
Basketball Association), spending time on such teams
as the Oakland Oaks and Denver Rockets. Devoted to
social causes in his retirement, he was then and
remains today an inspiration."* (Shocker's Alumni
Magazine)

My reason for wanting to make this proposal is not
simply to honor a great basketball player but rather (and
in addition) to put before students, teachers and families
a story that will continue to inspire.

Any direction you can offer me would be appreciated
greatly. I would be happy to make a presentation to the
Board, if that would be appropriate, and I'm sure I could
find local leaders who would do the same. I believe that
the implementation of this proposal—to whatever degree
is possible, i.e., field house or court—would be very
good for the community and very good for the city
overall.

Attached is a packet containing several essays and
tributes to Warren (along with essays Warren has
written). I hope you will have the time to read it—or
much of it—as it, too, (I believe) helps make the case for
what I am proposing.

I received no response.

Over the course of the next few weeks I left a couple of phone
messages for Mr. Smith (no response) and also remained in frequent
contact with Alex Ellison and Kennie Denman. Both Alex and Kennie
were, by this point, full collaborators in this initiative, providing
guidance and counsel on how we should proceed as well as providing
legwork to get it done.

It was Alex who suggested that I put myself on the agenda of the
School Board's Public meeting. Held once a month, the Public Board

PART II: Naming and Necessity

meeting allows individuals from the community to make proposals (as well as express grievances and concerns) directly to the Board. In late January, I called the School Board's Administrative Offices and asked to be placed on the March 12 agenda.

On February 15 I traveled to Kansas City to attend a game at the Field House—Central versus Lincoln—and to meet with Ed Corporal, the current director of the Interscholastic League Athletic Department. Mr. Corporal, with whom I had visited at length by phone and to whom I also had sent material on Warren's career, was extremely receptive to the proposal. He already had envisioned some sort of installation or trophy case honoring the players of the Interscholastic League, and, as well, had wanted to name the court in someone's honor. He also had heard any number of stories about Warren's high school career and those stories, reinforced by the material I had sent, convinced him that the court should bear Warren's name. He offered to help in any way he could.

The following night, February 16, Alex hosted a gathering at his house to discuss the proposal. Present were Alex, Kennie, Willie Stewart, Murvell McMurry, and Alex's brother-in-law. Though much of the evening was devoted to stories centering on Warren's legendary feats, the topic did turn to the March 12 Board Meeting and the best way to proceed.

> *Alex:* The proposal should be packaged as handsomely as possible, perhaps with statistics from Warren's career included. It wouldn't hurt to enclose a letter from the Kansas City Sports Commission (the group that inducted Warren into its Hall of Fame in 2003).

> *Kennie:* It would be helpful to get as many supporters as possible at the Board meeting; perhaps an ad in the *Kansas City Star*, certainly one in the *Kansas City CALL*. And also include a letter from Wichita State (which had inducted Warren into its Hall of Fame as well).

> *Murvell:* No thought should be given to separating Warren's basketball career from his commitment to social justice. That's who he is as a person. And that's one of the reasons we want his name on the court.

> *Willie:* Warren was the best, there's no question about that. The court should be named after him. No question.

Later that same week, I contacted Al Smith, a former ABA teammate and friend of Warren's, to ask for a letter of support and to get his advice on how best to proceed. Al—with records of his own in the ABA—was immediately on board, offering to write a letter and recommending that I call Fatty Taylor (another former ABA player) for contacts that might result in additional letters.

Over the course of the next two weeks—thanks to the phone numbers provided by Fatty Taylor—I talked to several former ABA players. And though initially it must have seemed that I was coming "from out of the blue," the moment I mentioned Warren's name there was immediate interest. Four letters of support resulted and were included with the proposal, as was the letter Alex was able to obtain from the Kansas City Sports Commission. (The letter from Wichita State—which Kennie obtained—arrived too late to be included in the proposal but is included below for the record.)

In researching the price of ads, Kennie discovered that the cost would be exorbitant. For that reason, he shifted direction, proposing to the *Kansas City CALL* that they write an article about Warren (and about the proposal); perhaps "a where are they now" piece. The reporter with whom Kennie discussed the article, a young woman named Tracy Allen, had never heard of Warren and wondered why anyone would care. There was, after all, Lucius Allen and Anthony Peeler; if Warren Jabali was so great, why hadn't she heard of him?

Kennie continued to visit with her and as support for his argument, sent her the packet that had been sent to David Smith and Ed Corporal. When Kennie last spoke to her, she was convinced. She did feel that a story was warranted and stated she would give me a call as a next step in the process.

Later that week, Ms. Allen called. We visited at some length about Warren's career, his contributions on and off the court, and why the Interscholastic League court should be named in his honor.

On March 8, the Friday before the School Board meeting and the day the article was to appear in the *CALL*, I received a call from Kennie: "The first thing I did this morning was get the *CALL* newspaper. I turned to the back section and no article! I was furious! She had promised! I threw down the paper and was about to phone my complaint to the CALL when I noticed Warren's picture on the front page. They placed the article on the front page!"

The *Kansas City CALL* has served the African American community in Kansas City for over 80 years. To place an article on the front page is no small matter and, for our purposes, ensured that far more readers would be reached than would have been reached though an ad alone. And while there were one or two inaccuracies in the article, (it was the court and not the building that we were seeking to rename), still the article served not only to alert the *CALL*'s readership to the Board meeting and proposal but also—whatever the outcome of the proposal— to educate (or remind) people of one of Kansas City's greatest athletes.

Excerpts from the CALL article are provided below:

Group Spearheads Effort to Rename Field House
After Central High ABA Star
by Tracy Allen
CALL Staff Writer

It was the early days in the mid-1960s and the new Field House was constantly filled to capacity as students and fans of the interscholastic League watched some of the best high school players in Kansas City do "their thang."

Of course, Warren (Armstrong) Jabali was the crowd favorite in those days, an incredible standout for Central High School who went on to play at Wichita State and with the Denver Nuggets of the American Basketball Association. Jabali has been considered by many as "the best" high school player to ever come out of Kansas City. But there will be those who argue that Lucius Allen, a Wyandotte High star, also should be mentioned as the area's best to grace a high school court.

There is an effort now by some of Jabali's former admirers to not forget his legacy as a prep basketball star in Kansas City.

Next week, on Wednesday, March 12, several of Jabali's admirers will petition members of the Kansas City, Mo. School District Board of Education, during their regularly scheduled meeting, to rename the Interscholastic Field House as the Warren Jabali Court, after the 1964 Central High School graduate and former professional basketball star.

"He had an all-around beautiful game," stated Thomas. "Too bad so few people knew of him. He was the real deal."

"Nobody wants to say anything to denigrate Lucius Allen but Warren was a slight notch above. He was always a step ahead. He directed the flow of the game… (and) was a scoring force."

The group behind renaming the Field House after Jabali believe his resume speaks for itself. It should also be a reminder of who from Kansas City made a national impact.

"We had never seen anything like him and never seen anything like him since," commented Thomas. "We've had really good athletes, but Warren had the great talent."

It would be a mistake at this point, however, to presume that there was agreement in the community on whose name should appear on the Interscholastic League Field House court. Indeed, both Alex and Kennie, following the article in the *CALL*, immediately encountered opposition: *Why should his name be on that court? There are others just as worthy—coaches, administrators, athletic directors. What's he done for Kansas City?*

Further, I had not received a response from the School Board president, and Alice Ellison (Alex's wife) had received a lukewarm response from him when, in the course of another conversation, she asked if he was going to support our initiative.

Even so, on Wednesday, March 12, the following proposal was presented to the Kansas City Board of Education. Alex Ellison, Kennie Denmon, Murvell McMurry, and Willie Stewart were present, as was an audience of approximately 150 people, though most of them had attended in support of other issues. Also present was Bill Boykin, a long-time friend and standout player at Paseo High School in the '60s. (I had not seen Bill in years, though one of the great pleasures of my life was playing basketball with him. We went to different high schools but played throughout the year whenever we could and always on the same three-man team in summer leagues. He had a beautiful game, and I learned a lot from him—and respected him greatly, then and now.)

The proposal was "packaged" as Alex had suggested, and for the purpose of this recounting, I include the letters of support although there was no attempt to read the letters to the Board. Alex made a few opening remarks introducing me and the proposal to the Board, suggesting that a precedent existed in the Board's recent past for ruling in favor of such proposals, and then stating that he thought naming the court after Warren Jabali *was the right thing to do.* He then asked rhetorically, *"If not now, when?"*

PROPOSAL TO THE KANSAS CITY SCHOOL DISTRICT
BOARD OF TRUSTEES
March 12, 2008

My name is David Thomas. I live in Omaha, Nebraska but I am
a product of the Kansas City School District, having graduated
from Southeast High School in 1965.

I am here to make a proposal, but in making it, I am not alone.
Seated throughout the audience are individuals in support of the
proposal.

The proposal is this:

> *that the Interscholastic League Field House Court*
> *be renamed the Warren Jabali Court*

For those of you who never saw Warren Jabali play or who do
not know his story, here is why we think this proposal is worthy
of your consideration.

First, the basketball side:

HIGH SCHOOL

Warren (Armstrong) Jabali, a 1964 graduate of Central High
School, is considered by many the best basketball player ever to
come out of the Kansas City area.

When the *Kansas City Star* examined the "greatest player"
question (in March of 1998), their leading contenders were
Warren Jabali, Lucius Allen, Anthony Peeler and JaRon Rush.
Concluded the Star: *"Many of the people who saw all four*
wouldn't necessarily admit it, but they sounded as if they'd give
a slight edge to Jabali."

For three years, Warren was All-City, for two years All-District
and as a senior, All-State and All-American. Said the *Kansas*
City Star in its review of the 1963 Missouri State Tournament
(held in the Field House and including Jo Jo White): *"...the best*
all around player (we) saw was Warren Jabali of Kansas City

*Central...only a junior, Jabali faces a great future if he
consistently exercises all his tremendous talents."*

It is hard to convey the excitement Warren brought to Kansas
City high school basketball. His explosiveness, the balance of
power and grace, the sheer beauty of his game; it was the first
time we had ever seen such a complete and extraordinary talent.
More than any single person, Warren is responsible for the
legendary, filled-to-capacity, early days of the Interscholastic
League Field House. The history of that court begins with him.

COLLEGE

Following his graduation from Central, Warren entered Wichita
State University where he set rebounding and assist records and
was, for a while, their fourth all-time scorer. He was a three-time
All-Missouri Valley Conference selection, ranking in the top 20
all-time at Wichita State in scoring, rebounding and assists. At
6'2", he led Wichita State in rebounding for three consecutive
years.

In 1985, Warren was inducted into the Wichita State University
Athletic Hall of Fame. At the time of induction he held the WSU
record for assists in a game, a season, and a career.

THE PROS

Following his graduation from Wichita State, Warren was
drafted by the Oakland Oaks of the American Basketball
Association (ABA).

His first year in the league, he was voted Rookie of the Year. His
sixth year, Most Valuable Player in the ABA All-Star Game, a
game that included Julius Erving, George McGinnis and Artis
Gilmore. That same year he was named First Team All ABA
Guard. He was four times an All Star.

Hall of Fame coach Alex Hannum, who coached championship
teams in both the NBA and the ABA, called Warren *the smartest
player he ever coached.*

Al Bianchi, also a veteran coach of both the ABA and the NBA, stated that Warren *may have been the toughest competitor he ever was around in a lifetime of basketball.*

When the ABA announced its list of the thirty greatest players, Warren was on it.

Al Smith, a veteran guard of the ABA, went further. In his assessment, the five greatest ABA players with or against whom he played were Julius Erving, Artis Gilmore, Moses Malone, George "the Iceman" Gervin, and Warren Jabali.

Warren's lifetime statistics: fifth on all-time ABA APG/average; sixth on all-time ABA 3-point list; ninth on all-time ABA assist list (5.34/game); 25th on all-time points list (17/game).

In 2004, the Kansas City Sports Commission inducted Warren into its Hall of Champions.

————————

That is the basketball side. In our view, Warren's career is remarkable, too little known and worthy of tribute. But there is another side that compels us to make this proposal, as well.

If students should ask: "Who is Warren Jabali?" they will learn of a remarkable basketball player, someone worthy of note on that basis alone.

But they also will learn of a remarkable individual, someone who did not believe that becoming a professional athlete meant that nothing else should matter. For Warren, there has always been "a duty that transcends the playing field."

In Warren's case, that duty has meant doing what he could to affect, in his words, *"the standing of African American people in the human community."* And this we have seen him do as educator, mentor, coach and scholar.

We believe that a successful education is measured (in part) by the extent to which it helps students understand that in the end, they must serve something larger than themselves.

Such an education requires examples, real-life examples; and if those examples can come from the community, then all the better. Warren Jabali is such an example.

We make this proposal because we believe it serves three important ends at once:

First, a great talent, perhaps the greatest basketball talent ever to come out of our city (no small matter), is remembered, acknowledged and honored.

Second, through that honoring students are reminded that *in this community greatness is possible*; reminded— whatever their advantages and disadvantages—that nothing compels them to settle for less than the best in themselves.

And third, by this honoring students and their families are put in dialogue with a story that calls them to the full exercise of their gifts *(while also discouraging them from ever concluding that they do not have something to give)*.

Warren Jabali knows nothing of this proposal. We submit it because we believe it serves the educational and inspirational interests of the community, and we thank you for your consideration of it.

Letters of Support

Mon., March 10, 2008

Dear Sirs:

I am writing this as a representative of the Pizza Hut Wichita
State Shocker Sports Hall of Fame and Wichita State University
Intercollegiate Athletic Association in support of the Committee
to name the Interscholastic League Fieldhouse "Warren
(Armstrong) Jabali Court."

Warren Armstrong, who later changed his name to Warren
Jabali, was an outstanding men's basketball player at Wichita
State from 1965–68.

Jabali was named a three-time first team all-Missouri Valley
Conference performer at a time when the conference was
regarded as one of the top leagues in the United States. He
averaged 16.7 points and 10.8 rebounds per game, tenth and
fourth-best all-time at WSU, respectively, while he ranks 11th
all-time in scoring with 1,301 points and is first all-time in career
assists with 429.

He led the Shockers in rebounding during each of his three
seasons before playing professionally in the American
Basketball Association from 1968–75. He was the ABA's
Rookie-of-the-Year in 1969 and MVP of its all-star game in
1973. In addition, he averaged 17.1 points per game during his
pro career.

At WSU, he was inducted into the Shocker Sports Hall of Fame
in 1985, and his name would be an outstanding choice to
represent the Interscholastic Fieldhouse and the Kansas City
School District.

Sincerely,

Larry Rankin
Kansas City Sports Commission and Foundation
McGuff Sports Center

February 28, 2008

Mr. Dave Smith
President, Board of Trustees
c/o Kansas City School District
Board of Education Building
1211 McGee Street
Kansas City, MO 64106

Dear Dave:

I am writing to express our support for the naming of the
Interscholastic League Field House basketball floor after Warren
Jabali. He was, without a doubt, one of the finest basketball
players ever to come out of Kansas City.

Mr. Jabali was All-City at Central for three straight years. He
earned All-District Honors as a junior and senior, and All-State
and All-American status as a senior. He went on to a tremendous
career at Wichita State University followed by the ABA where
he was Rookie of the Year. He was inducted into the Earl Smith
Greater Kansas City Amateur Sports Hall of Champions in 2004.

Remembering tremendous athletes like Warren Jabali is an
important part of our community. He has shown tremendous
leadership and has touched many lives over the years. This is
indeed a fitting tribute for a gifted athlete and one of the best to
ever play in Kansas City.

Sincerely,

Kevin M. Gray
President

March 6, 2008

Dear Mr. Smith,

I'm writing to you and the Kansas City School Board supporting the renaming of the Interscholastic League Field House Court to the Warren Jabali Court. You see, my first introduction to Jabali aka Warren Armstrong was my sophomore year in college on the basketball court (I'm a BRADLEY BRAVE). Warren was one of the most talented players I ever saw.

Jabali was a year ahead of me in college, and boy did I learn a lot in the two years I played against him. When Jabali became a pro player, I knew he would be one of the greatest, but like a lot of players a knee injury almost ended his career.

During this time Jabali and I lost contact. When we saw each other again, I was playing for Denver, Jabali was playing for Miami. His physical ability was limited. His first two years in the pros were ALL Star numbers. Maybe even Hall of Fame. Playing on one leg, Jabali was an ALL Star. When Jabali joined me in Denver, I got to see a great all-around player night in and night out. It was his intellect on the court that set him apart from most players. Don't get me wrong, he could still dunk on you. I didn't play against Spencer Haywood, and I only played against David Thompson a year and a half. With that said, my top five players that I played against in the ABA were George Gervin, Artis Gilmore, Julius Irving, Moses Malone, and Warren Jabali.

I think some of Warren's greatest accomplishments are what he's doing now. He is helping communities in Florida, Kansas City Missouri, and Kansas City Kansas. Jabali won't toot his own horn. He doesn't seek publicity or speak about all the people he's helped. He is a "doer." To me, well done is always better than well said. WELL DONE, JABALI! His athletic prowess and achievements alone should warrant this honor. His mentoring and community service should put it over the top!

Respectfully yours,

Al Smith
Former ABA player

Monday, March 10, 2008

Hello Dave!

It's nice to hear from you. I would be more than happy and willing to do whatever I can to expedite the Kansas City School Board naming the high school court after Warren Jabali.

I met Jabali when playing in the American Basketball Association. He was always a quiet, serious-minded individual off the court and somewhat a "general" on the court. He knew how to take charge and bring the team together to emphasize hard work, teamwork and fair play. While some considered him a "radical" at times, I found him to be an individual who was well ahead of his time. He seemed to have the foresight to know what would be best for the players in the long run. Now, in hindsight, we all see that he was right on many issues. He still evokes much leadership potential when we all attend the NBA Retired Players Association functions. He still has the quiet underlying spirit that seeks fairness for everyone including the many disenfranchised players as well. We are wishing that he will one day step forward and seek one of the board seats of our organization. He's still having the positive impact on many of the lives he's touching, both young and old. He doesn't seek notoriety, he just wants fair treatment for everyone and I will always respect him for that.

My wife and I were elated to learn that he was being considered for this honor! We were just honored at the NBA Retired Players Association Brunch during the NBA All-Star events. We were awarded the "Humanitarian of the Year Award" for our assistance with the Katrina evacuees in Dallas, Texas, and my wife as the Founder of HOPE HOUSE, an emergency placement center for children in foster care. My wife and I have been foster parents for 20+ years and she recently retired from the Dallas School District after teaching 28 years. We are really hoping and praying that they will allow this honor to be bestowed on Jabali. It's long overdue!

Sincerely,
Eugene "Goo" Kennedy
Former ABA player

March 11, 2008

Dear Mr. Smith,

I'm writing this note on behalf of Warren Jabali, a former high school, college, and professional basketball player from Kansas City, Missouri. It has come to my attention that a group of people from the Kansas City area, led by Mr. David Thomas, is trying to honor Warren's tremendous basketball accomplishments by having the Interscholastic League Field House Court to be renamed the Warren Jabali Court.

I am a former University of Colorado (CU) basketball player and graduate who also played in the American Basketball Association (ABA) and the National Basketball Association (NBA). I have known Warren for the past forty-one years.

I competed against Warren both on the collegiate and professional level. He was probably the most tough-minded player I ever had to play against. He would literally impose his will on the play of the game. He would be the guy you wanted to take the last shot either to tie or win the game. He played both forward and guard positions which was certainly unheard of for a player that stood only 6'2". Exhibiting an all-around game, Warren could score, dribble, pass, rebound, and defend. I dare say he would be a standout player in today's modern game.

Since his playing days, Warren has devoted his career to helping others and giving back to the community in which he lives. He is an educator, mentor, and coach who conveys strong character, values, and morals to the youth of his community.

To honor Warren with the renaming of the Field House Court to the Warren Jabali Court would be great recognition for a man that in my eyes is the greatest basketball player to come out of the Kansas City area.

Sincerely,

Chuck Williams
Former ABA/NBA player

Wednesday, March 12, 2008 1:39 PM

To: David Smith
President, Board of Trustees
Kansas City MO School District

Mr. Smith,

I have known Warren Jabali for close to 40 years and was
fortunate enough to play with him professionally for 3 years in
the former ABA. We played together in Oakland, where we won
a championship in 1968–69, in Washington and in Miami.
Warren came in as a confident rookie and played with the
energy, confidence and maturity of a veteran, which was integral
to our team success. Warren possessed great skills and was able
to shine alongside such greats as Larry Brown and Rick Barry.
He was a great teammate, very personable and humorous. He
always played beyond his years and was very mature and had a
great understanding of the game even as a rookie. I am honored
to have been able to play with him.

He has exhibited these types of personal skills the entire 40 years
or so I have known him. He is one of THE BEST if not THE
BEST guards I was ever able to play with. We have remained
friends all these years, and it is always a pleasure to see him and
re-connect. I wish we were able to see each other more often.
Warren is a great basketball player, but an even better person. He
is the consummate All American on and off the court. It is a
pleasure to be able to sing his praises.

All My Best,

Ira Harge
Former ABA player

Three minutes were allowed for presentation of the proposal (the limit for all public comments or presentations). I was told that I was given more time than that, but even so I was able to get through only half of the proposal. When time was called, I thanked the Board and handed copies of the proposal to the clerk. The audience responded to the proposal with applause.

Alex told me that the Board seldom comments on issues raised at Public Board meetings; a presentation is made, the Board thanks the presenter, announces (perhaps) that it will take the issue under advisement and then moves to the next item on the agenda. It was encouraging, therefore, when one of the Board members, Marilyn Simmons, after all public agenda items had been addressed, returned to our proposal and suggested that it merited further discussion. She said that something like what was being proposed (if not exactly) should be done; *"after all, there is a lot of history in the Interscholastic League that no one knows about and that history needs to be known."*

Unfortunately, Board members then began to recount that history, throwing out the names of favorite players, some—oddly—not even basketball players. Still, the topic remained alive for several minutes, concluding with a decision to consult Board policies for direction.

Following the meeting, Alex, Kennie, Murvell, and I went to Gates Bar-B-Q for dinner. The general feeling was that the Board meeting had gone well enough—especially given Ms. Simmons' interest in the proposal—to justify a degree of cautious optimism. In the parking lot after dinner, the following views were expressed:

> *Kennie:* I've said from the beginning that even if the proposal doesn't pass (and I now think there's a chance it might), that a service to the community has been performed. People now know that one of the greatest basketball players of all time came from Kansas City. I'm just happy about that.

> *Murvell:* Kansas City is a funny place. It's got a very short memory, especially when it comes to black folks. I'm a little more optimistic myself after tonight. This may be a start, and if we can make this happen then maybe it can open the way for the recognition of others who deserve to be recognized.

Alex: I was a little disappointed by the response of some
Board members, but like I said to the Board, there is a
precedent for this. When I was on the Board, we named a
school after a hero from the Hispanic community. It was
the right thing to do then, and this is the right thing to do
now in regard to Warren Jabali. And again, if not now,
when?

From the beginning, we all agreed that Warren should not know
about the proposal. He would not seek this recognition for himself, and
no one should have reason to think otherwise. It would be better for the
initiative if we could say (as we were able to say): "Warren knows
nothing of this proposal."

However, now that the proposal had been submitted to the Board
(and given the appearance of the article in the *CALL*), we thought
Warren should hear from us directly. After I returned home, I sent him a
note explaining our efforts and enclosing a copy of the proposal. In his
response, Warren expressed his gratitude and then offered the following:

> *If you communicate with the board any further, I would
> prefer that they consider using Armstrong as opposed to
> Jabali. I was Armstrong at that time and there are those
> who did not keep up with my professional career and
> therefore would not know the identity of Jabali. It is
> moreover my family name in KC.*

I communicated Warren's wishes to the group (Alex, Kennie,
Murvell, Willie). I also sent a follow-up e-mail to all Board members in
which I expressed my interest in furthering/assisting with the proposal in
any way I could. Then, on March 24, I received the following e-mail
from Murvell:

> *I had a chance to talk with Dave Smith (Board Chair) just
> this weekend. He said he is in support of the proposal that
> would allow Warren's name to be placed on the field
> house court. He did express some concern as to the
> financial burden, and who might cover that. We also
> talked a little about making the field house a place to
> showcase other IL players, a display case or something of
> that nature. I'll keep you informed of what I find out here.*

Murvell had mentioned the night of Alex's gathering that he and David Smith were friends and that when the time was right, he would speak to him about the proposal. David Smith's response was very encouraging.

I also received a call from Ed Corporal. He said that the Assistant Superintendent of the District had contacted him requesting that he set up a committee to pursue the proposal and asking when I might be available. I gave him a couple of dates in April, said I was looking forward to the meeting, and waited to hear back.

Time passed without a word. I made several attempts to reach Mr. Corporal—by phone and e-mail—but all were unsuccessful. When I did reach him, I learned that within a very short time, he no longer would be with the school district. I also learned that David Smith was no longer the president of the Board (though he remained a member-at-large), and that Marilyn Simmons was now the Board President.

After a couple of conversations with Alex and Kennie in which we discussed next steps, I learned that Alex, who knew Ms. Simmons, was planning to call her to get her sense of where the Board stood on the proposal.

I later received the following e-mail from Alex:

> *I spoke with Marilyn Simmons and she didn't seem to think it would be a problem naming the court after Warren, but didn't have a clue and/or give any indication as to the process (i.e., if a committee was necessary or what).*
>
> *To be quite honest with you, I really don't know what steps to take at this point with the district being in such disarray. No real leadership at the central office and/or on the board. The naming of the court probably isn't a top-priority item with all the other issues confronting the district.*
>
> *One suggestion might be to have Merv talk to Dave Smith to see if he would take it upon himself to be the "driver" behind the initiative. Dave will need to work with Marilyn and develop some bond, because he didn't support her for chair/president of the board. It's called politics, my brother.*
>
> *FYI, when I talked to Marilyn I indicated that our plan also included the development of some type of hall of fame that would recognize the outstanding players from*

the IL. This is a big selling point and will require some work to identify those players.

It was around this time that I developed an implementation plan (of sorts) for an Interscholastic League Field House Hall of Fame, thinking that such a plan might assist the Board in seeing how the court-naming initiative could proceed as an initial step in a process that eventually honored other players, coaches, etc. I wanted to avoid giving the impression that the entire hall of fame installation had to be done at once. Rather, the implementation plan called for phases, and the first phase—the least expensive and least complicated phase—could be done right away.

Implementation Plan:

PRESERVING AND HONORING THE HISTORY OF KANSAS CITY'S INTERSCHOLASTIC LEAGUE

Vision:

An installation located at the Interscholastic League Field House honoring the basketball players, coaches, athletic directors and administrators so instrumental in creating the rich history and tradition of Kansas City's Interscholastic League.

Phase I – Naming the Court

Following the proposal submitted to the Kansas City Educational Board of Trustees on March 12, 2008, the Interscholastic League court is renamed the Warren Armstrong Court. This occurs at a ceremony to be held at the Field House at which the unveiling of the court occurs.

The event is well publicized with articles in the *Kansas City Star* and *Kansas City CALL* with a press release inviting local media. Ceremony includes presentations by dignitaries, invited guests, and Mr. Armstrong.

It is at this event that the larger vision honoring the history of the League is formally announced to the community.

Target date: Fall 2008
Cost: To be determined

Phase II – Installation Honoring History of League
(Players/Coaches/etc)

Step 1 – As soon as possible, a coordinated effort begins to
identify the individuals and teams to be honored in the Field
House installation. Beginning with the 1963/64 season, the
following information is collected:

League Champions	All-City Honors
District Champions	All-District Honors
State Champions	All State Honors
	All America Honors

Key Administrators – Coaches – Athletic Directors

In addition, the following:

Newspaper accounts of key games and/or events important to the
history and development of the League; film footage of
Interscholastic League play; trophies, awards and artifacts
suitable for display; video interviews providing an oral history of
the league's outstanding players/ moments/etc.

Target date: Fall 2009
Cost: To be determined

Step 2 – Once the information gathering is underway, the design
of the installation is determined. This involves visiting other
similar installations, consulting with design professionals,
developing schematics for review by the Board, etc. A primary
consideration is cost. The important thing to remember is that the
installation can and will evolve but should start with a design
that is attractive, accessible and honoring of the history that is
displayed.

Target date: Fall 2009
Cost: To be determined

Step 3 – Finally, the installation is created. There is a ribbon-
cutting ceremony accompanied by a press conference at which

Board members and District officials explain and discuss the value to the community of the history displayed in the installation.

Target date: Fall 2010?
Cost: To be determined

NOTE: The above is offered as the roughest of sketches, to be elaborated into a complete vision and implementation plan by the committee created to take the initiative forward. The important point is that this is an initiative that can be done in phases, with Phase I (the naming of the court)—the easiest and least expensive phase—raising interest in and drawing support for Phase II.

(I should add that I did not imagine that I or others on the court-naming team would be involved with Phase II. We were on board for Phase I. Phase II—if it was to occur—would require considerable work and would need to be addressed by the District.)

When I next talked to Alex, he said that he had spoken again with Marilyn Simmons and that she had suggested that we get in touch with Ray Wilson, the newly elected Board member whose district included the field house. Mr. Wilson and I talked by phone on July 1. He was extremely enthusiastic about the proposal and said, "No problem, we will get this done." He also mentioned his interest in having the building named in Warren's honor, not simply the court. I told him that such an outcome would be wonderful and that I would send him the proposal and other information that I thought would be helpful to him.

That evening, I sent Mr. Wilson a packet of material including what I had written about Warren to date, Warren's essays, the court-naming proposal and the proposal to create an installation honoring Interscholastic League players and coaches. Concerning the latter, I emphasized in my cover note to Mr. Wilson that we move ahead with Phase I—Naming the Building or Court after Warren—and that we not wait just because we're not ready to do Phase II. I then called him on the July 3 to make sure he had received the material.

Over the course of our two conversations, I learned that Mr. Wilson had graduated from Central (1973), that he knew a great deal about Warren and, in fact, credited Warren (and others in Warren's years) with a change in the culture at Central. I learned as well that he had been present at the Board meeting the night the proposal was presented and had already met with Dave Smith and Marilyn Simmons to discuss how to implement the court-naming proposal.

In our second conversation, Mr. Wilson indicated that it was just a matter of figuring out how to do the court-naming process in the right way, that it was, from his point of view, *a done deal.* He also mentioned that the board policy to which I had referred in my e-mail had been created in recent years and that there might be reason to think it could be bypassed. He said that he was tentatively looking at a date in the Fall—October, perhaps November—for a ceremony but that he would be meeting with several individuals in the coming days. Through those meetings he hoped to get a better sense of what needed to happen and when. He promised to keep me informed.

On August 12 I again heard from Mr. Wilson. He called to say that he remained committed to the initiative and that the naming of the court after Warren was meeting with little or no resistance. The Board, in his view, was simply waiting on him for direction and next steps. He did mention, however, that there seemed to be an interest in naming the building after Coach Wilkerson, the long-time coach of Central High School, now deceased. He said that he wanted to form a committee of Interscholastic League athletes, have a breakfast perhaps to launch the next phase of the initiative and in general, as he had said before, "do the thing in the right way."

He added that the naming of the court after Warren was such a foregone conclusion that he had to stop the crew that was stripping and refinishing the court from painting Warren's name on it (as he wanted Board approval, however much that might be a formality at this point).

I asked him if he was planning to get Warren's actual signature to duplicate on the court. He said it hadn't occurred to him. I told him that I thought that is what is done in these instances and that it should be easy enough to do, and I added: *Warren put his signature on that court forty-five years ago, and this will make it literally so.* He liked the idea and said he would proceed with that in mind.

One month later, on September 11, I received the following e-mail from Alex:

> *I received a call this morning from Ray Wilson, who represents sub-district 5 on the KCMSD Board of Trustees, informing me that the Board approved the naming of the court (i.e., **WARREN ARMSTRONG**) at the IL Fieldhouse. The vote was 9-0.*

In that same note, Alex mentioned that Mr. Wilson hoped to hold a "committee" meeting on Saturday, September 20, to "get the ball rolling and to do some 'brainstorming' on the 'wall of fame'." Alex indicated that he suggested to Mr. Wilson "that we implement these in phases and the naming of the court would be phase one."

On that same day, Kennie called to check on the status of our initiative. Since he had not yet seen Alex's e-mail, I was able to deliver the good news. Later, I e-mailed Goo Kennedy, Ira Harge, and Chuck Williams, the players who had written letters of support, informing them of the Board's decision and suggesting they attend the dedication ceremony (whenever it would be held). I then called Al Smith. Al said that he had heard about the vote and was delighted. He also said that he would give some thought to who should be invited to the dedication. Finally, I contacted Len Trower, Jabali's long-time friend from college, to inform him of the vote and to encourage him to come to Kansas City for the dedication.

I imagine that a similar "spreading of the word" was occurring through Alex and Kennie, as well as through Murvell, Roger, Willie, and others comprising the initiative's core network as they learned the news.

CREATING THE EVENT

On Friday, September 19, I drove to Kansas City prior to Saturday's meeting to meet Kennie for a tour of the schools, parks, and neighborhoods that played a part in the development of Kennie, Warren, and any number of other outstanding players: Northeast Junior High School, the legendary court at Dunbar in Kansas City, Kansas, the court at 30th & Paseo in Kansas City, Missouri, and the court at Blessed Sacrament. It was Kennie who, in 1962, his senior year of high school, was told by his coach that he had been replaced on the All-City Team by the sophomore phenom from Kansas City Central.

> (Jack) Patterson and (Larry) Norris (of Southeast) were joined on the first team by Randy St. Clair of Westport, Tom McCaffrey of Southwest and Warren Armstrong of Central. Armstrong's selection was noteworthy, not only for its honor, but because the 6-foot-2 frontliner is a sophomore. The other first-team members are seniors... Other members of the second team are Preston Washington (of Southeast), Kenny Denmon of Lincoln and Melvin Estell of Central. (KC Star, Feb. '62)

Kennie remarked that he had never resented his failure to make the first team even though Warren was only a sophomore because he appreciated how good Warren truly was. On quite another note, however, he did mention that on more than one occasion when all-black Lincoln High School played all-white schools, the referees (also white) had indicated to him—in so many words—that the "calls" would not go his way. One referee called him back to center court after the captains met to say, "It better not be close in the fourth quarter, Mr. Denmon"; and years later, another referee apologized for the unfairness of his calls.

The next day, Mr. Wilson convened the meeting. Present were Alex Ellison, Kennie Denmon, Murvell McMurry, Roger Pendleton, Ed Corporal, and me. (Ed Corporal, as it turns out, did not leave the employ of the School District but remained as Athletic Director of the Interscholastic League with a continuing commitment to the court-naming initiative).

Several topics were discussed, but the basic outline of what was accomplished was this: December 6 (tentative until confirmed by Mr. Wilson) was chosen as the date for the dedication ceremony. It would occur at halftime of a Central High School game (as Alex had suggested would be fitting), and because that would not afford sufficient time for presentations and speeches, Murvell suggested a luncheon be held earlier that same day. Alex provided Warren's signature to Mr. Wilson who would have it stenciled and readied for placement on the court. Mr. Wilson and Mr. Corporal would see to the timing and logistics concerning the field house court (its refinishing and usage arrangements) and Mr. Wilson would confirm the date, finalize the financial arrangements (airline, hotel, luncheon, court costs, etc.) and begin the publicity campaign necessary to ensure that the event would be known to all who might want to attend. It was also suggested (by Alex) that a letter of appreciation be sent to the Board of Trustees thanking them for their support of the proposal.

Within the week, I drafted a letter and sent it to the Board:

Marilyn Simmons
President, Board of Trustees
Kansas City Missouri School District

Dear Ms. Simmons,

I learned recently that the Kansas City Missouri School District Board of Trustees voted in favor of naming the Interscholastic League field house court *the Warren*

Armstrong Court. On behalf of those involved in this
initiative, I want to say *thank you.*

The Board's willingness to make this decision means
that the best of our history—in one specific area—will
be made known to current and future generations passing
through the Interscholastic League Field House. They
can only be inspired and enriched by what they learn.

I would like to name the individuals involved in this
effort: Alex Ellison, Kenny Denmon, Murvell McMurry,
Roger Pendleton, Willie Stewart (and, in truth, many
others who continued to supply support to this core
group).

Together, we want to thank you, David Smith (president
at the time that the proposal was submitted) and, in
particular, Ray Wilson, who embraced this initiative and
kept it front and center in the weeks and months
preceding the Board's vote.

We also want to thank the entire Board for its
willingness to take this step and for speaking in a single
voice (voting 9 to 0) on behalf of the importance of
making sure that the best of our history is present in the
lives of today's students.

Sincerely,
David Thomas

On October 3 Mr. Wilson called to confirm the date of the
dedication ceremony (December 6), although he had not yet met with the
superintendent regarding budget and accommodations—something he
would be doing in the coming week. We talked about the importance of
inscribing Warren's signature on the court, which would cap a year's
effort and should be done artfully and with care, enhancing the court and
drawing the eye of the viewer.

From that point it seemed only phone calls and networking
would be required to make the event happen. Unfortunately, the Kansas
City School District continued to struggle with financial, programmatic,
and administrative issues far more daunting and of greater immediate

concern than the issues surrounding our initiative. As a consequence, it proved difficult even at this late date to get certainty on a number of issues related to our event, such as hotel reservations, publicity, and budgetary commitments.

During this time I suggested to Alex (and later to Mr. Wilson) that we have a proclamation declaring December 6 Warren Armstrong Jabali Day. (Actually, I called it a resolution. Alex corrected me, noting that the proper term is *proclamation*.) I told Alex I would write it, and he said he would contact City Council members who could get it to the Mayor for his signature.

On November 11 I drove to Kansas City to meet with Alex and Ed Corporal at the Field House. The court diagram that the district produced was not consistent with our vision, nor was it consistent with the Board's resolution (i.e., the District's diagram showed "Warren Armstrong Field House" stenciled on the court rather than "Warren Armstrong Court"). In addition, Mr. Corporal had envisioned other features that would enhance the court, and we wanted to understand and incorporate his vision without sacrificing ours. Later that morning, at Mr. Corporal's suggestion, Alex and I drove to Manual High School to examine their court, as it had some of the design features that Mr. Corporal wanted to include on the Field House court.

As we left Manual—and since we were downtown already—Alex suggested we have lunch at Harper's, a restaurant located a few blocks from Manual at the corner of 18th & Vine. While we were there, we agreed that Harper's was the perfect place for the December 6 luncheon. Eighteenth & Vine is the birthplace of Kansas City jazz: Count Basie, the Kansas City stomp, the early days of Charlie Parker. Since basketball has much in common with jazz and since Warren, by all accounts, was an "improvisational artist," this seemed the perfect location. (From the beginning, I should point out, our initiative was about Warren, his impact as a player and as a person, but it was also about Kansas City, about a time in the city and about a style that seemed unique to the city. Warren epitomized that style, but it was a style influenced by many factors: jazz, rock & roll, basketball, the larger currents of social change and certainly by the integration of Kansas City's inner-city schools where a mixing of races and cultures enriched the experience of students—and others—at the borderline of that mixing.) The idea was sealed when Alex told me that that Harper's was owned by Myra Harper, sister of Maurice Harper, a friend of Warren's and an All City selection (along with Warren) during Warren's senior year in high school.

Midway through our lunch at Harper's, Mr. Wilson joined us.

We went down the list of "loose ends," and with each one he agreed with our recommendations while continuing to assure us that despite the delays—delays that he, too, had experienced—everything would happen as planned. On our way to the car, Alex put his arm around Mr. Wilson and—as his senior and as a former member of the School Board himself—suggested that it is for moments such as this, when leadership and follow-through are required, that he was elected. Mr. Wilson was quick to agree. This was a brotherly gesture, friendly and honoring, but it was also coaching in the finest sense, a call for focus and renewed assistance now that we were down to the wire.

The following week, I worked on court diagrams, e-mailing them to Mr. Corporal and to Alex until we had the one that suited us. "Kansas City" on each of the baselines and the state of Missouri at center court, a star marking the location of Kansas City, free throw lanes and three-point circle lines in white, these were Mr. Corporal's wishes; for Alex and me, it was a matter of making sure that Warren's name would be sufficiently large and easy to read. At the last minute, in discussions with Mr. Corporal, I suggested we put Warren's name on the left side of the court rather than the right since that is the part of the court nearest the entrance and the first to be seen by those entering the facility's home court bleachers.

At the two-week mark and with the Thanksgiving Day holidays before us, we still did not have answers and support on some crucial issues. Alex, with whom I was in touch daily, began scheduling meetings with school personnel in order to keep the needs of our event front and center. He used his considerable interpersonal skills to help District staff address the completion of essential tasks. Hotel reservations, for example, had not been made for Warren and his wife (the person assigned this task on the previous Friday was no longer working for the District on the following Monday); hotel rooms at the District's discounted rate were not available for out-of-town guests (as we had hoped they would be); Harper's had yet to receive a down payment on the luncheon, and so on. During this time, Alex frequently began his phone calls to me by saying, "I hate to be the bearer of bad news, but..." On every occasion, however, Alex had found (or helped District staff find) a solution to whatever dilemma was before them. By the week of the event (the first week of December), everything was in place (and/or there was clarity on what could and could not happen).

At my end, there were three issues. First, I had been attempting to coordinate out-of-town invitations and several individuals—interested in coming—were waiting to hear about the availability of discounted rooms. By the week prior to the event, however, it was clear that discounted rooms would not be available. Thankfully, Len Trower and Carlton Lee (from Philadelphia) had already made reservations in case the discounted rooms did not materialize; and Al Smith (from New Jersey) was able to make reservations at that late date even though many events—the Big Twelve Championship game, for example—were scheduled for that weekend in Kansas City.

Second, while I had thought that the school district and perhaps the Board itself would design the court dedication ceremony, by the "one-week mark" that task had fallen to Mr. Corporal and me. I put together the barest of outlines and sent it to Mr. Corporal who, in turn, forwarded it to Andre Riley in the District's public relations office. With slight modifications, the outline was followed; I should add, however, that the District added a flair and degree of hospitality to the event that is to its credit alone (see below).

In addition, at Mr. Corporal's request, I provided a fact sheet recounting Warren's career for inclusion in the ceremony's program. It was from this fact sheet that the announcer read to begin the ceremony. Finally, one last change to the court dedication ceremony—and a good one—was Mr. Corporal's decision to have the ceremony not at half-time of the Central High School game but preceding it, making more time available for the dedication.

The last issue concerned the video interviews I had done some fifteen months before. While I had considered creating a DVD to be shown at the luncheon, I had dismissed the idea as simply too large an undertaking. Also, there was now an irony associated with the video project. While it had started out to be one thing—the stringing together of a series of interviews—it now seemed to be about something more: the court initiative itself. In a sense, it had given birth to the initiative, and in any event, I found myself feeling as though I would be missing an important opportunity if I did not enlarge the video to include the court initiative. At best, then, given this line of thought, I had only part of the necessary video footage; the rest awaited the event.

Still, I had done some editing and I had shown what I had done to a few friends. On one such occasion, three weeks before the dedication ceremony, I was encouraged to see things differently. The luncheon, in the opinion of my friends, was the perfect occasion to share at least a portion of the interviews, and that—it seemed to them and, increasingly, to me—would add to the event.

So, I set about trying to finalize what I thought would be a five-minute DVD but which quickly morphed into the entire video I had envisioned originally (though now seen as something that might fit within, or be a companion to, the video of the event itself). To accomplish the task of completing the video, I hired Adam Wiltgen. I had met Adam when he worked at the Apple Store. He had assisted me on other projects, and his experience—far greater than my own—meant that he could show me how to achieve the effect I was after.

In order to complete the video, one more trip to Kansas City was required. On the Friday following Thanksgiving, I drove to the field house in order to get footage of the final work on the court, particularly the painting of Warren's name. With that footage I could conclude the video at the point that the court dedication weekend begins.

An acceptable "rough cut" of the video/DVD was completed at 9:00 a.m. the night of December 5. Paula and I then left for Kansas City, arriving at the Hyatt Regency at Crown Center in downtown Kansas City at 12:30 a.m.

THE EVENT: SATURDAY, DECEMBER 6, 2008

As I understand it, the "event" began mid-week for Warren. He flew into Kansas City on Wednesday (to be joined later in the week by his wife, Mary). Between Alex, the school district, and other friends, several events had been scheduled: a gathering of former players and old friends at Gates Bar-B-Q, a presentation on Thursday to the Urban League, and on Friday a presentation to the student body at Central High School. I wanted very much to attend all of these events and get them documented, but work on the video made that impossible.

I arrived at Harper's shortly after 9:00 a.m. on Saturday morning. I wanted to make sure that the setup was in place for playing the video, and I also had told friends who were documenting the event that I would meet them at 10:30. Everything fell together smoothly: school district personnel arrived with DVD player and screen; my friends arrived with their cameras, the radio station technician arrived to prepare for the broadcast. At 11:30 guests began filing through the doors, in many cases surprise guests and/or friends that Warren had not seen in years.

The radio broadcast began at noon: the Reverend Nelson "Fuzzy" Thompson's weekly radio show, "Community Solutions," airing on 1590, KPRT-AM. (This, too, had been one of Alex's suggestions. Fuzzy was a long time friend of Warren's and the radio program a perfect way to provide background on the event while also announcing to a listening audience the dedication ceremony that evening.) Seated at the broadcast table were Fuzzy, Warren, Alex, David Whalen, an associate of Fuzzy's and his co-host, Councilwoman Melba Curls who, after opening remarks by Fuzzy, read the proclamation, and me.

Each of us in turn talked about the dedication of the court, how it came about, the roles we played, the importance of Warren and his great talent to our memory of that time (early '60s). Warren was given the last word and as part of his remarks offered the following:

When it comes to reflecting on the naming of the Interscholastic League Basketball Court after me, I can modestly say that I think that it is appropriate. And one of the reasons why I think it's appropriate is because people tend to have very short memories. And we who played during that time when the field house would be full to the rafters are getting to the point where, as Willie Stewart can tell you, we don't even recognize each other. We don't even remember each other.

In Miami, when I first got there in about 1976, I rode through the Black community and they were having a big funeral for one of their legendary coaches. His name was Nathanial Powell and his nickname was Traz. And I had been in the habit of sponsoring young boys—I'm a PE teacher in elementary school—to play Optimist football whose parents either couldn't or wouldn't pay for their registration fee. And there was one boy—I had paid for him for several years—and he had now gotten to the point where he was getting pretty good. He walked by the school one day and I called him in and asked him what was happening. He said that he had been selected for the All-Star team and that they were going to play in a game. I said, "Well, that's great. Where is the game going to be?" Now remember TRAZ POWELL was the man's name. They had named the stadium after him. So he told me that he was going to play at the TRASH PILE. I said, "Where?" "The TRASH PILE." "Well, where is that?" "Over there at the Miami Dade Community College." "Oh, you mean Traz Powell Stadium." So Traz Powell is already gone from the consciousness of everybody in Miami and the stadium is now the Trash Pile.

So when we recognize that Warren Armstrong used to play here, that is a tribute to all of us. Because in a very short time they are going to say, "Warren who?"—and have no idea who I was or who we were.

So we need to celebrate ourselves, and that is why I agree wholeheartedly with the naming of the court and give as much

thanks and accolades as I can to the people who were
responsible for making this happen.

Following the radio broadcast, lunch was served buffet style.
This meant that while people sat at tables they also were up and moving
about, mingling and visiting. While the majority were there because of
their history with Warren, I nevertheless had several friends (other than
the friends I had made through the initiative) with whom I wanted to
share the event and who were good enough—despite considerable
distance—to attend. Among them were Paula, of course, who had been
instrumental in helping me think through each step of the year-long
initiative; Randy Eccker, Ward Peters, and Doug Paterson from Omaha
(Randy and Ward with schedules that permitted them to stay only for the
luncheon), Don Mayberger and Phil Minkin from Lawrence, Kansas, and
Michael Herzmark from Los Angeles (Don and Michael documented the
luncheon and, later, the court dedication ceremony). The presence of
these individuals enriched the event enormously for me (see postscript).

After an hour or so of mingling I showed the video. Four of the
seven people interviewed in the video were present. Through their
interviews they reminded luncheon viewers not only of Warren's impact
on Kansas City high school basketball (and culture) but also of a time
that was for them—and for many of us present—both memorable and
important, a time when we were teenagers, imprinting to and acquiring
some understanding of the world outside family and neighborhood, a
time when we were awakening to differences and also eliminating
differences depending on the common ground we could find. This is one
of the reasons the field house was so important. It housed the basketball
court, and the court was our common ground. From the beginning, it was
Warren's court—and thus, the initiative to give it his name—but
symbolically it belonged to all of us, a place where we attempted to
demonstrate our uniqueness, witnessed and then tried to copy the best of
what we saw in others, played to win but within a refereed framework,
winners and losers at one level but all winners at another.

By 2:30, the luncheon was over with many planning to meet at
the field house at 6:00 p.m. for the court dedication. My wife and I were
the last to leave, and as we crossed the street to go to the Jazz and Negro
League Baseball Museums, Warren pulled up in his car. He was with his
wife, Mary, Len Trower and Al Smith. I asked him if he had enjoyed the
luncheon. "It was terrific," he said, "but it caused me to think about all
the people who deserve to be recognized but never are."

Al Smith joined us for a walk through the museums, and we
joined Carlton Lee (Philadelphia) and Dr. Herman Watson (Kansas City

physician and long-time friend of Warren). Carlton, "Doc," and Al are all jazz aficionados (as is Paula), familiar with the music and lives of many of the artists whose work is celebrated in the museum. Doc talked about something that had happened when he played at Drake University and went to New York for the NIT:

> We snuck out of our hotel to go to the Village Gate to hear Miles Davis. We paid $10.00 a ticket, fought through the crowd, got right up front and when Miles Davis finally came out he blew two notes and walked off stage. That was it! Ten dollars was a lot of money in those days, twice our per diem, plus we had risked getting in trouble with our coach just to be there. We went back upstairs and found Miles leaning against the building smoking a cigarette. We were just kids, nineteen or twenty years old, but we didn't have any problem speaking our mind: "Man, what are you doin?! That ain't right!" He put out his cigarette, turned to us and in his raspy voice said: "You right, you right." We all walked back downstairs. He played the entire evening. It was incredible! A great night! Of course, his decision to go back and play could have had something to do with the fact that my friend was 6'7" and weighed 250 pounds.

Before Al Smith was a basketball player—and eventually a member of Bradley University's All Century Team—he was a baseball player. Kennie Denmon, who grew up with Al (see Postscript), said that when Al was nine or ten years of age, everyone in their community had predicted that he would grow up to be a professional baseball player. This was Boonville, Missouri, in the late '50s. Each year, Al's father took him out of state where he could play baseball. When Al was eleven, his father decided that the Little League in Boonville should be open to his son. He approached one of the coaches and said that he would like for his son to play. There was a tryout and then—once they saw Al's ability (he was a pitcher)—a scramble among coaches to see whose team he would be on. That year, Al and three of his friends integrated the Little League in Booneville. His father "had wanted to show them that these kids could play." Al was drafted by the Majors out of the high school but he opted for college, playing baseball and basketball at Bradley University before entering the American Basketball Association.

Later that night, after the court dedication ceremony and the post-ceremony gathering at the Juke Joint, Al and I sat in the lobby of the Hyatt Regency where he told me a portion of his life story. He talked about growing up in Boonville above his father's bar in a predominately white community, the things he saw and later did; it's a story for another time and one that Al himself should tell.

After visiting the museums, we went back to the hotel and rested for an hour before heading to the field house. We were to arrive at 6:00 but were running late. When we arrived we found the parking lot full. The field house was packed, not by the standard established in the early days when Warren played, but nearly so. We discovered that a hospitality suite had been set up in another part of the field house and that Warren was already there holding court. The court dedication ceremony, scheduled for 6:00, did not begin until 7:30.

The students—cheerleaders, pep club, current players—formed a funnel that stretched from the opposite corner of the court to directly in front of the scorer's table. Mr. Wilson (school board member), Mr. Corporal (school district athletic director), Warren, and I were kept behind the bleachers as the announcer read Warren's bio of accomplishments. That was followed by Councilwoman Sharon Sanders Brooks' reading of the mayor's proclamation announcing that December 6th would be Warren Armstrong Jabali Day in Kansas City. We were then introduced and walked through the funnel of students to the area in front of the scorer's table: first Mr. Corporal; then me; then Mr. Wilson and Warren.

Mr. Wilson was the first to speak. He thanked the school board members for supporting the initiative and emphasized that this was just the beginning. He mentioned that this event was one step in an effort to help students in the Kansas City Missouri School District understand their history and that it would be followed by other steps, including a Hall of Fame honoring the other great players from this league. He then asked the students to do what they do best when they come to the field house: *"Make some noise!"*

The microphone was then handed to me, and I offered the following remarks.

I will be brief, but I cannot stand here without saying certain names. ALEX ELLISON. This event does not happen without Alex Ellison. Nor does it happen without KENNIE DENMON, MURVELL McMURRY, WILLIE STEWART, ROGER PENDLETON, and an ABA player with records of his own, AL SMITH.

Here is the history: Warren played in the first game ever played on this court. That night, and every night that he played, he put his signature on this court. Tonight culminates a one-year effort to return Warren's name to this court.

Warren Armstrong Jabali was an electrifying basketball player and more than any other person was responsible for the legendary, filled-to-capacity, early days of this field house. But we did not pursue this honor for Warren because of his basketball prowess alone.

In the future, when students ask, "Who was Warren Armstrong?" we want them to know that he was a great basketball player, that he came from this community, this league, this school district; but we also want them to know that he had a vision of service that went beyond basketball, that he was committed to issues larger than himself. We want them to know—as Rev. Nelson "Fuzzy" Thompson said when commenting on Warren: "It is one thing to be a great ball player, but it is more important to be a great person, to be someone who is respected for their principles and the things they stand for; and Warren is that kind of person."

So, for that reason as well as for his great achievements as a basketball player, it gives those of us involved in this initiative enormous satisfaction to know that this court—a court that has seen so many great players, so many great games—will be known from this point forward as the Warren Armstrong Court!

At that point, as arranged, the current members of Central High School's basketball team removed the covering over Warren's name on the court so he could see it for the first time. There was considerable applause and cheering, after which Warren spoke:

Good evening. As you can see, this is a great honor and I feel it as a great honor. But I don't think of it as an honor for me individually. I think of it as an honor for those that played during the time that I was playing. Because they, and they alone, know what this gym meant to us.

There will be those who say, "Well, why him?"

And I hope that the answer is because ARTHUR STROZIER says it should be him. CLAUDE HARDY says that it should be him.

*KENNIE DENMON, JOHNNY YOUNG, VERNON VANOY say it
should be him. RUSSELL WASHINGTON, JIM LAFFOON,
DAVE THOMAS, KEN CHRISTOPHER say it should be him.
And I'm sure BENARD STEVENSON, SCRAP IRON (ROBERT
FELLS) and BILL BOYKIN—the way we dogged them that night
when you all were still comin' in the door, they say the game was
over in the first quarter—I KNOW THEY WILL SAY IT
SHOULD BE HIM!*

*So all of those people who came after me that have such great
talent, they had their gyms. We couldn't go to our own gym; our
gym had a track on top of it and we couldn't even shoot out of
the corner. And when the field house opened, we were ecstatic.*

*So let it be known that all of those people who were a part of
basketball in Kansas City at that time, THIS IS FOR YOU!*

Even the students huddled in the far corners of the stands were
attentive when Warren spoke. And when he was done, enthusiastic
applause and cheering were provided by a crowd estimated at over five
hundred people, many of whom were from the time when Warren
played.

Mr. Corporal was the last to speak. He expressed his pleasure at
being part of the event, addressed Warren directly indicating that the
future of the Interscholastic League would make him proud, and then
invited the audience to *"GIVE IT UP ONE MORE TIME FOR MR.
WARREN ARMSTRONG JABALI!"*

The rest of the evening was taken up with visiting, watching the
game, and then later, a trip to the Juke Joint, a dance club where Warren,
his family, and a few friends finished out the evening.

IN THE PARTICULAR RESIDES THE UNIVERSAL

The names Warren mentioned in his courtside address had not been
heard in that field house for perhaps forty years. On any given night, few
in attendance would have known who they were. But in the minds of
many who played in Warren's time and who were present for the
dedication, these individuals constituted an array of archetypes,
categories of style and movement into which we could sort and make
sense of the players we later would see. This, I imagine, happens in
everyone's life; at some point, perhaps through a sport like basketball or
a game like chess, perhaps through the observation of friends and

acquaintances, an imprint of sorts occurs and a keener understanding of the various ways of playing or operating or moving in the world is acquired. Grace, power, touch, mental toughness, the role of confidence, all the ingredients get combined in various ways and against these combinations one assesses strengths and weaknesses (one's own and those of others) while also seeing for the first time new possibilities.

I made an effort to find out what had happened to the individuals Warren mentioned. (And, of course, there are others he could have mentioned and in fairness, though it was good of him to mention me, I cannot include myself in such a pantheon. I played; I loved the game; but he was talking about the stars or, as I am suggesting, the archetypes as they arrived or emerged in our community at that time.) So, with apologies to each for the sketchiness of my update, here is what I learned:

> **Arthur Strozier** played two years for the Kansas City Chiefs and now is an administrator in the Kansas City School District. **Claude Hardy** got off the homeless rolls in southern California and in recent years wrote a book on the role of black players in the history of basketball. **Kennie Denmon** retired from the Kansas City Power & Light Company after thirty-eight years and now pursues his interests in genealogy and golf while enjoying continued good health. **Johnny Young**, from what I understand, lives in Kansas City. Like the others listed here, he was a remarkable athlete. **Vernon Vanoy** played five years in the NFL (Green Bay, the Giants and Houston). He became a Rastafarian and now, so I am told, sells incense in LA. **Russell Washington** had a stellar career as an all-pro tackle for the San Diego Chargers, married a woman from Pata, Truk Island, in Micronesia and, according to what I could discover, lives there still. **Jim Laffoon** is a retired high school teacher living in Florida where he plays between 150 and 200 games of senior softball each year. **Ken Christopher** spent his working life in sales, is semi-retired, lives in St. Louis, and is an avid golfer. **Bernard Stevenson** lives in Kansas City. Beyond that I don't have any information about him, only that I imagine he continues to wrestle with the memory of the desperation shot that denied his team a trip to the State Tournament. **"Scrap Iron" (Robert Fells)**, sadly, is deceased. **Bill Boykin** is a State Farm Insurance Agent living in Kansas City and to this day remains unguardable.

CONCLUSION

I'm very proud of my involvement with this initiative. It was an honor to work with Alex Ellison, Kennie Denmon, Murvell McMurry, Roger Pendleton, Willie Stewart, Ed Corporal, Rev. Nelson "Fuzzy" Thompson, Ray Wilson, Kenny Wesley, Andre Riley, Derek Shelton (and for their participation in the video, Paul "Too Tall" Alexander, Coach Jack Bush, and Vicki Shelton). There were others whose names I no doubt am forgetting. We did it the right way. We were a team, each person playing an important part. It was a team that included Warren although he had played his part 45 years earlier. The important point is that when it came time for us to play our part, we did not drop the ball. And as a consequence, something that (in our view) should happen did— in fact—happen. Now, Warren's name is on that court and that means an important story will not be forgotten: Warren's story, but our story, as well.

Five weeks after the court dedication ceremony I received the following e-mail from Ed Corporal:

> Everything has been positive this year... We always start the games off saying: ***"Welcome to the Warren Armstrong Court!"*** It sounds so good. We just added new chairs on the bench and a new scorer's table that lights up. It looks like a college arena. We have a big game that is being televised Feb 20 on Metro Sports... Central is playing Lincoln.

Postscript II-A: Court-Naming Afterthoughts

- This event brought together individuals who had not seen one another for years. With no two people was this more true than with Kennie Denmon and Al Smith. The last time they had seen each other was in 1956, when Kennie was twelve and Al was nine. In that year Kennie's family moved from Boonville, Missouri, to Kansas City, Missouri. Kennie told me that he had wondered about Al, who had been an extraordinary baseball player even at that young age. Kennie said he had never associated the Al Smith of his childhood with the Al Smith he heard about in the ABA. When Al flew to Kansas City, Kennie picked him up at the airport.

- Warren had many friends in Kansas City, but there were three individuals who at their own expense traveled great distances to be a part of this event. They are not individuals who grew up in Kansas City, nor did they have anything to do with Kansas City high school basketball. Len Trower and Carlton Lee traveled from Philadelphia and Al Smith from New Jersey. All three met Warren during their college days. In the midst of their two to three days together, I'm not sure how much time these long-time friends got to spend with Warren, but from what I saw, not much. His time was spent with Kansas City relatives and friends. But Len, Carlton, and Al were not there to spend time with Warren—not first and foremost—but rather to stand in as witnesses to the honoring of a friend. And by their presence alone, they added to that honoring. Male friendship is a handsome thing when it is done in this way.

- I enjoyed a measure of this support as well. Ward Peters, Randy Eccker, and Doug Paterson traveled from Omaha. Seven hours of driving, and for Ward and Randy, only for the luncheon; and Doug, for the luncheon and part of the dedication ceremony. Phil Minkin and Don Mayberger came from Lawrence, Kansas, and Michael Herzmark traveled all the way from Los Angeles. All three lugged around the camera gear, and Don and Michael filmed the entire event: luncheon and dedication ceremony. None of these individuals knew Warren personally, though over the years they knew of my esteem for him and they certainly knew of the court initiative. It was a thrill to have them there. To speak at the luncheon and see Randy, Ward, and Doug in the audience, to see Michael and Don moving about doing everything they could to capture the event; it was dreamlike, a slight bending of space and time. And to see Phil at the scorer's table at the dedication ceremony—but not until I was in the middle of my courtside comments—was unbelievable, all the more so as Michael and Don circled with their cameras. It was Phil who, in an e-mail following the event, was kind enough to say that the event itself could be considered a *phenomenon sociologic,* i.e., an event recognized and responded to as meaningful by a community of people.

PROCLAMATION

Whereas, communities honor themselves whenever they acknowledge the exceptional individuals that come from within them; and,

Whereas, athletics enrich community life, providing enjoyment and life-lessons to participants and spectators alike; and,

Whereas, the Interscholastic League Field House has remained for over forty years the epicenter of Kansas City High School Basketball; and,

Whereas, no one is more responsible for the electrifying—and now legendary—early days of field house play than was Warren Armstrong Jabali; and,

Whereas, the Kansas City School District Board of Trustees has voted unanimously to rename the Interscholastic League Field House Court the Warren Armstrong Court; and,

Whereas, this honor is conferred not only in acknowledgment of Mr. Jabali's athletic achievements but also because of his commitment to education, lifelong learning, and service to the community,

Now, Therefore, I, Mark Funkhouser, Mayor of the City of Kansas City, Missouri, do hereby proclaim December 6, 2008, as

Warren Armstrong Jabali Day

In Witness Whereof, I have set my hand and caused the Official Seal of the City of Kansas City, Missouri, to be affixed this Sixth day of December, Two Thousand and Eight.

_____

Mark Funkhouser, Mayor
City of Kansas City, Missouri

Postscript II-B: Tributes from Across Town

In the spring of 1964, the *Kansas City Star* published the Missouri Writers' Association list of District All-Stars. Warren headed the list.

> Warren Armstrong of Central, regarded as one of the most talented basketball players ever to come from this area, heads the Kansas City District All-Stars that were announced last night by the Missouri Writers' Association. The 6-foot-2 Armstrong, who led the Blue Eagles to two successive third-place finishes in the state tournament, was virtually a unanimous choice among Class L coaches. In addition, most of them called Armstrong the most outstanding individual they had seen all season.

> Armstrong combined shooting, rebounding and playmaking to put a 3-way clamp on opponents with his amazing moves all over the floor. He averaged almost 30 points a game, and his rare jumping ability helped him average 14 rebounds.

Also named to the 1964 Kansas City District All-Stars team was Stan Slaughter of Lee's Summit. Stan went on to play at Southern Methodist University for two years and then to Rockhurst College, but the impact of Warren's play never left him.

Stan has spent his career as an educator focusing on environmental concerns: on green science and green practices. When he learned of Warren's death, Stan wrote the following piece, which was published in the *Kansas City Star* on July 16, 2012:

> I am deeply saddened by the death of Warren Jabali. He was the best natural athlete I've ever seen. I made the All-City first team with Warren and Lucius Allen. Though I only played one official game against him (and lost), I followed Central through the regionals in '63 and '64 as well as played in open gym games against him at Rockhurst in the summers.

> I'll relay two plays he made that I've never seen by anyone else of any size at any level. At the Ruskin gym in our regional final, after Ruskin beat our Lee's Summit team, he stole the ball from a very good player, Don Draper, and took off on a break away to the basket. He jumped at the free throw line, cocked the ball behind his head and smashed a monster dunk with two hands.

Then with cat-like quickness he switched the position of his two hands holding onto the rim and swung down, turning his body so that he ended up at the end of his swing facing back down court looking through the clear backboard over the rim. He then swung back down, released the rim and landed near the free throw line again and ran down the court without any show that he'd made the most incredible play in the world. The feeling of seeing that play still gives me chills. He did it so that he wouldn't crash into the stage and the three-deep crowd there.

The second dunk came at Southeast Field house later that year as Central played St. Louis Christian Brothers. The scene is a Central free throw with Warren in second rebounding position on the right. There were two 6'6" burly white guys from CB in first position. The Central player missed the shot hard against the left heel of the rim so that the ball bounced directly toward Warren but maybe 12 feet high. He soared straight up, caught the ball with two hands, drew it backwards and threw it down powerfully without touching the guy in first position. I was so shocked that I wanted to go outside and let what I'd seen sink in.

He was smooth, powerful, quick and friendly. I had never been around African Americans, being from a small farm out in the country. The awe I felt for his abilities carried over to his entire race. I figured that if a black man could be so superior in that field, there was nothing that black people couldn't do in any field. He was a great ambassador and went on to help many children in his working life.

Mike Thiessen played high school basketball in Kansas City in the early to mid-1960s as well. He attended Pem-Day High School and in 1964, as a junior, was named to the second team All-District team. The following year, his senior year, he was a first-team All-District selection. Following high school, Mike played for the Air Force Academy. It was Mike who was quoted in the *Kansas City Star* article referenced earlier: *"I played against Elvin Hayes and Don Chaney in college, but Warren was better than them. He did things in high school that Michael Jordan does now."*

Today, Mike is a practicing attorney. Like so many of us, he remains grateful for the opportunity to witness Warren in action and also play against him in high school. When sending me pictures of Warren from Mike's Pem Day Yearbook, Mike offered the following:

How many high school yearbooks do you think have dedicated four photographs concerning their basketball team to an opposing player? Ours did my junior year, Warren's senior season. This may not seem all that significant to some people, but I think it is nothing less than extraordinary.

We had a good team, not as good as my sophomore year, but we were 20-8. I averaged 20 pts and 15 rebs a game. But I think we had more photos of Warren than me. And appropriately so.

And no one, including me, thought anything of it then. That was due to the absolute respect we had for him, our genuine appreciation that we had the opportunity, indeed the privilege, to compete against a man of such talent, skill, class and presence. It may be that such a tribute has never been accorded to an athlete from an opposing school.

It should also be noted that at the time this yearbook was published Pem-Day was all white. We were not integrated until later that year, in August of 1964, the summer before my senior year. It was in this circumstance that a black athlete was accorded this recognition.

Part III

The Nature of the Game

As much as anyone I have known, Warren Jabali was interested in the "nature of the game", the larger game, the game he would play with increasing adeptness the rest of his life.

As a result of the Jabali tribute published on the "Remember the ABA" website, I developed a correspondence with James Owen, a.k.a. Jimmy Legend, an individual with much to say about "the nature of the game." I never met James, and I know very little about him beyond the fact that he had big dreams and a big heart. When I attempted to reconnect with him to say that I wanted to include our correspondence in this book, I learned that he had passed away the year before.

I first heard from James shortly after the posting of the Jabali tribute. He wrote the following:

> I have just finished reading your tribute to Warren Jabali I found on Remembering the ABA… It—and Mr. Jabali's letter that you enclosed—is the best of Basketball journalism I have ever read. It was historical, informative, inspirational and fulfilled the 3 pre-requisites of transcendent prose, namely it gave MEANING to our past, illuminated VALUE for the present and projected HOPE for the future. GREAT WORK, and without going into details, BASKETBALL was my life in NYC as a player, coach and student of this great game from 1969 to 1980, and there was nothing I didn't read or know about basketball the world over.
>
> I put your article at the top of everything because of its transcendent and universal message. Also, I am profoundly impressed with Mr. Jabali and his powerful intellect (who else in the NBA today would know of the word 'onus' and its meaning?) as revealed in his letter to the KC Star. You ended your article with the words, "…myself included, were enriched by it." Let me proudly say I am greatly enriched by your noble effort to bring this story to life and its royal sentiment has made my spirit soar!
>
> —James Owen

James was very generous in his comments. But he always made it clear, often in poetic riffs that he had thought a great deal about the nature of the game.

I posted the following to the "Remember the ABA" chat room. My exchange with James follows:

> Many of you are probably aware of a book of which I was unaware until today. It's called *Hoop Roots* and it is by John Edgar Wideman. Here is how it begins:
>
> > We went to the playground court to find our missing fathers. We didn't find them but we found a game and the game served us as a daddy of sorts. We formed families of men and boys, male clans ruled and disciplined by the game's demands, its hard, distant, implacable gaze, its rare, maybe loving embrace of us: the game taught us to respect it and respect ourselves and other players. Playing the game provided sanctuary, refuge from the hostile world, and also toughened us by instructing us in styles for coping with that world...
>
> Wideman adds:
>
> > Rather than a set of rules for playing the game, there is an instrument, the court, and the point of playground hoop is to coax music from it.
>
> There have been so many who have "coaxed music from it"— Bill Russell, Oscar Robertson, Elgin Baylor, Jerry West, Dr J, Magic Johnson, Larry Bird, Michael Jordan, Kobe Bryant—so many, and what I am suggesting is that Jabali was one of them.

———————————

dave...

thanks for telling us all about the book "Hoop Roots"... i definitely am going to look for it. your comments and insights are a slam dunk... thanks for sharing them. for me, basketball was not only "coaxing" the "music"... it was a way for me to "PLAY" and create my own music... all "REAL" ballplayers are really musicians and that is why basketball of all sports seems to have the most intimate affinity with music...ITS ALL IN THE SOUL, MAN! YOU CAN FEEL THE GAME AND THE MUSIC AS YOU PLAY IT... ESPECIALLY WHEN PLAYING

WITH OTHER GREAT HOOP VIRTUOSOS! ITS LIKE
COLTRANE AND ARMSTRONG AND MARVIN GAYE
AND JAMES BROWN ALL TOGETHER... (I KNOW YOU
KNOW WHAT I MEAN!)

> "sometimes i feel so good i jump
> back...wanna kiss myself..i got
> soul..and I'm superbad"
>> james brown

without getting into details the greatest influences in my life
were my grandmothers, basketball, and music... my grandparents
gave me love and support...but music and hoops gave me "MY
LIFE". its inspiration and imagination rescued me from the
despair, apathy, boredom of adolescence...it gave me something
to do...to create and grow into... they both gave me a "GAME"
to play in the world...

> TO BE...OR NOT TO BE...
> I WANTED TO BE!...
> as we all do...
> but its got to be something that was
> REAL and I had TRUE FEELING
> for... hoops and music...
> they were it for me...

of course, i didn't know any of this at the time of being a 15 year
old kid listening to music and playing ball on the streets of NYC
in the late 60's and early 70's...but its so CLEAR now...now i am
playing "another game"...what i think is the greatest "game" of
all...which is helping other players to be great "ballplayers" and
to "dunk the world"...but once again you and your insights have
inspired and reminded me of the "MAGIC" that is basketball and
music...thanks...and keep on playing the "GREAT BALL" and
"GREAT MUSIC"

> i see it...i hear it...i feel it!
> ROCK STEADY BABY... WHAT IT
> IS...WHAT IT IS...WHAT IT IS!

best wishes
jimmy legend nyc

James,

In high school, we talked non-stop about the "great move" – the ability to create, pass, shoot, increasing the capacity of others.

We would look everywhere for great moves and talk about them when we saw them. *Higher than the life of art is the art of life* (Will Durant). That's what we thought we were seeing, the art of life—like your comments on the nature of the game.

Please do stay in touch, James…it's my honor to know you.

DAVE,

It's not many people that can "bring inspiration" or bring "LIFE" to the world and i greatly recognize your brilliant insights and awareness of the "game". Each person in the world has to find something to "CONNECT" with…some "GAME" larger than themselves…

This "REMEMBER THE ABA GROUP" gives individuals who found it something special and wonderful in this "basketball" experience—a way to express and reveal and share the romance and collected memory of their "connections of the heart"… (which i think is the greatest thing in the world because it "CONNECTS" to life and the FEELING of being alive.)

Basketball, music, dance, art, words, film etc. are all ways we try and communicate and participate in this "feeling" and affirmation of life… "the real, the heart, the truth" of the "game"…what is called "SOUL"… because it goes beyond just the communication of facts and ideas and words and things…to the communication of "FEELING"…and all the great "music" and "ball playing" in the world originates from this authentic universal creative force and "feeling" which i call LOVE… that force and power within one's soul that desires LIFE…to participate and play and excel and share victory and success...and survive temporary defeats and loss. You once said something a long time ago i never forgot... "to let your spirit soar"...

My wish for you, ...and all the people who read this...

"MAY YOU ALL FIND AND PLAY
THAT GAME THAT CAN LET YOUR
SPIRIT SOAR and ALLOW YOU TO
DUNK THE WORLD EVERYDAY."

THANKS TO THE BENEVOLENCE
OF DIVINE PROVIDENCE I AM
FORTUNATE TO BE ABLE TO
"HAVE A GAME" and "DUNK THE
WORLD"...and each day can walk down
the street and sing...

"I DONT NEED NO MONEY,
FORTUNE OR FAME...
I GOT ALL THE RICHES BABY ONE
MAN CAN CLAIM...
I GUESS YOU SAY WHAT CAN
MAKE ME FEEL THIS WAY... MY
GIRL... MY GIRL... TALKIN 'BOUT
MY GIRL. oooohhhoohhh
MY GIRL...THATS ALL I CAN TALK
ABOUT IS MY GIRL"....

... "my girl" for me is "my world"...
may everyone get a piece of the world...
we all own it...and there is plenty to go
around!

jimmy legend
nyc

Part IV

The Odyssey of Black Men in America:
A Kansas City Perspective

In my experience, the "Sixties" did not arrive all at once. Rather, it arrived gradually and at different times for different people (and, of course, meant different things to different people). For me, the "Sixties," by which I mean the shake-up in consciousness that took so many forms but nevertheless began to permeate the time, did not begin until the second half of the decade. During the first half I was largely oblivious.

I remember the events of the day, certainly—the Cuban missile crisis, gunshots in Dallas, the Beatles on Ed Sullivan, Freedom Riders, Vietnam—but I had no real understanding of the time. I had a vague sense that change was perhaps occurring, but nothing more.

Politics were not discussed in our home. I do remember that my dad read a book or two about Thomas Jefferson and he offered to give me five dollars if I would memorize the Gettysburg Address. Still, as I recall, the health of the nation, the health of its various parts, the societal meaning of the events noted above, were not discussed.

My family was focused on "family" and on making ends meet. As for myself, I lived in my own bubble, a high school bubble with basketball and adolescent concerns at its center.

—

Warren may have had a similar experience. According to his two oldest brothers, Greg and Reggie, and his sister, Sheree, Warren had a normal childhood. Everyone knew each other in the Kansas City, Kansas, neighborhood where they grew up, and to a considerable extent, the same was true of their neighborhood in Kansas City, Missouri. Neighbors knew and looked after neighbors.

In order to address the needs of eleven children (Warren was the oldest), Warren's father worked both a full-time and a part-time job for much of his life. According to Sheree, their father was "a quiet, soft-spoken man who nevertheless carried a big stick," while their mother "was more outspoken, involved in the PTA and with neighborhood and community concerns." According to Greg, neither race nor politics were discussed at home. For Warren, said Greg, the focus was on basketball from an early age.

Kennie Denmon, who met Warren when the Armstrong family moved to the Missouri side of the river, did say that for some time he did not like Warren. Warren, he said, often told him that he was not "street" enough. And the Reverend "Fuzzy" Thompson, who grew up with Warren, offered a similar view: "He was rough around the edges... He would come into your house and open the refrigerator door: *'What's to eat?'* But always there was basketball. He loved the game. And he got better at it. All the time, he got better at it. You'd see him bouncing a ball up and down the street, 9:00 or 10:00 at night."

For Warren, as with so many at that time, the change in his set of concerns came with college.

—

Because of his basketball prowess, Warren received scholarship offers from around the country. The day he committed to attend Wichita State, the airline ticket to UCLA arrived.

Warren chose Wichita State, he said, for two reasons: First, he knew black players who had gone to WSU. He had spent time with them and felt comfortable in their presence. In particular, there was Ernie Moore, one of the truly great players to come from the Kansas City area. Warren greatly admired Ernie's game. He once told me that Ernie was one of the few players he would actually pay to see play.

The second reason Warren chose WSU was because, as he put it, he did not believe he had the social skills necessary to operate at a bigger school or with middle-class blacks. He was more at home with the players he knew at WSU.

So, in 1964, Warren entered Wichita State University and began a WSU Hall of Fame career. That same year he met Len Trower-Mfuasi.

In an e-mail I received from Len, he recounts his first meeting with Warren. "I came to Wichita from Philly, heard about this baaddd dude with a basketball, went to one practice, but came away unimpressed. Made the mistake of telling one of his homeboys that I wasn't that impressed (after all, I grew up with Earl Monroe). Next thing I know, there's a knock on the dorm door, a booming voice, and a 'proud walking' Warren strolls through the door, asking, *'Who's the man who said he wasn't impressed with my game?'"*

That meeting began a lifelong friendship. Len, already steeped in thought concerning the extremes of racial injustice, guided Warren to literature, to teachers, and to various national movements. At the core of what came to be their shared philosophy was the notion of self-determination; namely, that the individual, indeed, the community of which the individual is a part, can take responsibility—complete responsibility, if it must—for the realization of the potential residing within it.

Black nationalism in the form articulated by Maulana Ron Karenga, the founder of Kwanzaa, affected them deeply and served as foundation for their view. Self-reliance and service to the black community remained its hallmarks, as did their belief in the resourcefulness of the black community, its capacity to transform societal structures or create new ones.

At the same time, both Warren and Len continued to develop their own perspectives on matters of race and social justice. They read widely, exposing themselves to an array of literatures, from philosophy, psychology, and economics to history and the arts. They also steeped themselves in continuous dialogue—dialogue with one another and with others, like-minded or not.

—

They were not alone. WSU recruited basketball and football players from around the nation. Many of these recruits were black men from urban centers: Philadelphia, Chicago, St. Louis, Dallas. These players came to WSU with a set of concerns, a set of life experiences, a consciousness different from the consciousness and life experiences possessed by most of the students from central Kansas.

Kenny Lee (who for a while held the record for the number of carries in a major college football game – 53), Melvin Reed (a member of WSU's 1965 Final Four team), Ron "Slim" Washington (a basketball player and later a labor organizer and president of the Black Telephone Workers for Justice), Mansa Moussa Abdul Allahmin (a football player who would become a Black Panther and then, deciding he must work within the system, a social worker), Mohamed Sharif (also a member of WSU's 1965 Final Four team and later, a curator of traditional African Art from tribes all over the African continent): These individuals and others, along with Warren and Len, formed a subculture focused on friendship and consciousness raising. Their daily give-and-take on matters of race and social justice affected them deeply. Years later, the members of this small group would talk about how they raised one another.

—

With the support, then, of this circle of friends, and through dialogue and study, Warren's consciousness changed; and so, too, his sense of identity. He was a young African American man, a basketball player blessed with enormous physical gifts, but he was now, as well, a young man committed to the struggle of African American people.

This newly acquired sense of identity never left him. A few months after his death, Mary Beasley, Warren's wife, reflected, "If you were involved in trying to make things better in the African American community, Warren would help you in every way he could. But if you weren't involved in trying to make things better, he wouldn't give you the time of day."

Of course, how best to serve the African American cause was an evolving discussion, as was the notion of what it meant to be a man in service to that cause—indeed, what it meant to be a man, period.

———

At Warren's sixtieth birthday celebration, his long-time friend and prominent Kansas City physician, Herman Watson, commented that the thing he most appreciated about Warren was his toughness. "Yes," he said, "Warren was a great player, but it was his toughness that I liked."

Fatty Taylor, whose first year as a pro was spent with the Washington Capitols of the ABA, said, "Here's how tough Warren was: Bob Travaglini, the trainer for the Caps, told me that there's not a man alive that could have played on his knees. And he never complained. Never said anything about it."

Taylor continued, "All I can say is that Warren Jabali was a man's man. And he was a hell of a ballplayer. He could do everything: shoot, pass, drive, rebound, play defense, and he didn't take nothin' off nobody."

Taylor then related the following incident:

I'll tell you a story. My first year in the ABA was with the Washington Caps. Jabali and I were close. We lived in the same apartment building. I may have been his only friend on the team. He kept to himself, but when he was on the court he was the best teammate you could have.

Anyway, that summer there was an outdoor league. Tough players. *Really good players.* I'm from D.C. and I knew those guys.

Jabali's team was playing for the championship. Cars were parked for blocks and everybody was watching the game through the fence. I arrived late, and for some reason the game was at a standstill.

As it turns out, Jabali had been called for a fifth foul. He didn't think it was a foul and he refused to leave the court—in fact, he sat in the middle of the court preventing the game from proceeding.

"You better get your boy." That's what I was told the minute I arrived, told by the brother of the referee who had called the foul. *"We'll kill that .....! You better get your boy!"*

So I walk out to the middle of the court. Everybody is watching to see what will happen. "Hey, Warren, what's going on, man?" He tells me what happened and that he's not getting off the court. "Warren, these are some tough dudes. Somethin' bad is gonna happen. These boys don't mess around."

All I can tell you is that Warren didn't move. Twenty minutes later they reversed the call so the game could continue. Warren's team won the championship.

Taylor concluded by relating a story told to him by Bernie Williams, then a member of the San Diego Rockets of the NBA:

Alex Hannum, then coach of the Rockets, was walking through the Rockets locker room as his players were hotly debating who was the toughest player in the NBA.

Finally, Hannum interrupted: *"You guys don't know what you're talking about. The toughest player in basketball (referring to Jabali) is in that other league."*

It was in this interview that Taylor offered the comment that is quoted at the beginning of the book: *"If he would have played in the NBA for any length of time he would have been among the 50 greatest players of all time. No question. You can take that to the bank."*

—

In 2004, I received the following e-mail from Warren:

Nothing much new on this end. I have not lost very much weight but my appetite is changing and I don't eat as much or as badly. I hurt my back playing basketball and it has taken about 6 months for it to get back to a point where I feel confident about exercising again.

There was a nice article in the Oakland Tribune with comments from Rick Barry, Larry Brown and myself. Rick made the statement that I was a racist because I didn't pass him the ball. Larry described it as my having a difficult time getting along with white folks. He added that we never had a problem on the court.

I never gave much thought to what impression I made on people back then. I decided to write a little piece on the subject but lost motivation because there is really nothing to do with it.

I may be going to KC for our 40-year graduation activities. That is an amazing number to look at in print.

I read the piece in the *Oakland Tribune* and encouraged Warren to write his response. I doubt that he needed my encouragement, however, as within days I received his response to the article.

The *Oakland Tribune* article follows, as does Warren's response. I should add that Warren's response (more appropriate perhaps to call it an essay) also appears in Mary Beasley's book.

Brief stay in Oakland produced ABA championship for Oaks

by Dave Newhouse
Oakland Tribune, Friday, January 23, 2004

They were the Oakland Oaks, who won the 1969 American Basketball Association championship and then were gone by the next season.

"It's part of history," said Rick Barry. "It was a bush league, not unlike being in the NBA, which wasn't a great bargain then either. It was a stone age."

Well, at least, the NBA had Bill Russell, Wilt Chamberlain, Oscar Robertson, Jerry West and Elgin Baylor. The ABA, at the time, had Barry, and that was about it for superstars.

Then when Barry tore up a knee 18 games into his first active season with the Oaks—legally he had to sit out one season after jumping leagues from the then San Francisco Warriors—the team needed a new identity.

"We had a lot of depth," said Larry Brown, the Detroit Pistons coach who was the Oaks point guard. "And we had a phenomenal coach in Alex Hannum."

The Oaks were a curious mix. A minority owner was Pat Boone, the 1950s pop singer and movie star. Hannum replaced Bruce Hale, Barry's then father-in-law, as coach after leading the 1968 Philadelphia 76ers to the NBA title.

The Oaks then traded Steve "Snapper" Jones to New Orleans for Brown and Doug Moe, the ABA's top scorer. The Oaks signed two exciting rookies, Henry Logan and Warren Jabali, who then went by his birth name of Armstrong.

Ira "The Large" Harge was the center, with Logan, Garry Bradds and Jim Eakins the top three reserves. When Barry went down, Bradds took his spot and the Oaks didn't lose any momentum, continuing on to a 60–18 season.

Jabali was ABA Rookie of the Year, but not without incident. He kicked Jim Jarvis of the Los Angeles Stars in the head and was suspended 15 days.

"Rick was getting 16, 17 free throws, and I was getting killed," Jabali recalled. "Jarvis snatched my arm and snatched the ball. I knocked him down and stomped him. It's something I regretted, but it's the only time I had a real confrontation."

This was a militant time in sports, and Jabali not only seemed moody to teammates, but racist.

"I had a teammate who wouldn't pass me the ball because I was white," said Barry, alluding to Jabali.

"He had a hard time dealing with people of my color," said Brown, "but we never had a problem on the court."

Thirty-five years later, Jabali defended his social position.

"Those were class issues, not race issues," he said. "I came out of a segregated situation (in Kansas City, Kan.). I didn't go to the University of Kansas because I wasn't comfortable with upper-class blacks. I went to Wichita State because I was more comfortable with blacks who were from my situation."

Thus, Jabali identified with Logan more than his other Oaks teammates. But Jabali was an absolute force on the floor, and his game soared in the ABA championship series against the Indiana Pacers, led by Roger Brown and Mel Daniels.

The best-of-7 series was tied at 1–1 in Indianapolis with seconds left when Jabali received an inbounds pass and made a remarkable 35-foot turnaround jump shot that sent the game into overtime.

"There was no pressure," said Jabali. "It was a real easy shot."

Jabali had 30 points that night as the Oaks won. He then scored 37 as the Oaks took a 3-1 series lead. The fifth game was in Oakland on May 7, 1969. Jabali poured in 39 points as the Oaks won 135–131 before 6,340.

"That was one of the greatest years of my life," said Brown. "I hadn't played in two years, and the ABA gave me a chance to play again. I played with a great group of guys and a Hall of Fame coach. It was about as much fun as it gets. I loved that area, and almost came there seven years ago (to coach the Golden State Warriors). My wife is still mad at me over that.

"There were a lot of wonderful things about that league. The players from different teams went out with each other. We stayed in the same hotel as the referees."

What wasn't wonderful was the ABA's red, white and blue basketball.

"I hated that ball," said Barry, "not because it was red, white and blue, but because it had abrupt edges and it was slick. It didn't have a nice feel in your hands."

"Those Who Carried Us Away Captive Required of Us a Song . . . Those Who Wasted Us Required Of Us Mirth"
Warren Jabali

A writer from the *Oakland Tribune* called me recently to get my thoughts on being a member of the 1968–69 American Basketball Association champion Oakland Oaks. That team boasted members such as Larry Brown and Doug Moe who later became NBA coaches. The team also included Gary Bradds, an All American from Ohio State, Henry Logan and me. In addition, we had Rick Barry, who played only in the first 18 games of the season due to a knee injury.

During the interview the writer told me that Rick had stated that I was a racist and was a teammate who would not pass him the ball because he was white. I do not know if these quotes are accurate but they nonetheless deserve examination. They deserve examination because those of us who came into adulthood during that time have never openly and honestly had any discussion about the dynamics of those days. There are sure to be opinions held by all that have yet to find expression.

It would seem to me, however, that Rick would put forth something a little more substantive than I wouldn't pass him the ball. The preponderance of evidence contradicts his assertion since I was second behind Larry in assists, and it would have necessitated my passing only to Ira Harge and to myself since we were the only black starters. I fail to see, with all of the other possible subject matter, why this should be his focus. We could not have gone 68–13 and become ABA champions with that kind of animosity on the court. A more gracious person would have commented perhaps about the high expectation which existed for him to lead the Oaks to higher attendance and a championship, how his injury cast doubt upon that goal, how the team coalesced without him and how I surprised most people by averaging 33 points and 12 rebounds in the championship series and 28 points for the entire playoff. These are, of course, the type of numbers which would have been recorded by him had he played. Can it really be that what Larry and I remember as fondly as a great and wonderful time can only be commented upon relative to one's feelings about the texture of the ball and not receiving it enough?

There is nevertheless a modicum of validity to Rick's charge related to race, although it certainly has nothing to do with passing a basketball. The 1960s was an explosive decade with regard to race in America. Although it would be a misnomer to call the period the beginning of the end of active white racism and terrorism which had been directed toward blacks for centuries, it was certainly a decade which witnessed acceleration in black assertiveness. The actual beginning was of course when the abolitionists, Sojourner Truth, Frederick Douglass, Paul Robeson, Bayard Rustin, Luizo, Swerner, Goodman and others made their stands. The racism which these outstanding Americans targeted was the "racism which is the scientifically unsubstantiated belief that each human race is characterized by distinctive attributes which determine behaviors and capacities, and that a particular race is inherently superior." I did not maintain a belief that white people possessed any attributes or capacities that were inferior to mine. I did and do maintain however that white people exhibited behaviors toward black people which were despicable and disgraceful. Since it was impossible for me to know whether a white person was harboring such attitudes and behaviors, I chose to cast a wary eye toward all.

As far as I am concerned and given my background, this was the prudent thing to have done. The socially acceptable thing to do, according to some, was for me to continue in the vein of proving to white people that we were their equal. I saw that as placing blind faith in the hands of strangers. A passage from the Bible illustrates the dilemma faced by those of us who began the integration process.

"Those who carried us away captive, required of us a song; those who wasted us, required of us mirth." This is the sentiment of the Hebrews during their captivity. The "captives" allude to the arrogance and the ignorance of those in the ruling classes with respect to their attitudes toward those whom they subjugate. The rulers demand that the subjugated "not worry and be happy" and never display resentful, discontented nor hostile countenances.

The aforementioned sentiment compels blacks to project what Franz Fanon called "Black Skins, White Masks." W.E.B. DuBois called it "twoness." Listen as DuBois expresses his point of view. "It is a peculiar sensation, this double consciousness, this sense of always looking at oneself through the eyes of others, of measuring one's soul by the tape of a world that looks on in amused contempt and pity. One ever feels his twoness—an American, a Negro; two souls, two thoughts, two unreconciled strivings; two warring ideas in one dark body, whose dogged strength alone keeps it from being torn asunder."

Dubois' insight and the Hebrew lament are accurate reflections of the feelings of most African Americans up until at least 1970. Although all groups of people have their "Edward G. Robinsons," that is to say they have accommodationist strands, most African Americans were about the business of redefining their relationship to white people particularly during the late sixties, and did not relish the role of being required to make white people feel comfortable when the setting was mixed.

This accommodationist relationship was one in which blacks had to look the other way and give no apparent significance to events such as the killing and mutilation of Emmett Till, the Ebony Magazine yearly count of black men lynched and burned in America, the four little girls killed by a bomb while in church, James Meredith being shot while attempting to enroll in college, the assassination of Martin Luther King and the assassination of Malcolm X. All of these things and infinitely more were being done by white people.

The relationship had also forever been one whereby blacks had to be an "example for the race" and not make any blunders that would jeopardize the opportunity for other blacks to get a chance. This relationship of course had been based upon the African American's relegation as an inferior and as an intruder into white affairs. History reveals that sports have been the main instrument of integration in this country. Paul "Tank" Younger, the football player from Grambling, and Jackie Robinson, the baseball player from UCLA, were the cross bearers for black folk. They had to be highly skilled athletically and socially and are to be commended for the sacrifices that they made. Many other black men became highly skilled and highly sought after by the sports industry, but not all of them had the "social skills" of Younger and Robinson. Fortunately, they did not have to.

More and more blacks got opportunities as owners of professional teams acted upon what would later be an Al Davis admonition: "just win, baby." By the time I began playing professional basketball it was no longer required that black men be like Younger or Robinson. The only actual requirement was to be better that most of the non-starting whites on the team. Very few if any black men sat on the far end of the bench. Black men were playing and starring. Consequently the attitudes of the black players began to change accordingly. My attitude reflected the indifference that I saw in the attitudes of whites toward me. The burden had not been transferred to me of carrying the banner of the race. The white world did not extend an invitation to me and I sought none.

My introduction to this world took place in college at Wichita State University where the majority of blacks on the campus were athletes. We saw whites in the classrooms and student center and interacted with whites on the practice field and in games. We did not go to the same parties or clubs and did not chase girls together. Sometimes we had relationships with white girls, but those relationships were clandestine affairs carried out under cover of night.

We got precious little training in dealing with the larger society because we did not get invited to activities where personal interactions were occurring. I was one of those who had no experience socializing with whites and consequently had no desire to make social acquaintances of white people. This condition existed not because I disliked white people but rather because I had been segregated from childhood through my senior year of high school and in addition was also taught to fear white people. (Emmett Till had been murdered for speaking to a white girl.) With all of the things that were happening to black people at the hands of white people it simply never occurred to me that they were awaiting my entry into their world with open arms. So I felt no obligation to step into the abyss and ascertain where the bottom might be.

Rick Barry's accusation of racism has to be weighed with the events of the time. Rick is operating from the point of view that is understandable for him. Most Americans are uninformed and ill informed about race relations in this country. Consequently, the opinion that he held during that time, and the one that he continues to hold, is incomplete and erroneous. His opinion does not take into consideration key social and racial realities.

Rick did not consider that in 1964 when Bobby Mitchell left Cleveland and signed with the Washington Redskins that he was compelled by management to sing "Dixie" at one of their functions. Earl Faison and Ernie Ladd had a gun pulled on them and were promised that they would be shot if they attempted to enter a club in New Orleans. That event prompted the black players for the American Football League to boycott and have their all-star game moved from New Orleans to Houston.

Rick never experienced treatment such as that. Rick was not only a member of the dominant group, he was also one of its princes. His attitude was that professional basketball provided him with a wonderful opportunity for fame and wealth and that anyone with such an opportunity should maximize it, as he did. He seems to have failed to realize that black players could not do what he was able to do. During our playing days a comment was made and attributed to someone in management that there were too many black players in pro basketball. Good white players were highly prized. Rick promoted himself well and saw pro basketball as a marketplace that anyone could exploit, but he underestimates the double standard that existed.

His self-promotion, as expert as it was, does not however qualify him as an expert on the psychology of race relations in America. My opinion is that he thought black folk should have been so satisfied with arriving in professional basketball that nothing else should have mattered. Rick and white people in general assumed that blacks and whites being teammates and "league mates" should have or could have somehow eradicated the realities of black life in America. I already knew that whites and blacks playing on the same team did not directly correlate to off court relationships.

During my time at Wichita State University not one of my white teammates invited me or any other of the black players to join in any of their activities off the court. I never met any of their parents, and I never took any trips to their hometowns. I had no idea who their girlfriends were. If they lived off campus, I could not have located them in case of a team emergency. Life was such that we didn't expect them to include us in what they did and it never occurred to us to extend such invitations, thus off court camaraderie was never an issue.

People found my attitude inscrutable because I did not subscribe to the conventions of the day. I had learned from reading and studying about the Black Struggle that the integrating of black and white societies was a one-way street. It was the black person who bore the brunt of the responsibility for "getting along." We were expected to demonstrate a cordiality that would allow white folk to feel comfortable enough to relate to us. If we did not happen to have the experience and exposure to relate culturally and intellectually, we usually resorted to humoring. If a black man chose not to initiate exchanges on any of these avenues, he was assumed to be hostile, angry or someone who "hated" white people. What crime is it to be "indifferent" to white people?

I typically let statements concerning attitudes and opinions about me go unchallenged. I have accepted that very few people got to know me and that the description of my being enigmatic, as far as they are concerned, was essentially correct.

This time around, however, surprise overtook me. Surprise not by the comment but by the commentator. Rick has always been a person whom I have admired and respected. My most lasting impression of Rick came as I worked with the organizers of the first Indiana Black Expo. (It is continuing to go strong now after some 30 years.) I was put in charge of recruiting players to play in a nationally televised Martin Luther King benefit basketball game. I called Rick and asked him to play. He had a previous commitment on the East Coast but said that he could arrange to come in to play the first half and then run to the airport to complete his connection. I think most people would have just said that they were too busy. This was not something that I felt that he did for me, but rather for the cause of civil rights, and with that act he gained my respect. He obviously doesn't know these things; therefore I decided to take an opportunity to inform him, as well as give some clarity to the larger issue.

With concern to the larger issue, I think we Americans are severely myopic. Why does the issue have to be whether Warren Jabali liked white people as opposed to did white people like Warren Jabali? I was a member of the victimized class and as such should not have been expected to react with anything other than suspicion. The fact that white people felt no requirement to demonstrate to me that they were not one of those who would "waste" me, means that I was to step onto the plane having to experiment by extending my emotions in hope of gaining approval. Remember, as a child of the segregated '50s and a teenager in the tumultuous '60s I saw white people as oppressors and mean spirited people. In my mind the question should have never been "Did I like white people?" but rather "Do white people like me?" With a backdrop of James Meredith being shot for trying to enroll in college, the four little girls getting bombed while in church and the murder of Martin Luther King, just to point out a few atrocities, the greater question has to be "Why on earth should I have liked white people?" What have they done that I should put down my guard and embrace them? If one looks at white folks as I did, which is as a monolith, then they were to be as despised as the Egyptians were by the Hebrews. Certainly there were "individual" white people who were committed to the cause of human rights, but I didn't grow up with any. To this day only Jim Eakins,

Claude Terry and their wives have demonstrated the humanity that compels me to share mine with them. Jim Eakins is the only white player, from college or professional ball, who actually sought to understand and challenge my thinking on the subject of race in America. A former high school opponent of mine has turned out to actually be a good friend. We exchange thoughts and ideas.

In retrospect, most of these issues were class issues. They were issues of education, exposure and experience. Steve Jones was the perfect example. Steve was smart, well versed on a lot of subjects and dealt with white folks on a level plane. Steve ended up as a national broadcaster for the NBA.

We can see today that when black kids grow up in the more affluent neighborhoods and go to better schools the aforementioned racial issue is ameliorated. Issues of race have not disappeared, but wealth and opportunity are great equalizers.

The professional players of the days of blatant segregation and discrimination constantly look back and measure their responses to the great issue of their day, mostly with pride for the things which they "took" or which they "stood" for. The black professional players of today should draw from the examples of Jim Brown, who created the Black Economic Union, and Magic Johnson who believes in investing in urban areas. Up until this point the black athlete has had an historical importance that transcended the playing field. If the current and future African American athletes are only going to be measured by what they do on the field, then they will have abandoned their historical calling. As long as they have not witnessed an end to the social, political and economic problems of their race, what then is "required" of them?

My friend Bill Tuttle, a professor of American Studies at the University of Kansas, had expressed considerable respect for Warren's essay, and he was not alone. Not long after the essay was posted, I received the following note from Bill Noack:

> Dave: Just read the outstanding piece on Warren Jabali on the ABA website. I played basketball at Michigan State in the 1960s and, like most white players of that era, had no understanding or appreciation of the social pressures that my black teammates faced. Do you happen to have an e-mail address for Warren as I would like to drop him a note. Thanks much. —Bill Noack

I provided Bill with Warren's e-mail address and on November 8, 2007, Bill sent the following note to Warren:

> Dear Warren: I just read on the ABA website your outstanding letter in response to (the Oakland Tribune article). I played basketball at Michigan State in the mid-'60s and later lived in Indianapolis where I became a follower of the ABA. I remember many nights at the Indpls. Fairgrounds Coliseum when you caused the Pacers a great deal of grief.
>
> What struck me about your letter was how well it was written and how completely it outlined a very complicated subject: race relations in American sports, particularly in the '60s and '70s. When I was at MSU (my last year was '63) most of my teammates were totally ignorant of social issues. Mostly, they wanted to get laid or get drunk or just watch TV. That applied to whites and blacks alike. I don't recall many intellectuals. I roomed with a guy named Pete Gent, a good basketball player who was drafted by the Dallas Cowboys and played 6 years in the NFL. Since then, Pete has written some good novels, including *North Dallas Forty*, about some of his adventures as a Cowboy. I stayed with the program and got a degree in journalism from MSU.
>
> Concerning the dumb racial remarks I heard from players I knew... most were made out of sheer stupidity and ignorance rather than outright meanness. Hope you're doing well and, again, it was a pleasure to read your fine letter.
>
> —Bill Noack

The Odyssey of Black Men in America:
A Kansas City Perspective

On August 29, 2010, Warren's sixty-fourth birthday, I called to wish him well. During the call I mentioned a project that my friend, Bill Tuttle, had suggested to me a few years before. Bill is the author of several books on American history, including *Race Riot: Chicago in the Red Summer of 1919,* and he had been very impressed with Warren's two essays on his playing days in high school and the ABA. In the course of discussing these essays with Bill, an idea emerged: to write a book focusing on black men who had taken a principled stand on social justice during the '50s, '60s, and '70s but who, generally speaking, were not well known. These men deserve to be known, however, and their stories are important to the historical record and their lives, if known, would enrich and expand the array of role models available to black youth and others. This was Bill's idea, and it was this idea (and project) that I mentioned to Warren.

Warren was enthusiastic about the idea and began suggesting names, largely from the world of sports. When I asked how we might proceed, he suggested that we encourage Len Trower—a long-time friend of Warren's—to travel from Philadelphia to Kansas City over the Christmas holidays and that the four of us (Warren, Len, Bill, and I) meet to discuss the project and perhaps outline our next steps.

I then called Bill to share Warren's response. Although Bill had initially been enthusiastic, the size of the proposed undertaking had begun to sink in. Originally, when Bill had suggested the idea, he was active in the Department of American Studies at the University of Kansas and interested in finding a last project to which he might devote himself prior to retirement. By the time I proposed the idea to Warren, however, Bill had retired and was enjoying a new chapter in his life. The prospect of undertaking a project of this scale now seemed daunting. Thus began our search for a scaled-back version of the proposal.

A number of discussions concerning our proposal occurred by phone and e-mail during the months of September and October. On October 25 I sent the following e-mail to Warren:

> Here is what I would like to propose: that we have a
> gathering when you are in Kansas City over the
> Christmas holiday and that we invite Len Trower, Al
> Smith, Fuzzy Thompson, Doc Watson, Alex Ellison,
> Murvelle McMurry, Kennie Denmon, Willie Stewart,

Roger Pendleton and anyone else you and others think
should be invited; and that we have a seminar (of sorts),
a discussion or recounting of stories, all centered around
the topic of "The Odyssey of Black Men in America."

I've wondered for some time what Part III of our book
(if it is to be a book) should focus on. We have the
following:

> Part I – "Race and Athletic Greatness in America"
> Part II – "Naming and Necessity: Calling a Thing by
> its Proper Name"

And now, perhaps,

> Part III – "The Odyssey of Black Men in America"

Part III would tell the story—the individual odysseys
of—a cohort of friends who, for the most part, grew up in
the Kansas City area during the same time period. It
would be your story but it would be theirs as well, and the
attempt of course would be to identify and express what
goes beyond this specific story to whatever might be so
generally.

This is what I would like to see us do, with the video of
the event potentially serving as an educational video on
history, race, and cultural awareness.

But there are reservations that should be discussed.

Bill Tuttle called the other day saying that he had visited
recently with an African American academic whose focus
is, in fact, "the Odyssey of Black Men in America" and
that he (Bill) found himself wondering if two white guys
have any business involving themselves—as we have
been discussing—in such a project.

Originally, Bill was thinking that the project might
involve specific individuals from around the country—as
you and I had discussed on the phone—and not, as I am
proposing now, a focus on Kansas City and your cohort

largely. Still, the issue he raises remains relevant and one I have wondered about, as well.

When we were involved in the court-naming initiative and several of us had gathered at Alex's home to discuss our plan, I asked if it would be better to have an African American in the role I had assumed. The consensus was that it was fine the way it was and that I should continue. Still, the topic we are considering now is on another level. So, Bill and I thought we should ask you and get your assessment. Are we out of place? Should we back off, leave this topic alone?

For my part, should we proceed, I imagine myself in the role of coordinator and documentarian. I would write/edit Part III (if that is to be) and I would edit together a video (if the footage we get seems to warrant it—I still think we're making a movie of some sort). I would want to make a couple of remarks about how the event came about and I would want to identify—along with you, Bill and others—some questions that would be before the group as the discussion develops, but beyond that I imagine myself as observer.

As for Bill, I have never seen him in any situation where he did not have a great deal to contribute but he emphasized over and over on the phone his reticence about the presumption implicit in what we are proposing and that he had too much respect for the topic—and too much interest in it—to compromise it in any way.

So, what do you think? Should we back off, proceed with the gathering, or modify it in some way? Whatever you think is the way we'll go—

What we have done together has evolved so organically it's hard to know what's next. The gathering described above seems right to me but I could be wrong, and regardless, whatever we do, we'll take it one step at a time to see if something unanticipated calls on us to go another direction.

Let me know what you think and we'll go from there.

On October 31, Warren responded:

> As long as the information is accurate, any criticism can be withstood.
>
> As for me, I think that a national exploration is good, but in order for it to be "absolutely accurate" it must result from a compilation of local efforts of the type which you have described. I will participate in the KC connection but not a national one. I am really interested in friends getting together and "kickin' it."

With that, we began to put the event together. The first issue was where and when to hold the event. Next, we needed to decide whom to invite. One of the first people I called was Dr. Herman Watson, Kansas City physician and Warren's long-time friend. I had met Dr. Watson briefly and had been impressed when I heard him speak at Warren's sixtieth birthday celebration in Miami. I had not been aware of Dr. Watson's career as a basketball player. He had gone to Drake University where he was captain of his team, voted most valuable player and, according to the United Press and Associated Press, the best defensive guard in college basketball during his senior year in college.

"Doc" Watson was very gracious and expressed his willingness to participate. He added, "I always tell my son, 'You can't be average. Average will not get it. Not in this world and not for a young black man.'"

I also called Alex Ellison and Kennie Denmon. At the luncheon honoring Warren on the day of the court dedication, Alex had remarked that while I had driven the bus, he had served as navigator. That was certainly true. At every turn in that initiative, or whenever we got stuck, it was Alex who suggested the route through. We would not have reached our destination—and the court-naming initiative would not have been a success—without Alex.

Alex recommended several individuals whom he thought should participate, and he suggested that we consider holding the event at the Bluford Library, which is located at 3050 Prospect in the heart of the African American community. It is named in honor of Lucile H. Bluford, a journalist who spent her adult life working for the cause of civil rights. In 1955, she became the editor of *The Call,* Kansas City's African American newspaper, a position she held until the end of her life in 2005.

Alex also suggested that we secure the services of a capable moderator, someone who could handle the strong personalities who would be participating. He suggested Carl Boyd. Although Carl was born and raised in Chicago, he had been living in the Kansas City area for some time and was the host of a local radio program focusing on the civil rights movement.

When I was able to get in touch with Kennie Denmon, he promised to attend if his recovery permitted. Recent surgery on his hip and knee had curtailed his activities considerably. Kennie was accustomed to physical activity. I knew that he had been a highly regarded athlete in the 1960s—an All-City basketball player who had gone on to be a quarterback in college—but I had never seen him play either basketball or football. I never will forget, however, my friend Bill Boykin saying that Kennie was *"a bad boy!"*...an assessment that impressed me greatly, given that Bill was in that category for me.

In late October, I drove to Lawrence to pick up Bill en route to Kansas City where we had an appointment with Leon Dixon. Mr. Dixon is the author of *Future in Our Hands: Institution Building for Supplementary Education* and is a co-founder of the W. E. B. Dubois Learning Center, an enrichment and tutorial services program for Kansas City students that has been operating continuously since 1975. Mr. Dixon is a friend of Warren's and a long-time student and scholar of the Black struggle. Warren thought that Mr. Dixon's involvement was very important to our event.

We shared with Mr. Dixon the outline of our event, saying who was "on board" and asking for his participation. He said he would be happy to participate. He recommended other individuals as participants and he, like Alex, recommended Carl Boyd as a possible moderator. As for a location, he suggested the Bruce Watkins Cultural Heritage Center.

Our visit with Mr. Dixon lasted two hours. During that time he provided us with a treatise on African American history, concluding his summary by saying: *"Given the roles that black people must play in this society, as far as I am concerned, every black person I know should be given an Academy Award."*

At one point during our visit, Mr. Dixon told us a story about Kansas City Royals Hall of Fame baseball player George Brett. Brett had been voted to the All Star Team but was required to play not at third base (his normal position) but in right field. Uncharacteristically, Brett made two errors during the game. When asked why he had made those errors, Brett replied that it was because he was "playing out of position."

That was precisely what we (Bill and I) did not want to be doing, so we immediately asked, "Is there any way in which we are playing out of position?" Mr. Dixon replied, "Yes and no." He said that the event was underway and that the topic was worthy. We had done considerable work and should carry it through. He added, however, that the direction the event would take would need to be determined by the participants, as would any follow-up that might result.

As we left, Bill commented on Mr. Dixon's recounting of black history by saying, "He has the history correct." Then he added, "That's a very wise man."

The Dubois Learning Center is located two blocks from the house where I grew up. This meant that Bill was required to take the tour of "my neighborhood," including my boyhood home (actually, the lot where the house had stood); Swope Parkway, the route I had taken each day to Mark Twain Elementary School (which also had been torn down); and then Southeast High School and the Interscholastic League Field House where so much history had been made. Bill had been unable to attend the court dedication ceremony and I wanted to make sure he saw this historic building and saw, as well, Warren's name writ large on the court.

From there we drove to the Bluford Library to see whether it might serve as a location for our event. The library had a general meeting room that we felt would accommodate the number of participants we imagined attending. Overall, the Bluford seemed to be an acceptable venue. Our plan was that Bill would contact several acquaintances at the Kansas City Library in the hope of securing the Bluford meeting room for the afternoon of December 28.

After leaving the library, we drove back to Lawrence. It was raining, and traffic on the interstate highway had slowed to a crawl. This meant that we were able to have an extended conversation about a number of topics: people we both knew, our *Odyssey* initiative, Bill's career, and other topics ranging from the personal to the philosophical. I asked the following questions, and Bill responded:

> What do you think is your particular gift as an historian? *I think I can write well, say things clearly...bring a story to life.*

> I remember when you went to Stanford in the early '80s. While there, you looked into the field of psychology for a school of thought that might augment your work. What did you find that proved helpful? *When I was at Stanford, the psychologist Eleanor Maccoby told me that the field of psychology that I would find most helpful would be*

cognitive psychology. I was dubious at the time, but she was right. Beginning with Jean Piaget himself and moving to Lawrence Kohlberg and his student Carol Gilligan (author of In a Different Voice*) as well as studies in political socialization, I did find this literature to be extremely helpful. I also found very valuable the writings on psychosocial stages by Erik Erikson as well as studies done in social learning theory in the 1930s–'40s, the work by John Dollard on class and caste, the work of Robert Sears, and others.*

I always thought you were a very good father, but do you think that had you known about the work of the cognitive psychologists that you would have been a better father? *In some respects, I do. Their work made me aware of how fragile the developmental process is, how easily it can be distorted and how important a father's guidance and support can be. I knew this, of course, but their work drove it home.*

At the end of your last book (*Daddy's Gone To War: The Second World War in the Lives of America's Children*), you suggest that the variables that most determine individual development and shape social change are age, culture, and history. Do you still see it that way? *Yes, I do. That's why I think historians and social scientists should work together. All three variables are at play in a person's life. A given historical event affects each person differently depending on his or her culture and whether or not he/she is a child, an adolescent or an adult—to speak about it very generally.*

And what about that crazy question we all ask from time to time: Do you think that some kind of individual consciousness continues after the "biological container" falls away? *Yes, I do, but I don't know how it works.*

We also talked about *Tuttlefest*, a remarkable event held in downtown Lawrence and attended by 350 people. *Tuttlefest* was a celebration of Bill's career. A series of speakers—colleagues and former students—discussed Bill's contribution to them and to the field of American history. It was a joyous event. Adding to the festivity—and extending it through the weekend—was the fact that a lecture in Bill's honor was scheduled for the next evening. The lecture was given by Bill's long-time friend and colleague, Leon F. Litwack. Dr. Litwack is a general editor of *The Harvard Guide to African-American History* and author of *Been in the Storm So Long: The Aftermath of Slavery,* for which he won the Pulitzer Prize. His talk was entitled "Fight the Power," a title borrowed from the rap classic by Public Enemy. It was the inaugural lecture in what would become an annual lecture series: The Bill Tuttle Distinguished Lecture in American Studies.

The day following our trip to Kansas City, I met Alex Ellison, Leon Harden (a friend from high school), and Ralph Brown, owner of the Sportman's Barber Shop, for lunch at Gates Bar-B-Q. Warren had recommended that I contact Mr. Brown because Mr. Brown had followed the Kansas City sports scene for many years. His barbershop is renowned for its clientele, for the conversations about Kansas City's best athletes, and for the pictures of athletes that hang on the wall. For a while, according to Leon, Warren's picture was the only picture of a high school athlete on Mr. Brown's "wall of fame."

Leon and I had been good friends in high school but had lost touch after graduation. Later I learned that following high school Leon had attended Texas Western University (now Texas–El Paso University), played football, and later played briefly in the NFL. During his freshman year Texas Western, led by Bobby Jo Hill, David Lattin, Nevil Shed, Harry Flournoy, and Willie "Bitter Wolf" Cager, beat the Pat Riley/Louie Dampier-led Kentucky Wildcats for the National Championship. I remember where I was when I watched that game, in which five African American players defeated an all-white Kentucky team in what was considered the game that changed college basketball.

> "Kentucky was playing for a ring or watch," Lattin says.
> "We had something to prove. People didn't think we were capable of winning because of the color of our skin.
> Coach Haskins gave us the opportunity to do that. I still remember Coach Haskins telling us Coach Rupp had made a comment in a press conference right before the game that five black players couldn't beat five white players. If you add gasoline to a fire, it's going to burn harder."

According to the news report from which the above excerpt was taken, "it still bothers Flournoy...that the players from the two teams never shook hands afterward." (See Endnote 1.) In 2002, the "game that changed college basketball" was the subject of the film *Glory Road*.

Leon was friends with the players on the Texas Western team, particularly Bobby Jo Hill (*"He loved life and life loved him,"* according to Leon), and currently is involved in contacting Texas Western/Texas-El Paso University athletes for University Homecoming events.

During lunch, Alex, Leon, Mr. Brown and I discussed the planned event and began to list the names of individuals who should be invited. Among those mentioned was Ollie Gates, the founder of Gates Bar-B-Q. Alex felt that an event that potentially reached into the history of Kansas City would gain an important contributor if Mr. Gates were to participate.

About that time, Arzelia Gates, Mr. Gates' daughter, walked into the restaurant. We described the proposed event to her, and she said it might be something her father would be interested in knowing about, if not attending. Since the Gates Bar-B-Q international administrative offices were across the street, I decided to stop by and see if I could meet Mr. Gates and personally invite him. Unfortunately, he was not available. I did, however, follow up with a written invitation, and I made sure that he received the flyers announcing our event. I also sent him background material, including the story of our effort to name the Interscholastic League Field House Court in Warren's honor. I indicated in my cover note to Mr. Gates that Warren's career and the small piece we added to it by naming the court in his honor is a Kansas City story and that on the 28th we hoped to look more directly at the Kansas City story itself.

Unfortunately, Mr. Gates did not attend our event. Thanks to Alex, however, we made sure that Mr. Gates was aware it and was recognized for his role in the history of Kansas City's black community.

After returning home, I e-mailed Warren, Len Trower, and Doc Watson, catching them up on the planning for our event and concluding with the following comments:

> In the next couple of weeks, we should lock-in our times
> and finalize our location. As for panelists—though in a
> sense all who attend are panelists—we have the three of
> you and Leon Dixon; and then some old timers yet to
> commit. I have invited everyone I have talked to not only
> to attend but also to feel free to contribute.
>
> I will work on a description of the event, but for now I
> have told everyone that the title is: "The Odyssey of
> Black Men in America: A Kansas City Perspective"

At some level, it seems to me, the underlying question to be addressed by the panel (and others) is: "<u>What don't we know that we should know</u>?" In particular, what are the unique challenges that black men face in their effort to find "wholeness" in a culture set up to deny them that right? What is it that black men must address, overcome, transcend, etc. in order to actualize their inherent possibilities—socially, politically, economically, spiritually?

And by "we" I mean young black men, women, white people; *what don't we know that we should know.*

Let me know if I'm not moving in the right direction here.

THE EVENT TAKES SHAPE

Not long after returning home I received an e-mail from Leon Dixon indicating that he had talked to Carl Boyd about the *Odyssey* and that Mr. Boyd would be willing to serve as our moderator. I contacted Mr. Boyd and formally invited him to serve in that role He confirmed that he would be delighted to do so.

Also, prior to leaving Kansas City, I had been able to visit the Bruce Watkins Cultural Heritage Center to see whether it might be a possible location for our event (even though Bill had been successful in securing the Bluford Library). Given that our event was beginning to gather momentum, it seemed that the Watkins Cultural Center would give us more flexibility and certainly more room than would the Bluford Library, so I applied for its use. Fortunately, nothing was scheduled for December 28 and we were able to secure the facility (again, I must thank Alex Ellison for his assistance).

It was time to send out flyers announcing our event (we had compiled a mailing list of approximately thirty individuals). I had envisioned a series of flyers that would keep the event uppermost in everyone's mind, given that the holidays are a busy time. The first two flyers, which follow, were e-mailed a couple of weeks apart. Along with the second flyer I attached Warren's essays.

First Flyer:

The Odyssey of Black Men in America:
A Kansas City Perspective

<u>Date</u>:   December 28, 2010
<u>Location</u>:   The Bruce Watkins Cultural Heritage Center
                 3700 Blue Parkway
                 Kansas City, MO
<u>Time</u>:   2:00 p.m. to 5:30 p.m.
<u>Moderator</u>: Carl Boyd

<u>Format</u>:   A moderated discussion on the odyssey of black men in America as viewed by former athletes (and others) from the Kansas City area. There are several parts to the discussion:

Part I: Former athletes—from the '40s, '50s, and '60s—share their stories: where they played; who they played with; their coaches; their idols; their experience as black athletes in Kansas City at that time.

Part II: These same individuals and others interested in participating are invited to reflect on the odyssey of black men in America; on what should be known (or appreciated) that is not known; on what young black men should know; on what the larger culture should know; on manhood and the issues and obstacles that must be addressed in order to achieve it.

Part III: As this event has evolved, several individuals have expressed an interest in outcomes or possible "next steps." We want to leave time for this topic to be discussed, if interest in it remains.

As mentioned previously, if you are receiving this e-mail, you are welcome to invite spouses, adult children, friends, and interested others.

There are several individuals to be thanked for their role in making this event happen: Warren Jabali, William Tuttle, PhD, Alex Ellison, Leon Dixon, Leon Harden, Ralph Brown, Herman Watson, MD, Murvelle McMurry, Len Trower, Carl Boyd, and others who have provided names/contact information.

For those receiving this notice that I have not met, I was a member of the group that succeeded in getting the Interscholastic League Field House Court named in Warren (Armstrong) Jabali's honor. This event is, in part, an expansion of the dialogue that grew out of that initiative.

More detail on this event in coming days.

Second Flyer:

The Odyssey of Black Men in America:
A Kansas City Perspective

Date:	December 28, 2010
Location:	The Bruce Watkins Cultural Heritage Center
	3700 Blue Parkway
	Kansas City, MO
Time:	2:00 p.m. to 5:30 p.m.
Moderator:	Carl Boyd

How did this event come about?

Two factors were at play. First, there was the initiative that resulted in the Interscholastic League Field House Court being named in honor of Warren (Armstrong) Jabali. Out of this initiative came a dialogue and set of friendships in support of a follow-up initiative, if a meaningful one could be found

And second, a dialogue formed involving Professor William Tuttle (retired professor of American Studies from the University of Kansas and author of *Race Riot* and other books on black history), Warren Jabali, and myself. Professor Tuttle had been very impressed with Mr. Jabali's essays on his playing days both in Kansas City and in the ABA (see attached essays). In the course of discussing these essays, an idea emerged; namely, to write a book focusing on black men who had made a principled stand in the course of their lives (often at some considerable cost to themselves) but who, generally speaking, were not well known. Men, however, who deserve to be known, whose stories are important to the historical record of the past sixty or seventy years, and whose lives, if known, would enrich and expand the array of role models available to black youth and others.

Warren expressed interest in this project and proposed that the three of us, along with his long-time friend, Len Trower, meet in Kansas City over the holidays to discuss it. As we continued to discuss the project, however, the ambition of it seemed beyond what might be available to us in the way of energy and resources. So the idea was scaled back until, eventually, we hit on the notion of the gathering we now have scheduled for the 28th.

The Odyssey of Black Men in America: A Kansas City Perspective is billed as a discussion of two, maybe three, parts. What will Part I be about?

The men participating in Part I are Kansas City athletes from the '40s, '50s, and '60s. These men know better than anyone else an important slice of Kansas City history because they lived it and, in fact, helped create it. It's the history of athletics in Kansas City (Kansas and Missouri)—at least a part of that history. We want to hear from these men, their stories, their biographies, en route to understanding an important influence and an important time in the life of Kansas City.

We will ask these men to tell us what it was like to be an athlete growing up in Kansas City, who inspired them, what it was they admired in fellow players and in their coaches, where they found their support and what arose as challenges. This will be the focus of Part I.

(Next time—if there is a next time—perhaps we will focus on artists, musicians, businessmen, etc., but this time it's through the eyes and experience of athletes that we will remember and honor an important part of Kansas City's history.)

What will Part II of the discussion be about?

Part II focuses on some of the themes we anticipate emerging in Part I. In an essay entitled, "Black Identity," Cornel West wrote:

"The basic [problem concerning Black identity is] on at least four levels—existential, social, political, and economic. The existential level is the most important because it has to do with what it means to be a person and live a life under horrifying conditions. To be a black human being under circumstances in which one's humanity is questioned is to engage in not only a difficult challenge but also a demanding discipline."

Part II invites those present (those participating in Part I and others who wish to participate) to talk about this "demanding discipline," to speak about what is required in order to navigate the issues and obstacles of the larger culture so as to keep one's identity intact, to find wholeness, to channel one's anger, resentment, heartache, and rage into actions that benefit self, family, and community. Part II is on manhood, on what it is and on how it is achieved. For insight into such matters, communities turn to their elders as well as to other knowledgeable individuals, and that is what we will be doing in Part II.

What will Part III of the discussion be about?

At the end of our discussion, we want to leave a few moments should anyone want to discuss possible follow-up steps/topics/initiatives. If not, the discussion will close with Part II.

More to follow in coming days.

After the second flyer went out I had a phone conversation with Warren in which he told me about the Commemorative Wall that had been created in honor of the players who grew up playing on the Dunbar Courts in Kansas City, Kansas. He said he planned to visit the Wall the morning of our event, and the more we talked, the more it seemed as though we ought to make the opportunity to visit the Wall a part of our event.

At Warren's suggestion, I called Bill Robinson, a former Kansas City, Kansas, basketball player who had gone on to the University of Nevada where he starred in the early 1960s. Mr. Robinson had been quite involved in the creation of the Commemorative Wall. When I called he was very cordial and happy to make arrangements for access to the exhibit for those who would be interested in stopping by. He also indicated that he would contact a number of players listed on the Wall and personally invite them.

One of the legendary individuals on the Wall is Ernie Moore. I first learned of Ernie from the Reverend Nelson "Fuzzy" Thompson. Ernie was a high school All-American who had gone on to Wichita State where he starred in the late '50s and early '60s. "Ernie did everything beautifully," said Fuzzy, "and he was so quick. *And what a dresser!*" (Warren once mentioned to me that while his [Warren's] style was about power, Ernie's was about art.) "Ernie even looked good when he was falling," said Fuzzy, *"If you were going to fall, you wanted to fall like Ernie."*

I called Mr. Moore to invite him to our now expanded event and he said he would plan to attend. When I mentioned that some people thought he might be the best player to come out of the Kansas City area, he chuckled and said, "Well, arguably." He went on to say that he didn't know why but he had been given considerable range. He could shoot with accuracy from well beyond the three-point line, though of course in those days there was no three-point line. Unfortunately, Mr. Moore was unable to attend our event.

About this time, I contacted Michael Herzmark and Don Mayberger. Both had attended the court-naming event and were, in fact, the reason that the event got videotaped. I asked if they would come and videotape this event. It was asking a lot. There was no money in this venture and a full day's labor. Don, at least, lived in Lawrence, an hour away. Michael lived south of Los Angeles and would bear a sizable expense just getting to the event. Both said they would be there.

From my point of view, this was no small matter. Don is a local Kansas City celebrity. Along with two colleagues, he has traveled the country doing the camera work and narration for "Rare Visions & Roadside Revelations," a locally produced public broadcasting program capturing the rare and often inspiring visions of America's folk artists. "Rare Visions…" airs on Public Broadcasting Stations around the country, and the fact that it is locally produced is a source of considerable pride for many in the Kansas City/Lawrence community. For their efforts, Don and his colleagues have been awarded nine regional Emmys (though, as Don is quick to retort: *"Who's counting?"*).

Michael is semi-retired, having sold his LA-based company a few years ago. He and his wife (and business partner), Melissa, produced movie trailers—an art form all its own—for the Disney Company. In 2009, while traveling through the South, Michael and Melissa went through Selma, Alabama and were reminded of the events that had taken place on the Edmund Pettus Bridge some forty-five years earlier. They have since devoted themselves to documenting the life of Selma, revisiting the event known as Bloody Sunday, interviewing those who were there on that fateful day as well as others who can tell the story of Selma since that event. The result is a documentary entitled, "45 Years Across the Bridge – The Battles of Selma," the intent of which is to tell the story of one community's effort to deal with the racial tensions that erupted throughout the United States in the 1960s.

Michael committed himself to videotaping the *Odyssey,* but in the course of making plans wondered if there might be a way to show his documentary to our audience and others. The first person I called was Alex Ellison. Alex suggested the Kansas City Public Library as an ideal place for the showing the documentary but thought the prospect of securing an auditorium unlikely on such short notice.

The Kansas City Public Library has become an important educational institution in the Kansas City area, providing a venue for nationally known writers and hosting discussions on topics important to the community. Alex said he would ask the director of the library— someone Alex has known for some time—if it would be possible to have the library host Michael's documentary. Even though the time was short and the likelihood of securing a place in the library's schedule dim, Alex said he would see what he could do.

Within a day, Alex called to say that arrangements would be made and that library staff would be in touch to finalize the details. Thanks to Alex, Bill Robinson, Crosby Kemper, the Bruce Watkins Cultural Heritage Center staff and others, our schedule for the 28th was in place. Shortly thereafter, a final flyer alerting everyone to the expanded schedule was e-mailed.

Third Flyer:

*Our lineup of events for **Tuesday, December 28th** has expanded.*

The Commemorative Wall

Location:	Faith Lutheran Church
	530 Quindaro Boulevard – KC, KS
Time:	**10:00 a.m. to 11:00 a.m.**
	Tuesday, December 28th

The Dunbar Courts were Kansas City's version of New York City's Rucker Park Courts. The best players in Kansas City, Kansas, played there, their games and styles shaped by the high caliber of competition. A wall now commemorates those courts and the players who played on them from the 1930s to the 1970s.

Players honored on the commemorative wall and others are welcome to gather for photographs and recollections. Special thanks to Mr. Bill Robinson.

The Odyssey of Black Men in America: A Kansas City Perspective

Date:	December 28, 2010
Location:	The Bruce Watkins Cultural Heritage Center
	3700 Blue Parkway
Time:	2:00 p.m. to 5:30 p.m.
Moderator:	Carl Boyd

As indicated in previous notices, this is a discussion in three parts. Part I focuses on Kansas City's athletic history, on who some of the players were, on how they inspired us and inspired one another, on what it was like to be an athlete growing up in Kansas City in the '40s, '50s, and '60s. Part II focuses on the odyssey of black men in general, on navigating the demands of the larger culture so as to emerge with one's identity intact, on manhood: what it is and how it is achieved. Part III provides time for a consideration of next steps/topics/initiatives.

"45 Years Across the Bridge – The Battles of Selma"

Location: Helzberg Auditorium – KC
             Public Library
Time: 8:00 p.m. to 10:00 p.m.
             Tuesday, December 28th

Kansas City natives and Los Angeles filmmakers Michael Herzmark and Melissa Wayne spent much of 2009 and 2010 in Selma, Alabama. The result is **45 Years Across the Bridge – The Battles of Selma,** the first of a proposed series (**50 Years Across the Bridge**) of six annual one-hour programs documenting Selma's 45-year journey from an infamous past to an uncertain role in the 21st century.

The location of 1965's "Bloody Sunday" beating by law enforcement personnel of unarmed civil rights marchers on the Edmund Pettus Bridge, Selma was once one of Alabama's richest cities. Today it is one of the poorest. Struggling to overcome its racist past, solve deep economic and education woes, and span a vast political divide, her future is up for grabs. Many of the problems Selma faces, notes Mr. Herzmark, mirror the greatest current challenges through much of America.

Mr. Herzmark will host the showing of this one-hour documentary with time following for feedback and discussion.

Please note: There is no charge for any of the above-listed events. Anyone with an interest in the above events—whether they are receiving this e-mail directly or not—is welcome to attend.

THE RADIO INTERVIEW

In advance of the December 28th event, Mr. Boyd asked me to be a guest on his radio program. Here is his description of the program:

> The name of the program, 'The Last Mile of the Way', connotes traveling the last half (i.e., the final fifty years) of one's journey, and features guests who came through the Civil Rights era and who now have historical reflections to share and a legacy to pass on. As you can see, the outline you have written, relative to The Odyssey, has a theme that fits the format of the radio program. I am, certainly, interested in interviewing guests who have the history, and the "authenticity," if you will, of this nation's Warren Jabalis. Some of the December 28th participants will have already appeared on the show.

I was reluctant initially to be on the program (feeling that Mr. Boyd's audience might be expecting a bit more depth than I would be able to offer), but in order to get the word out about our event, I agreed.

Mr. Boyd began the interview by providing the time, location, and a brief description of our event. We then discussed its history, its genesis in the court-naming initiative, in Warren's essays and Dr. Tuttle's interest in them, and in the willingness of several who were involved in the court-naming initiative to work on another project if one could be found. I then emphasized that no one involved with our event was pretending that we were initiating anything new. What we were proposing was a gathering that—if it went well—would complement the efforts long underway by others.

Mr. Boyd then asked for my own views on the event, what I thought it was about and why I was involved, a non-African-American man. I stumbled around looking for my response, mentioning again some of what had been said already (my interest in Warren's career, the court-naming initiative, my interest in Kansas City). I then offered the following—though not as smoothly or as coherently as I would have liked.

> *I said that I believe that every birth is the birth of someone with far more potential than they usually are able to realize, because potential and opportunity get obstructed along the way, sometimes from a very early age. I added that as far as I know there are few groups for whom more obstacles exist than black men...obstacles of the severest sort and for a lifetime. Any*

*individual who navigates these obstacles and emerges integrated
and whole has a lot to teach the rest of us. The black man as
teacher—that, I suggested, is what our event is about.*

*I also mentioned that I had heard Emanuel Cleaver, the former
mayor of Kansas City and now Congressman from Missouri's
Fifth District, say that "pain is a terrible thing to waste." Our
society wastes the pain it has caused, I suggested, and loses
insight into how it might be used when it fails to learn from those
who have suffered that pain, whoever they are, black men,
women, the poor. Our event will be attended by men who have
turned the pain and struggle implicit in what it means to be a
black man in America to the advantage of themselves, their
families, and their communities, and we hope to hear their
stories and to learn from them.*

*I also mentioned that our event will be a reunion for many
attending: athletes from the '40s, '50s, '60s, and '70s telling
stories of their "glory days"—"lies," as Warren is fond of
saying.*

The interview closed with an invitation to the audience, male and female,
to attend if they were interested in doing so.

DECEMBER 28, 2010: THE COMMEMORATIVE WALL

The building housing the Commemorative Wall was once home to Faith
Lutheran Church. It now is a neighborhood center—a medical clinic,
among other things—serving the immediate area. Bill Robinson was
there when I arrived. We walked in together and he began explaining the
Commemorative Wall, its history, the effort to acknowledge the many
exceptional players who had played on the Dunbar courts, courts that no
longer exist. Of the many questions I asked Mr. Robinson—his name
among the many names on the Wall—was: *"Of all the players listed
here, who was the best?"* His response: *"Probably Jabali."*

By 10:00 a.m., eighteen individuals had joined the gathering:
men in their fifties, sixties, and seventies, one gentleman in his eighties.
Their lives had gone in a variety of directions, but they nevertheless were
bound together by their playing days on the Dunbar Elementary School
courts.

What was being honored in this gathering was the fact that the
Dunbar courts were for Kansas City, Kansas, what the Rucker Park

courts were for New York City. Here the game was being created. Said one of the men in attendance: *"The coaches would come down to Dunbar to see the basketball talent from throughout the area, from Rosedale, from Sumner, from Wyandotte, from Northeast. If you wanted to improve your skills, you came to Dunbar."*

A rich discussion ensued, only part of which is captured here. On the great Ernie Moore, Bill Robinson remarked: *"Ernie knew every crack on the Dunbar courts. Some of the shots Ernie made you couldn't believe. He could use the backboard, he could jump, and what I loved most about Ernie is that he fed me! [Laughter] The truth is God had blessed Ernie Moore."*

Several gentlemen commented on the now legendary game between Central High School (Kansas City, Missouri) and Sumner High School (Kansas City, Kansas) in 1963, in which Warren had scored 44 points. *"I tell my children about that game,"* said one gentleman. *"I even tell my grandchildren about it. There wasn't a 3-point line in those days, but if there had been, Warren would have scored 60 points!"* Added another gentleman: *"I was at that game. I sat in the stands and I was fuming. I'll tell you one thing, if I had been guarding him he never would have scored 44 points!" [Laughter]*

(I had heard a great deal about that game, about how Warren had gone into Sumner's gym—Sumner a perennial powerhouse—and scored 44 points. No one who was at the game, so I am told, will ever forget it. Kennie Denmon was there: *"If you didn't get to the Sumner gym early, you couldn't get in. I got there at 5:00 p.m. and the gym was already packed."* The Reverend "Fuzzy" Thompson: *"Nobody goes into Sumner's gym and drops 44 points on them, but Warren did. That was something to behold!"* Willie "Sparkles" Stewart: *"We had a gathering place up on Troost, a little place called Smacks. We were scheduled to play Central the next night. Some of the Lincoln players came in and started talking about how Warren had just scored 44 points against Sumner. 'He did what!? Oh, no, we can't have that!' We started bragging about how we were going to stop him, how we were going to shut him down. I was one of them doing the talking, I'll admit it. And I'll be darn if he didn't score 42 points the next night against us!")*

Warren reminded everyone of what he felt they were forgetting: namely, that the year before, when he was a sophomore, Central had been *"run out of Sumner's gym."* *"That was the team with Richard Dumas, Herman Watson, Red Starks."*

As the discussion continued, many names were mentioned: Leonard Gray, Rufus Cruthers, Henry Smith, Zig Johnson, Butch and Nolan Ellison, Monte Owens. Said one gentleman: *"I used to see Larry*

Drew dribbling the ball past my house. I knew he would be pretty good, but I never dreamed he would go on to the University of Missouri and then the NBA and do the things he did."

"We even had a commentator on the Dunbar Courts," said Warren. *"J.B. Hill, he'd stand out on the court and report the goings on. He should have had his own television show."*

Warren added: *"I would go so far as to say that the Dunbar Courts not only influenced basketball in Kansas City, Kansas, but that they influenced basketball in Kansas City, Missouri, as well. When I moved to the Missouri side I couldn't find anything comparable to the Dunbar Courts. And a lot of players who did begin to define basketball on the Missouri side had come from Kansas City, Kansas, and had played on the Dunbar courts."*

"Even when integration came in, in '55 and '56," said another gentleman, *"and we were all required to go to different high schools, we nevertheless came back to Dunbar to play."*

With apologies to those not listed here (as many more are listed on the wall than are listed here), the Commemorative Wall includes the following names:

Lucius Allen (see Endnote 2) — UCLA, Milwaukee
   Bucks, Los Angeles Lakers, Kansas City Kings
Johnny Battles — Pittsburg (KS) State University
James Caruthers — Bradley University, Bradley
   University Basketball Hall of Fame
Benoyd "Butch" Myers Ellison — Kansas University
Nolan Ellison — Kansas University, All Big Eight
   selection
Daryel Garrison — Missouri State University
Paul Graham — Head Coach, Washington St University
Leonard "Hughie" Gray — Seattle Supersonics,
   Washington Bullets
Craig Hall — Coach, Sumner High School
Ronald Hamilton — Tennessee State University,
   member of team that won three straight NAIA
   Championships
Dennis Hill — Southwest Missouri State University,
   Head Coach for Pittsburg State University
Warren Armstrong Jabali — High school All American,
   Wichita State University Basketball Hall of Fame,
   voted one of the thirty greatest players in the history
   of the ABA

Ernie Moore — High school All American, Wichita
    State University Basketball Hall of Fame
Monte Owens — Armed services basketball team
William "Big Dipper" Robinson — University of
    Nevada, led University of Nevada in scoring
David Verser — First round draft pick, Cincinnati
    Bengals
Herman Watson — Drake University, considered best
    defensive guard in college basketball his senior year
    at Drake by United Press and Associated Press
Charles Weems — Rockhurst College

Hoop Roots, the novel by John Edgar Wideman, opens with the
following passage:

> "We went to the playground court to find our missing
> fathers. We didn't find them but we found a game and
> the game served us as a daddy of sorts. We formed
> families of men and boys, male clans ruled and
> disciplined by the game's demands, its hard, distant,
> implacable gaze, its rare, maybe loving embrace of us:
> the game taught us to respect it and respect ourselves
> and other players. Playing the game provided sanctuary,
> refuge from a hostile world, and also toughened us by
> instructing us in styles for coping with that world."

Wideman's statement is not true in its entirety for those who
played at the Dunbar Courts. Many, perhaps most, were from intact
families. But there is an element of truth in it. Why else create a
Commemorative Wall? Why else return some forty or fifty or sixty years
later if not for the fact that something substantial happened on those
courts? A community of peers dispensed a sense of identity and readied
its members—as communities are supposed to do—with a knowledge
and a pride they might have been unaware they were acquiring.

As for the names on the Commemorative Wall...Bill "Big
Dipper" Robinson...Leonard "Hughie" Gray...Warren Armstrong
Jabali...Ernie Moore...they are not so much names as they are poems,
part of the lore that establishes and deepens a sense of place.

The Wall—a work in progress, with other names still to be
added—honors a slice of Kansas City history. For those who can read
between the lines, it tells the story of a time in young men's lives when
they were being made into what they would become. Not entirely but

partially, and indelibly. This same process occurred in other locations in
Kansas City but perhaps nowhere in a more concentrated and prolonged
way than at the Dunbar courts.

DECEMBER 28, 2010: The Odyssey of Black Men in America – A Kansas City Perspective

I drove directly from the Commemorative Wall event to the Bruce
Watkins Center, arriving around noon. I was met by Michael and Don,
already in the process of unloading cameras and equipment. *"Setup is the
best part of any event,"* said Michael. We spent the next hour and a half
setting up cameras, checking sound, arranging the room...a few chairs in
front of the stage facing a loose arrangement of theater-style seating.

The Bruce Watkins Cultural Heritage Center opened in 1989 and
is named for Bruce R. Watkins, "a political and social activist interested
in preserving the artistic, cultural and social history of the African-
American experience." The Center serves as a "living museum...a tribute
to the legacy of Kansas City's African American pioneers." (Watkins
Center website)

The plan was to open the doors at 2:00 p.m. so that those
individuals who came early and had not seen one another for years would
have time to visit. The program would begin at 3:00 and last until 5:30.

By 2:00 we were ready, all except for refreshments that I had
forgotten about completely. However, Bill, on his way from Lawrence,
made a last-minute stop so we could have a table of food, water, and soft
drinks. In the meantime, I met in a side room with several young men
who, by previous arrangement (thanks to Reverend Willie Baker, a
mentor to a number of African American youth in the Kansas City area),
agreed to form a "human sculpture". My hope was that the young men
involved would be able to create an image, a sculpture, that would make
vivid the obstacles young black men face when they set out to realize
their hopes and dreams.

At 3:00 the chairman of the Watkins Center's board of directors,
Archie Williams, welcomed everyone to the Center and to our event.

I then gave a brief history of our event—born out of Dr. Tuttle's
interest in Warren's essays, born also out of the court-naming
initiative—and I mentioned the other events of the day: the gathering—
already held—at the Commemorative Wall, and the event that would
take place later that day at the downtown library, the showing of "45
Years Across the Bridge—the Battles of Selma."

I also mentioned the names of the individuals who had worked to make our full day of events happen: Warren Jabali, Bill Tuttle, Mr. Leon Dixon, our moderator Mr. Carl Boyd, Michael Herzmark, Don Mayberger, Murvelle McMurry, Leon Harden, Mr. Bill Robinson, the staff of the Watkins Cultural Heritage Center, Crosby Kemper and the staff of the downtown library, Dr. Herman Watson (though his schedule did not permit him to attend, his name associated with the event was extremely helpful), Rev. Willie Baker, Mr. Ralph Brown, and of course, Alex Ellison, who—as with the court-naming initiative—had been instrumental in helping us secure our venues and in making our event happen.

Part I: The Odyssey of Black Men in America -- Kansas City's Athletic History

The best way for me to convey the content of Part I is simply to report, with minimal editing, what each person said. I should add that no one involved in the planning of our event presumed that we would be reviewing in any comprehensive way Kansas City's athletic history. Rather, this was to be whatever slice of that history could be remembered and shared, put on the record for the pleasure of those attending and those who might care to read about it later. This was a gathering of older men happy to talk about their youthful powers and their glory days.

Before turning the microphone over to Warren who would lead off Part I, I related what Kennie Denmon had said to me some two years earlier. Kennie had grown up with Warren, had lived in the same neighborhood, and had watched Warren's development both as a person and as a basketball player. *"I'm 63 years old,"* said Kennie, *"and I feel lucky in my life to have seen Jim Brown, Muhammad Ali, Michael Jordon, Tiger Woods and Warren Jabali." "And many of us,"* I added, *"feel exactly the same way. This event,"* I continued, *"would not have come together were it not for the respect and appreciation that so many feel for Warren Jabali. So with that..."*

Warren hesitated—only for a moment—and then offered the following:

> *My interest for today is in duplicating what we do with*
> *the retired ABA Players Association. The retired players*
> *get together annually and I enjoy those gatherings*
> *immensely because we sit around and do what Dave just*
> *did...embellish the truth. There's no way my name*

*should be in the same sentence as Jim Brown,
Muhammad Ali...I mean, that don't make sense! And
that's what we would do all night long at the retired
players gathering. We would sit up and tell lies like that,
and it was fun.*

*So I thought there's some people in Kansas City that I
haven't seen in a long time and my interest is in catching
up, in hearing what you did, what you wanted to do, who
did it better than you. I remember, for example, Arthur
Strozier. Though Strozier played basketball, he was a
better football player and I remember seeing him do
something I haven't seen since. Some player started to
run around his end and Strozier picked him up, moved
him to one side and dropped him... just like that. I
remember thinking: "That ain't fair!" And, of course,
Strozier went on to play at K-State and then the NFL.*

*So I'm sure you all have stories you can tell. I'll just
start it off with myself, as some people might be
interested in what I perceived when I came from the
Kansas side to the Missouri side. The first thing I
noticed was there weren't any basketball courts on the
Missouri side, at least none that I could find. Nothing
like the Dunbar courts in Kansas City, Kansas. I also
found that there wasn't much of a basketball tradition at
Central. At Central High School, all the players on the
basketball team were either track stars or football
players. After a year or so, people got interested in
basketball and that became the impetus for a lot of the
great things that happened after that in Kansas City
basketball. The year after I left, Central won the State
Championship, something that we never did. But if credit
is to be given, a lot of it needs to go to the Dunbar
courts, as a lot of players came over from the Kansas
side to the Missouri side who had played on those
courts.*

*I enjoyed my playing days at Central. The only game I
didn't enjoy was the semi-final game of the 1963 State
Tournament when we played against Jeff City. I had hurt
my ankle in a previous game and Jeff City had a pit bull*

*named Charlie Brown. They told Charlie Brown to go
out there and bite him and scratch him and do whatever
you have to do. And he was doing that. He did things I
never saw done in a high school game. I went up for a
jump shot and he would hit my elbow. So I got upset and
I threw the ball in his face and I got a technical foul.
That was the only game I did not like playing. Even
when we lost games I enjoyed playing.*

*We lost to Manual once. They had a monster over at
Manual. They had people on their team with names like
MANFRED SASSER. I mean, he sounds like he could do
things to you! I remember the first time we played
Southeast. They had Russell Washington and his
brother, Preston. They had legs as wide as this podium. I
was scared of them! But it was a lot of fun.*

*So I don't want to take a lot of time. I prefer listening to
you all. I think we should start with the oldest person,
the person who graduated in something like 1956!*

— Laughter/Applause —

D'Morris Smith:
*I graduated from Lincoln High School in 1956. In 1954,
integration started. May 17th, the Supreme Court said
you must come together. Separate is not equal. As a
result, in 1955, Manual and Lincoln combined for its
football. This was the first impact of integration in
Kansas City.*

*We played all of our football and basketball games at
Lincoln High School. In 1956 Lincoln came in second in
the league in basketball. The only team we lost to was
Northeast High School. They had Jim Hoffman, a big
center who went on to Kansas University. And we lost to
Manual High School.*

*In the summer, Lincoln was closed so we had to practice
in Parade Park on a dirt court. There was a tree on the
court and a fire hydrant, as well. And when it rained,
gullies formed and when they dried out, you had to learn*

how to dribble around the gullies. That was a basketball court! Finally, Brooklyn Center was developed and we had a full court to play on.

Kansas City was very supportive of sports. The churches had basketball leagues. We played at the YMCA where you had to learn how to shoot under the track that ran around above the court. We played baseball in Parade Park. You had to fight to get on the field. You needed a permit to get on the field. You played one or two hours and there were teams waiting to come on as you got off. Today, the fields are empty.

At that time, we talked about the boundaries (of the black community): East was Indiana Street; West was Troost; North was Ninth Street; South was Linwood Boulevard. No blacks at Central High School, no blacks at Southeast High School, at Westport or Paseo. We knew everyone our age and even two or three years older and younger. We competed against each other and yet, we lived next door to each other. We were very fortunate.

We had no baseball in high school. We played in the summer months in the American Legion League and also in the Jackie Robinson League. We had the support of the community. The churches, store owners, everyone who could contribute, did so, and this gave us the opportunity to play. And then Don Motley was able to get us sponsors and as a result we became the first all-black American Legion team in the United States. We have not been recognized for that fact, and yet it happened.

This was the first time, ladies and gentlemen, that when we went out to play as an American Legion team that there were no restrictions. We could go to the restroom, do whatever we wanted to do. Prior to this we couldn't go out to Independence, north of the river or south. We also played in Andre Park under the lights. And if we didn't have money to pay for the lights, we would pass the hat.

I was the first black selected on the All-City Basketball Team. I went to Texas Southern on an athletic scholarship where I played football, basketball, and baseball. And after my second year at Texas Southern, I signed with the St Louis Cardinals organization.

My father, Hilton Smith, played for the Kansas City Monarchs from 1937 to 1948. In 2001, he was inducted into the Baseball Hall of Fame, and I'm very happy to say our family was able to attend. I was even able to bring my father's sister, 93 years of age, to the ceremony.

— Applause —

At this point, the microphone was passed to our moderator, Carl Boyd.

Carl Boyd:
On March 3rd I will be 69 years old. One more elder than myself (addressing Mr. Dixon): *Permission to speak?* (Mr. Dixon nods approval.) *Thank you, sir.*

My name is Carl Boyd. I grew up on the South Side of Chicago. If you asked in the City of Chicago the best basketball team in the history of Chicago, they would say, "DeSalvo, 1954. Paxton Numkin, Brother McMillan." And if you said, "Where did you play ball?" I would say I played on 71st Street because that's where all the ballers played...except that wouldn't be true.

When I played for Lindbloom, my very best friend, Robert Tops, use to call me Judge because I spent all my time on the bench. So I was not one of those ballers like you mentioned. But I have found that the older I get the better I was. So I would like to find out if there is anybody in the city of Kansas City, Missouri, or from the city of Kansas City, Kansas, or from anywhere who thinks you have known somebody badder than Billy Harris from the South Side of Chicago who was a sure-enough ballplayer.

*Let's hear the stories that were told at a gathering place
called Smacks or at the barbershop or in the parking
lot...*

Maurice Copeland:
*Warren Jabali was the greatest, always will be the
greatest, but we used to say down on 27th Street, "When
is he going to come and face the wall?" It was a place
on 26th & College, a car wash. The goal was on the
wall. Now when you play basketball you sometimes have
momentum and you go under the goal. Not here. You
went against the wall! This man right here (Jabali)
mastered the wall! He mastered all kinds of dunks.
Everyone played there. Edward Tivis...Willie Stewart.*

— Applause —

Leon Dixon:
*I'm going to take issue with brother Jabali. Let me back
up. When I was growing up nobody knew people's
names. They only knew their nicknames. I don't know
who D'Morris Smith is; that's Mickey. I don't know who
Elvis Gibson is; that's Sonny. Charles Mathews, that's
Apple Jacks. Those three guys were ahead of me in
school. A lot of those guys played when schools were
segregated. Mickey talked about his father but one thing
he didn't say: his father was the one who scouted Jackie
Robinson. All of us need to know that.*

*We were talking about who was probably the first to go
pro. I could be wrong, but according to my recollection,
it was Josh Gratner. This is before my time. You grew up
hearing about this. When you were in the neighborhood
you heard these stories. I heard about Josh Gratner who
played for the Harlem Globetrotters. He went to Lincoln
High School.*

*Mickey talked about the first year that Lincoln High
School was integrated. I was a sophomore. Let me back
up. I was told that at that time the Interscholastic
League had three places you could play basketball:
Southeast, East, and Lincoln. I was told that they figured*

we [Lincoln] would be mediocre and average. Well, in
football we might have been average, but basketball was
a different story. Mickey points out that we lost two
games that first year. For the record, after that Lincoln
went three years undefeated in Interscholastic League
play. That needs to be known, too.

Now, talk about the Field House where the court has
been named after Jabali...Story I heard back in the day
is that the reason they built the Field House was so they
could get Lincoln out of their gym!

There's something else I wanted to point out. Mickey
talked about how his father played for the Kansas City
Monarchs. A lot of us don't realize the role that athletes
like the Monarchs played. They coached Little League
baseball. And when the Monarchs traveled around the
country they went to those colleges and got to know
those coaches and when they would come back they
could recommend kids to get scholarships. That's a story
that goes untold about the Monarchs. And I think as a
community we should realize that because a lot of young
boys in Kansas City got a chance to go off to college
because the Monarchs could make recommendations.
Someone mentioned Don Motley. Don Motley's
reputation was such that I remember a couple of guys
that went to Tuskegee off his word. This is part of the
history that goes unrecorded. There's an African
proverb that says, "When an elder dies, a library is
burned." Mr. Smith is no longer with us. All that
knowledge he had is gone. Josh Gratner is no longer
with us. Those of us might know about coaches like
Harry Kirpatrick, Jack Bush, Coach Wilkinson, Coach
Banks. I'm choking up because these men are people we
looked up to and admired. They could tell us to sit down
and shut up sometimes when our parents couldn't and
wouldn't. The community was a community back in
those days.

Even when the schools were segregated—there was
Lincoln, Sumner, and R. T. Coles—they had to travel to
Oklahoma and St. Louis just to play. You couldn't have a

season with just Lincoln, Sumner, and R. T. Coles. Those a few years younger than us need to know what their predecessors went through.

And then, once these schools got integrated, we watched them come in and refinish the floor, put up fiberglass backboards, and don't think we didn't know that.

(Mr. Boyd moves next to Mr. Gibson to signal time.)

They're calling time on me. And there are some other stories. We need to understand where we came from. I'm talking about Lincoln High School, but I'm sure the same thing went on over at Sumner. So, I'm going to...(pause) I'LL BE BACK!.

— Laughter/Applause —

Carl Boyd:
I may be from the South Side of Chicago but there was no way I was going to say, "Sit down and shut up" (to Mr. Dixon).

Chester Owens:
I'm from Kansas City, Kansas. I would just like to say something that most persons have never heard. There was a Sumner Junior College and a Lincoln Junior College. Sumner closed in 1951. I happened to be on that last team. And that's part of a history that people don't know. Probably the greatest celebrity to come out of Sumner Junior College was Johnny McLendon (see *Part VI: The Sumner Connection* for more on John McLendon). *Johnny Mac went to Sumner Junior College and they called him, interestingly enough, the Judge. I think Lincoln Junior College and Sumner Junior College is part of the history that is missing in this area and it's something we need to work on. Bill Carter is still alive, Robert Brooks, I think one of the Bergetts went there, but that's a history we need to work on.*

— Applause —

Bill Robinson:
I'm 70 years old. I came out of Sumner in 1958. I played on the Dunbar courts. We would come over here and play Manual and Lincoln. You know what happened, don't you? We smoked Manual and split with Lincoln. Lincoln had Jackie Gilbert. We won at home and they won at home.

I was blessed to do what I did...and that young man sitting up there (pointing to Jabali), that's a class act right there. Amen. Everything that I did when I had a chance to play basketball... I played against Dissinger, Rick Barry, Nelson, these were All Americans and I had to guard them as a freshman in college. I went to the University of Nevada, the Wolfpack. Three years in a row I was First Team All Conference. Bill Harrah owned Harrah's Club at that time and I sat on the podium with him because I was selected by the Sierra Nevada as their Outstanding Athlete two months in a row. I went as high as number three in the nation in scoring back in my day.

That's just to say that in Kansas City, Missouri and Kansas...I met a lot of basketball coaches and they said some of the best talent in the United States at that time came right out of these two cities. We were playing at National College down on 15th Street against the Kansas City Steers every Sunday and we would smoke 'em. George Unseld, Wesley's brother, he was at KU, Bill Bridges... every Sunday.

— Applause —

Michael Walker:
I went to Central High School, class of '79. I want to talk a little bit about the past. I go to a lot of high school games around Kansas City and one of the things I notice more than anything is that the kids don't realize that they are walking among legends.

When I was a kid, I knew who everybody was. I didn't know who Warren Jabali was to see him, but I heard all the stories. And it wasn't just him. It was guys like Martinez Denmom, Clay Johnson... I knew who these guys were. They couldn't come in the building but I knew who they were: "Hey, that's Clay," or "That's Martinez." Ray Ray Strozier, the Washington brothers from Southeast. That's one of the things kids don't realize, that these guys are right there with them.

I'd like to tell one story. I went to Martin Luther King Junior High School. Mr. Bergetts was our gym teacher and he had this picture on the wall. It was of the '73 All-Metro Team. It was Clay Johnson, Terry Blanks, Larry Coles of Central, and a couple of other guys. I always told myself, "I'm going to be on that picture, I want to be on that picture."

It was five years later. I was at Central. I was a junior. It was late at night after practice and I was walking down Indiana, around 35th, and here comes this guy. He's like 6'8". I'm like: "I know this guy." "Hey man, are you Larry Coles?" He said, "Yeah, I'm Larry Coles." I was excited. I started talking to him. I told him who I was, that I played on the team. And he said, "Yeah, man, I've heard of you. I know who you are." And it made my day.

And that's one of the things kids don't realize nowadays... that they are around guys who have played. They're just walking right past them. And the guys who have played don't know how to respond to them because there's no connection.

— Applause —

Carl Boyd:
Before Archie takes the microphone, let me reassure you. When Bernie Glaman brought the Kansas City Sizzlers, the CBA team, to Kansas City, Sam Lacy and I had a pre-game show together. Sam Lacy, Clay Johnson, and the owner, Bernie Glaman, knew who you were, brother, and they had some glowing reports about this young man [Michael Walker] so it is an honor to hear from you as from the others who represent this history.

Archie Williams:
It was legend over in Kansas that Warren could snatch a rebound off the top of a wooden backboard. I think I'm limping now from my effort to replicate that feat.

I came up following under some basketball legends like Lucius Allen, who lived down the street from me, and the Ellison brothers, Butch and Nolan. The caliber of basketball they played was awe-inspiring to me. And it inspired my brother.

My brother, Walter, when it came time to go to high school, he went to play for Wyandotte High School. Walter played for a coach named Walt Schubloom. He would kick you square in your pants on the court if you made a mistake. I asked my brother why he would want to play for a man like that when he could go play for Sumner. But it worked out well because all three years that he played up there, '67, '68, and '69, they took big school championships. I remember the time in Allen Field House when they played Wichita. Wichita had a center at 6'11" named Randy Canfield, and Walter was only 6'4", and I don't know if he was inspired by Warren or not but he played a heck of a game and Wyandotte wound up winning by two points.

The name of Warren Armstrong—at the time—or Jabali as it is now, with respect, rang loud and clear over in Kansas and there was a lot of folks who tried their best to emulate his accomplishments.

So I need to ask: Is it true that you snatched a rebound off the top of the backboard? I need to know that so that I can.... Is that true? 'Cause I'm walking with this cane and I need to know if it was truth or fiction. But I thank you for the legend you represent.

— Laughter/Applause —

Warren Jabali:
In the 1973 ABA All Star Game, I think that's when Julius Erving dunked from the free throw line. But I

think I was the first person that ever dunked from the free throw line. (Applause) Now hold it. It was in college. We were playing in Bradley. The Bradley Braves. So I went to the hoop and I went up and I looked up and there was a dude named Willie Betts... and I looked over him and there was a dude named Eddie Jackson... and I looked up over him and there was another dude, and all three of them were scratching for the ball, trying to knock it up into the stands. So the next time I got the ball, it was on a fast break. So I was going down the court and I looked back and I saw them three dudes coming at me. So I took off from the free throw line to get away from them. I got up in the air and said, "How am I going to get down from here?" 'Cause my feet... I was flying like that. I hit the rim and my feet came back under me. I dunked from the free throw line because I was scared!

— Laughter —

Archie Williams:
But did you pull the rebound from the top of the backboard?

Warren Jabali:
No, man, can't nobody do that!

— Laughter —

Eb Effrant:
In 1956, 95 black students integrated Central High School. I was one of them. In order for us to go out for sports we had to call the NAACP. And they came in and they investigated why is it you won't let these black guys play ball? And the coach said the white kids were here last year and we're going to give them a chance to try out and the blacks will have to wait. And after the NAACP finished negotiating with them, they decided to let us come out for the team. So I made the varsity. I was in the tenth grade. My coach told me, "You are going to sit on that bench until splinters come up in your behind just for

causing all this commotion." That's what I had to go through.

— Applause —

Carl Boyd:
That is a precursor to what we will be getting into during our discussion of the Odyssey.

Joe Lewis Mattox:
I just wanted to mention the Boot Heel. The Boot Heel is below St. Louis, Cape Girardeau, Sikeston, New Madrid. Thinking of my team, segregated, segregated so badly that we had to play teams in West Memphis and up to Cape Girardeau because we could not play white teams. One of the people that is a legend in Kansas City that was the first coach in Washington High School in Crothersville, MO, was Jack Bush. Jack Bush was my coach, and I am so proud to have known that man. At the same time, other coaches from African American schools, Lincoln University, the things they inspired in athletes is something that we carry in us. My track team of 1957... we won several straight championships. When we came back from the State we did not get anything from the Kiwanis Club, the JC's, newspapers or anything else. We just faded away.

— Applause —

Mike Thiessen:
I'm a 63-year-old white guy from Nebraska. So you might wonder why I'm here. Well, I moved to Kansas City when I was ten. I was from a small town of 120 people. No blacks in that farming area. I went to the old Pem Day. I'm here today and I say this with absolute sincerity: I became a much better basketball player playing against Vernon Vanoy at Lincoln, Russell Washington at Southeast, Mr. Jabali at Central. The sons of guns (Central) beat us three straight years by two or three points, but that's amazing because (Jabali's) team his junior year was populated with amazing athletes and he was at the top of them. But I became a

*much better player playing against these guys; I became
a much better human being playing against these
players. I read Warren's essays. I don't know how to say
this: I learned so much—I knew this as a young man,
sports meant a lot to me—but I learned far more from
sports than I ever did in the classroom. And I learned it
from people like you, and I'm here today to thank you
for that but also to tell you that I also learned from
Coach Bush and Coach Wilkerson. I worked with them
for three summers. I was a lifeguard. They were the
bartenders at the Kansas City Country Club. A black
could be a bartender back then. My high school coach
got them the job.*

*One quick anecdote: This is a true story, no
embellishment, the most embarrassing moment of my
basketball career. In our gym, we're trying to beat these
guys* (Central); *he* (Jabali) *would not remember this. I'm
here* (in the first block); *they're shooting a free throw.
Mr. Armstrong is next to me. I'm a good player, I'm
pretty tall and I'm a good rebounder. The ball comes off
hard. He goes up over me, rebounds the ball and jams it!
Have you ever seen that done before? He did that to me.*
(Someone yells, *"You're not the only one he did that
to!"*) [Laughter] *It's a privilege to be here and to be a
part of this.*

— Applause —

Norman Pendleton:
*I played in 1968 at Lincoln. Going back to the records
that Armstrong set at the field house… I think he set (the
scoring record) against Lincoln. Three friends of mine
broke your record. First was Ronald Steel. He broke it in
'68. He scored 44 points. I saw that game. He had 22
field goals. Then I saw Martinez Denmon break it in '69.
He was a teammate of mine. I saw Curtis Washington
break his (Denmon's) record. He scored 50. But they all
broke the record against East High School! Scoring is
scoring, but East at that particular time was not a good
school.*

*Also, we played Southeast one time. Our star got hurt. I
had 18 points the first half. I looked up and said, "I
might get Armstrong's record." But I had four fouls. I
ended up with 20 points. That was my career high. But
we all looked to try to break your record. So you put
something up there for us to do.*

— Applause —

Elvis "Sonny" Gibson:
*I think everyone in this room is my junior. In 1948,
Lewis Dudley went to the Harlem Globetrotters. He was
good—an excellent basketball player. But in my time, in
the early '50s, that gentleman sitting right over there
with all that snow on top of his head, Charles Mathews
(Apple Jacks), was one of the greatest basketball players
at R. T. Coles. But with him was Maurice "Poncho"
King. (He) went to Kansas University. And in the
summer months... the first time I saw Wilt Chamberlain
I had to look up at him cause he was down at Paseo
Park with another guy who was an exceptional
basketball player, Clarence Bell from Lincoln High
School. And they were scrimmaging with Goose Tatum,
Marcus Haynes, Josh Gratner. That was an awful long
time ago. Sixty years ago. I was not particularly athletic,
but I was there because of the enthusiasm and the skill I
was able to see. Maurice King was with several
professional teams. Maurice "Poncho" King, a very,
very, very exceptional basketball player from Kansas
City in the '50s, and I will stand on my record by saying
that.*

— Applause —

Will McCarther:
*I went to Central High School. One of my jobs was to
guard Warren in practice. Coach Wilkerson recruited
me because I'm from Leeds. In Leeds we were known as
boys who were willing to defend themselves. So my job
was to beat up on Warren. Kick him. Push him. Same
thing Charlie Brown did to you. So I beat up on Warren.
I'm not going to tell you no lie. I bumped him and beat*

him and all that.

One thing that's not mentioned... back then there was no organized sports growing up in my neighborhood in Leeds. We all played in the fields or whatever we did. The irony is—out in Leeds—I didn't even know white people. I had never seen white people—this is the honest truth—until I went to Central High School in 1959. And when we went there, it was just like Little Rock, Arkansas. They beat us up, chased us, ran us home. So we had to learn how to fight.

To make a long story short, Central was well known at that time for all kinds of sports... a school of courteous, competent champions. We won so many track championships at Central High School... Track-wise, there was no one in the State of Missouri (who could compete with us). I was a coach at Central... we had three or four boys and we won the State Championship. A kid named Randall... they changed all the State rules behind this kid named Kenny Randall. He won the 100, he won the 200, he won the 440; he anchored all the relays and they all won. He did everything. Everybody knows Kenny Randall if you're from Kansas City. The boy was outstanding. Now you can participate in only so many running events, so many field events, because he did it all.

In football, I was All-Metro, All-City. That was my sport. Got to play against Art Strozier, played head up with him, Russell Washington, head up with him. It was a good thing. The only thing I had going for me is that I was hard-nosed. I didn't know what I was doing. The coach said, "Go through and get the quarterback," and that's what I did. At that time we were taught to put them out of the game. We went in to hurt them and that's what we did. And... I'm sorry, Warren, if I hurt you a few times.

— Laughter and Applause —

<u>Carl Boyd</u>:
Thank you so much. Please give all of yourselves a round of applause.

[Break – end of Part I]

During the break the discussion continued as people gathered in the aisles, in small groups scattered throughout the auditorium, and in the large room just outside the auditorium. Getting people back in their seats was not going to be easy.

Mr. Boyd asked everyone to return so we could begin Part II. There was no response. He made the request a second time, again with no response. Then—in what I consider a stroke of genius—Mr. Boyd began singing:

I'VE GOT SUNSHINE ON A CLOUDY DAY *(pause)*
WHEN IT'S COLD OUTSIDE, *(a slight pause)*

I'VE GOT THE MONTH OF MAY

(a few scattered voices joined in)

WELL, I GUESS YOU'D SAY
WHAT CAN MAKE ME FEEL THIS WAY?

(still more voices joined in as people took their seats)

MY GIRL,
TALKIN' 'BOUT MY GIRL

I'VE GOT SO MUCH HONEY, THE BEES ENVY ME
I'VE GOT A SWEETER SONG, BABY, THAN THE
BIRDS IN THE TREES

(By this point, everyone was in their seat and singing along)

WELL, I GUESS YOU'D SAY
WHAT CAN MAKE ME FEEL THIS WAY?

MY GIRL...

(Ninety men were singing "My Girl" with just the right mix of female voices. It was stunningly beautiful.)

With Mr. Boyd's magic, Part II began.

Part II: The Odyssey of Black Men in America: A Kansas City Perspective

As with Part I, the most appropriate thing for me to do is report what each person said. Here, however, more editing is required. Comments were of greater length and at times emotionally charged. I have tried to do justice to the themes that emerged.

Carl Boyd:

As we resume, the title of our program today is "The Odyssey of the Black Man" from a Kansas City perspective. There are those who will associate the Odyssey with the epic poem by Homer who talked about Odysseus after the Trojan War taking ten years to get back to Ithaca. So the poem is called "The Odyssey." But if you look in the dictionary you also will see "odyssey" defined as a long journey, particularly as it relates to trials and triumphs. So, Warren Armstrong Jabali has given us an opportunity to—in an almost whimsical fashion—recall many of the triumphs. Dave Thomas, who has convened this gathering, also appreciates the trials. So we will engage in that discussion after Dave Thomas introduces Dr. Bill Tuttle. And it will be in one sense a more serious discussion but equally as enlightening as we have experienced so far.

Dave Thomas:

One of the reasons that I was so honored to be a part of this event is that some of the individuals I admire most are in this room. Dr. Tuttle is one of them.

Dr. Tuttle's first book was entitled Race Riot: Chicago in the Red Summer of 1919; *he edited a book of the writings of W.E.B. Du Bois; he wrote a book entitled* Plain Folk: The Life Stories of Undistinguished Americans; *and his most recent book,* Daddy's Gone to War, *was nominated for the Pulitzer Prize. Bill Tuttle...*

With that, Dr. Tuttle walked to the podium and presented the following speech, written for the occasion.

Bill Tuttle:

It's really a pleasure to be here, and good afternoon to all of you. This is all a tough act to follow, so I'm not sure how well I will do, but I'm going to keep it brief, as brief as I can. I want to thank Dave for that very kind introduction and again, it's such a pleasure to be here.

As Dave mentioned, he and I have been talking about this topic for several years, the topic of the odyssey of black men in America. On the surface what sparked our respective interest in this topic was different, and yet there was an important similarity. Dave's interest began with his deep admiration for Warren Jabali, and not only how he played the game of basketball, but also how he carried himself as a man.

I grew up not in KC, but in Detroit. But Detroit, too, was rigidly segregated, and it was brutal in its treatment of black men, particularly the "justice" handed out by the Detroit Police Department, which was still 85 percent white at a time when the city had a majority black population. My public high school of 5,000 students was all-white. There was a vast expanse between the races; I didn't know any black people.

In fact, it wasn't until the early 1960s, when I spent three years as the training officer of an Air Force bomb wing, that that changed. A very close friend was Captain Woody Farmer, a black B-52 pilot who was killed in a mid-air explosion of his airplane. My commanding officer, Captain David Taylor, also was black. He and I talked a lot, particularly about his boyhood in the South, his dreams for his own children, and the promise of the Civil Rights Movement to change America.

Like Dave Thomas, I deeply admired both of these men and not only how they did their work but how they carried themselves as men.

In fact, by word, deed, and example, these black men— like Warren Jabali—had become our teachers.

At one time, Dave and I talked about co-authoring a study of black manhood in America based on chapter-length biographies of ten or twelve men whom we considered to be heroes, such as Warren Jabali, Bob Moses of the Student Nonviolent Coordinating Committee, and Geronimo ji Jaga of the Black Panther Party. But we soon realized that perhaps two white men should not be the authors of such a book.

There is no telling where our discussion this afternoon might lead us—perhaps to such a book, or to a video documentary, or to a series of subsequent discussions such as the one today. Above all, we need to find a way to share the insights expressed today with young black men who are currently defining their manhood.

Again, there is no telling where our discussion might lead us, but I am very excited about the possibilities.

While I was thinking about what I might say today, I have been reading a fascinating book entitled After the Glory: The Struggles of Black Civil War Veterans, *by Donald Shaffer.*

In this book, I read a letter written in 1864 by James Monroe Trotter, a sergeant in the all-black 55th Massachusetts Infantry, who communicated the essence of what black soldiers were fighting for in the Civil War. "It is a great Principle," Trotter wrote, "that for the attainment of which we gladly peril our lives—Manhood & Equality."

Theirs was a battle not for freedom in the abstract. No, they fought for freedom and for the occasion to actualize that freedom by gaining for black men the same opportunities, rights, and status enjoyed by white men.

Though we now live in the 21st century, historians have come to recognize that the quest of black men for manhood was a significant theme much earlier in the history of African American men, including even during the long, sorry era of chattel slavery

*For example, one noted historian, Herbert Gutman, has
discovered that even during slavery, when marriages
between slaves were outlawed by the slave codes, the
practice of naming children for their fathers was
common. "It strongly disputes frequent assertions that
assign a negligible role to slave fathers...." In the*
Freedmen's Bureau Papers *at the National Archives in
Washington, Professor Gutman also found hundreds and
hundreds of applications for marriage licenses in
1865—evidence that these men and women, who already
considered themselves married, wanted to formalize
their relationship legally when they at last had the legal
opportunity to do so.*

*It is clear that during the Civil War, black soldiers in the
Union army went almost overnight from the abject
subjugation of slaves to the exercise of manly power as
soldiers.*

*And manhood meant many things to these black soldiers:
pride, dignity, respect, citizenship, autonomy, bravery,
and fraternal solidarity, not to mention political power
and economic opportunity. For these men, it was
important that their rights be comparable to those of
white men. It was this sense of parity that was the aim of
their quest for manhood.*

*During Reconstruction, which W.E.B. Du Bois and other
historians have recognized as the boldest social
revolution in United States history, black manhood with
all its rights and responsibilities seemed within reach.
Sadly for the country, however, that "revolution" was
short-lived.*

*As we know only too well, Reconstruction was followed
by the betrayal of America's African American citizens.
This was the period which one historian has called
America's "capitulation to racism." The 13th, 14th, and
15th Amendments were overturned by the Supreme
Court, most notably in 1896 with* Plessy v. Ferguson,
*which legalized racial segregation in all facets of
American life. Blacks also lost the right to vote through*

*such devices as the literacy test, the poll tax, and the
grandfather clause. Lynchings soared to over 200 a
year; race riots erupted throughout the country.*

*And slavery was supplanted by a corrupt, incredibly
racist criminal justice system. Because of debt peonage,
the crop lien system, and the chain gang, thousands of
formerly enslaved men became not free men, but
"criminals." Moreover, many of these new "criminals"
were not men, but children 12, 13, and 14 years old.*

*Black manhood had come to mean, among other things,
the ability to provide for and protect black families. But
now that, too, was increasingly problematic.*

*Although black men have served in all of America's
wars, racial exclusion and segregation remained the law
of the land. This was true after the Spanish-American
War and World Wars I and II. Racial desegregation was
finally implemented in America's armed forces during
the Korean War and after.*

*But it took the Civil Rights Revolution of the 1950s and
1960s to bring substantive change to America and to
complete the social and political revolution of
Reconstruction. Indeed, as many of us remember, the
Civil Rights Movement was called America's Second
Reconstruction.*

*And black men, and black women, were central to the
success of this revolution. I think of Bob Moses, John
Lewis, James Chaney, and so many other courageous
men, as well as courageous women such as Diane Nash,
Ella Baker, and Fannie Lou Hamer.*

*The resurgence of black nationalism also highlighted the
crucial political and intellectual roles played by black
men such as Malcolm X, Fred Hampton, and Maulana
Karenga. Indeed, as we celebrate Kwanzaa this week,
we acknowledge Karenga's contributions. In 1966,
Karenga not only created Kwanzaa but also established
the US Organization devoted to social change and*

educational reform. As Karenga stated, the US Organization provides "a philosophy, a set of principles and a program which inspire a personal and social practice that not only satisfies human need but transforms people in the process, making them self-conscious agents of their own life and liberation."

And now we have a black President, and he's doing an outstanding job. But—sadly again—some of the America's age-old problems persist.

Let me conclude by sharing with you a poem that I recently read for the first time. It's entitled "I Am a Black Man," and its author is the poet and musician George Edward Tait. I want to read the last three verses:

> I am a black man
> An Afrikan man
> Acknowledge my strength
> Offer me not prizes for weakness
> Do not encourage the superficial
> Tempt me not with diversion
> If you are my friend—
>   fight by my side or heal my wounds
> If you are my enemy—confess
> I am a black man
> An Afrikan man
> Detained
> But not destroyed
> Enslaved
> But not extinct
> Conquered and Oppressed
> But not for long
> I am a black man
> An Afrikan man
> Fighting for the future/heading for home
> Manhood -- Be my momentum
> Nationhood -- Be my challenge
> Familyhood -- Be my reward

— Applause —

Following Bill's presentation, Mr. Boyd suggested that we bring the young men on stage and form the sculpture. Twelve young men took the stage, ages twelve to twenty. (Our discussion thus far had taken place on the floor of the auditorium. The chairs, as mentioned earlier, were in front of the stage, not on it. With the use of the stage, these young men could be seen—head to toe—by everyone in the auditorium.)

Mr. Boyd asked me to share what we would be seeing. I did so by first thanking Rev. Baker who had been good enough to pull this group of young men together and then thanking the young men for their willingness to participate. I indicated that we asked these young men to sculpt with their bodies the feelings they experience in the face of the obstacles that confront them in the outer world, to illustrate with their bodies in a frozen image what those feelings/experiences look like. The young men, on cue, moved into their images, holding motionless the "sculpture." The immediate response was silence as audience members examined the various images within the sculpture.

Carl Boyd:

In the introduction to our program I indicated that "The Odyssey" is an epic poem. And I think that to some degree there is a poetic element to the journey we are discussing today. *Some of us are old enough to have actually witnessed the unsolicited humility of a Joe Louis and the honest arrogance of a Mohammad Ali. Some of us were around to actually see the Julius's and Jabali's. But, as these young men depicted, some of us also—if we have lived for a moment as a black man in the United States of America—have suffered some of the trials... in some cases leading to the triumphs. As Steve Harvey says, some of us grew up speaking to our boys. So when we are bragging we are talking to our boys; but when we're discussing this serious topic we're talking to our young men as well as to our boys.*

This is what we are considering: What is required in order to navigate the issues and obstacles of the larger culture so as to keep one's identity intact? What does it take to find wholeness... to channel one's anger, resentment, heartache and rage into actions that benefit self, family and community? Manhood: what is it and how is it achieved?

Leonard Edward Jones, Sr.:

What I would like to say concerning the subject of manhood... I had a pastor, Rev. Stanley Long, he described five specific principles that speak to being a man. Sacrificial love—which is the willingness to make a sacrifice for the benefit and well-being of your family. Consistent faithfulness—faithfulness is displayed because of your character, it's who you are; to love and provide for your family, never putting them down, never being negative in your judgment of them or pointing out faults but a loving, considerate and giving attitude to your family's total well-being. Responsible cooperation—being willing to be counted on to take care of your family; taking responsibility for your family by displaying a willingness to provide for them, meeting their needs, putting that first. Ever-increasing maturity—putting away childish things; men a lot of times talk at you, not to you, about you, not with you.

I want to say that the one fault I have as a parent is that I do not know how to nurture my sons. I'm 65 years of age. The models I had shaped me. I give credit to my mother and my uncles. They gave me background on the do's and don'ts. But the nurturing factor is not in many of us. A lot of times we don't give our sons the answers that deep down inside they want.

What I would like to say is that grown men walk with God. That's another thing that grown men don't share with their sons. The higher authority from deep within means something. It gives you a foundation.

I grew up in a single-parent family. My mother is about 4'5". My mother asked me to wash some dishes and because I had my friends with me I turned toward the door. Do you know what a Vess Cola bottle is? My mother hit me with that sprinkler bottle, knocked the wind out of me. My mother had given me something to do and I thought my friendships meant more. I learned something that day. Follow directions. Listen to your parents. Be willing to put something into your family setting.

*Find you a place where you can discover what God
means to you. A church, a parent, a relative; for me, it
was a coach. Jack Bush, Bill Heron, Bill White,
Sylvester Harris, all of these men were like surrogate
parents to me. I don't have a college degree. My boy
graduated from Morehouse. I have a daughter who
graduated from UCLA. I have one from Long Beach
State, one from USF. I'm proud of that fact. I'm a
grandparent now. My sacrifices* (allow me to) *see my
kids as citizens.*

— Applause —

Ron McMillan:
*I'm a street advocate... trying to stop all the homicides
and murders for the last twenty years around here. As I
sat here I saw that the magic that must be shared
between us older folks and the younger folks is all in
how we live. And we have not shared how to love one
another, how to care for one another.*

*I hope that when we walk out of here we might walk with
a new understanding of who we are and what we must
do as we move forward. Athletics plays such an
enormous role in America. It shaped America. You know
where all that came from? The plantations. We used to
compete with each other. I would send my Negro to your
plantation. The first man who won his way to freedom
was this guy named Tom. The whole athletic industry of
fighting came out of the competition on the plantations.*

*People don't know, but for the first one hundred years
the Kentucky Derby never had a white jockey. They were
all black until horse racing became a lucrative sport;
then they* (black jockeys) *had to go. Same thing
happened with the other sports. The one book* (I
recommend)...Forty Million Dollar Slaves *(by William
Rhoden)... he tracks the role of athletics in making
America what it is today.*

*God bless us all. To the young people: Read your
history. It will make you noble.*

— Applause —

Joe Louis Mattox:

I was named after Joe Louis. I would like to speak out on behalf of the army, the military. So many black men have found themselves and found their manhood coming out of slavery and the Civil War when they put eagles on their buttons and they marched for freedom. There have been only a few times in African American history when we have had mostly black men in the homes. So many black men have been raised without fathers in their homes. It was the army and other men who taught them how to be men.

The other thing I want to speak out on behalf of is college. If your parents can get you to go to college or you find that you go to college, you are going to find people there who want to make you great, who want to make you assets to our community.

And I want to speak out on behalf of all African American fraternities. If you are able to become a member of a great African American fraternity, those people in that fraternity are going to make you men. Sometimes it's rough, sometimes it's easy, but when you join a fraternity you are going to learn how to be an asset to your community.

The other thing is fatherhood. "Fathering" sometimes comes easy to black men. But the responsibility of fatherhood *is something you have to learn to do, and most of the time you learn it from another man.*

So, what I am saying is that sports can make you money. I was a track champion but now I'm in history and I love it. Many of you will not become pro athletes but if you take a look at the military, at college and learning something about a fraternity, you will become an outstanding asset in your community and to your family.

— Applause —

Carl Boyd:

Interestingly enough, in the 1980s Joe Louis Mattox and I had a conversation that dealt with fraternities. He, a Phi Beta Sigma, and I being a Kappa Alpha Psi actually found young men in California joining fraternities based upon gang colors. The Bloods wanted to become Kappas and the Cribs wanted to become Phi Beta Sigmas. And I appreciated Joe Louis Mattox, being a journalist, calling that to the attention of those who would hear it.

Will McCarther:

Currently, I'm a hospital administrator, but for 27 years I was a public school educator. I have a PhD in education administration from the University of Iowa.

The opportunity to read the essays that Warren wrote... I thought I knew Warren, but I learned a lot about Warren from reading those essays. There were some things in the essays that came out to me. One of the things... that is extremely important and needs to be repeated is the importance of being mentored, being advised, being guided by responsible adult role models.

I came from a very humble beginning. As I mentioned, I came from Leeds. Seven kids in my family; we all lived in one house, seven kids in one bedroom, mom and daddy in the other. We didn't even have sewers or indoor toilets growing up in Leeds. I'm talking in the '60s; I'm not talking about way back when. The sewer line came through Leeds in 1962. We didn't have paved streets or anything like that. I didn't know how poor I was until I went to Central 'cause everybody in Leeds was poor and we didn't know we were poor because everyone was just alike. So when we came to Central, people were very, very cruel. Kids let you know. Kids are cruel. They let you know very quickly that you are different than them. They laughed at your clothes and made fun of you. I guess that's why I had a chip on my shoulder.

But back to this role-modeling: One of the things we did have in Leeds—in that segregated environment—was some very, very dedicated, committed teachers. These were teachers who told us that we were somebody, that we were important, that we were smart, that we had to be twice as good as the white man in order to get ahead. And they told us that we were going to learn no matter what.

But our parents were also smarter than we thought they were because they gave their children away to those teachers and said, "I don't have an education—my daddy went to the third grade--but I want you to listen to those teachers because all I don't know, they may know and that may help you get beyond your current circumstances." So I had some role models early in life that told me that one of the things that I had to learn was the English language and learn how to write it and speak it and use it, and also basic mathematics.

When I went to Central High School in 1959, I had the fundamentals. Schoolwork was never hard for me. Even so, my high school coach was not a role model. He only had me out there to do bodily harm to other human beings. But he never gave me any advice that I can remember, that I can carry or that was useful. This individual never helped me. He never got me a scholarship to college. He never encouraged me to go to college.

But there were a couple of people up there (at Central)... Coach Banks put me in his car, drove me down to Lincoln University and said, "Boy, you going to go to school down here." He was only about this tall, but he would reach up and hit you in your chest. The man did it to me and said, "Boy, you going to go to school!" Miss Banks is living today, I love her dearly, a wonderful lady, almost 100 years old I believe, and to this day she grabs me and hugs me and calls me "boy." I love her. She was a role model. When I was in Lincoln, they came down to Lincoln. Not only did they put me in school, but they came down and checked on me... checked on me!

When I got out of Central, I had a scholarship to Pittsburg and I had a scholarship to Lincoln. I went down to Pittsburg; there was nobody down there who looked like me. So I went to Lincoln. Best decision I've ever made... I'm talking about Historically Black Colleges now. I got down there and had some other individuals, safe, adult role models who assumed the responsibility of counseling and advising me. They didn't counsel me on being a good athlete, but they counseled me on getting a good education and how important it was in getting ready for the next level. I got my PhD at age 27... I'm just saying to you it's because those people convinced me that I was smart and I had something to contribute.

So one of the things that's missing is that we don't have a defined community any more. We don't know what our community is. These young people don't have that support system that we had because of segregation. The irony of segregation is that we did have a community and we did have a support system and our parents gave the rest of the community permission to discipline us. We grew up at a time when white folks didn't care if we got an education or not. So I'm saying to you we need to know what our community is, we need to redefine our community; we need to take a look at our support system, redefine the support system that these young people need; take a look at education, redefine it, define what it should be and is. And we need to identify role models to help counsel and advise our children; and I think if you can't get but one kid, you should identify one kid—one at a time—that you can counsel and advise (outside your immediate children) *and help get beyond his current circumstances.*

— Applause —

Ronald Harland, Sr.:
I am a graduate of Sumner High School, 1967. I am a proud business owner in this city. When I start looking for potential employees for my company and I'm looking for African American males I'm having a very difficult

time finding them with the proper education and with the right attitudes. This is disturbing. I'm not only seeing it but I'm a member of the local Minority Supplier Counsel that represents over 200 African American and minority-owned businesses in the greater metropolitan area. We're all having the same problem. So I want to hear from the youth: what do they really see as a major barrier for them progressing and moving along with their career? Case in point: when I was growing up, African American men worked in the construction industry. Today, I go through areas where they're building buildings and houses and I don't see any African American males on any of these job sites. What is the future for our African American men? How will they take care of their families? I would venture to say that many of us do not live in the communities where the African American youth live. How can we find one to work with? And what do the youth see as their barrier to education and employment?

— Applause —

Marod Kareen:
I'm a Muslim. I was a member of the Nation of Islam, and I still embrace that philosophy. When I saw the images of those young men who stood on the podium, all of them had a unique image. Some were in a prayer position, some were in a fighting position, some were angry. But it came to me that every one of those youth could work themselves out of those situations just by thinking. Just by taking time to think, "Here I am. How do I get out of this position? What do I do in order to get out of this position?" If you use the proper method of thinking—I like to call it accurate thinking, correct thinking, mathematical thinking—this will help you get out of the situation you're in. And when we come back in six months, we won't see those poses. We'll see happy poses, joyous possess, gleeful poses, because the thinking has changed. And once you're thinking changes, then you are able to change.

*Like I said, I'm a Muslim. I joined the Nation of Islam in
1961. I came to Kansas City in 1972. I was traveling
with the Delfonics: "Didn't I (Blow Your Mind this
Time)," "La La (Means I Love You)," "For the Love
that I Gave," "How Are You Going to Break Your
Promise." These brothers were Muslims as well.*

*I heard Brother Tuttle. He's from Detroit. He could not
have overlooked* (he would know of) *the contribution of
the Nation of Islam in Detroit and Chicago.*

*I had nine children in Kansas City. All of them went to
Central High School. All of them came under Coach
Bush, my sons as well as my daughters. I'm well familiar
with Coach Bush and his contribution... and the help he
gave me in raising my children. But I can't overlook
what the Nation of Islam contributed to society,
especially to education. To see my children, to see other
children, going to school in an orderly manner...young
boys with bow ties, shoes shined, young girls with long
dresses. Very organized. And they were willing to learn
knowledge not only of society but knowledge of the
universe... the schools were called the Universities of
Islam. I heard Malcolm. I heard Ron Karenga. People
that I know are a direct result of the teachings of the
Honorable Elijah Mohammad. I'm not saying that
people should go out and become a Muslim. I'm just
asking you to look at the simple philosophy that works in
the life of young men and young women. It works on the
street, it works in schools, it works in the penitentiary. It
works everywhere that you apply good moral and
rational teaching.*

— Applause —

Maurice Copeland:
*I'm not going to take too long because it's a very heavy
subject. When I saw what was going to go on here today
and when I saw Mr. Jabali's name attached to it, I knew
all I had to do was send him one e-mail with some of my
thoughts on it and he remembered. He came up and said
something to me. That's an honor.*

I got an e-mail from a young lady that alerted me to this event. She said, "Copeland, you've got to be a part of this." And I saw some of the names associated with it and I said, "Well, I don't think I would really be welcome." She said, "I don't care. You need to be a part of it." So I sent an e-mail to Mr. Thomas and said, "If invited, I would come." He sent it back saying, "Come on." Well, first of all, I want you to know that the first shock I saw today was Mr. Thomas himself. Yeah, I appreciate that. After the stuff that I write... I mean, come on.

What you see and what I saw when I was growing up was some very dignified people. This is a man (Jabali) *that I respected because I saw exactly what it is. When I read his essays, I said, "Yes, this is what it's about." So with this, let me tell you, it's time for us to take on the posture of Warren Jabali. It's time for us to man up!*

These questions that we have about what's going on with the youth... It's our fault. We did it. We're the ones that did not lay the path. We did not man up when our brothers and sisters were being discriminated against with the unions not getting apprenticeship programs. Along the line we said, "Oh, man, you should have seen what we had to go through. These are just the trials of life." No, you're here now. Stand up for these kids... in the construction industry, the tooling industry, all these industries. We have to man up. We can do this over and over again, but until we man up and let these kids know who we are and how we got here... I'm a fourth-generation veteran. My people have fought in every war you can talk about. Not only that, one of my ancestors died with John Brown...died before John Brown, hanging on the gallows at Harper's Ferry. Now it's time for us to stand up like men and not just talk about these issues but act. If you want to know why I'm here: I need your help! Watch what goes on in Kansas City around you and if you're ready, Man Up!

— Applause —

Elvis "Sonny" Gibson:

*Everybody in this room who views themselves as
successful is lucky. You're lucky because you slipped
through the line. Now this is to these youngsters here:
The social reality of black insanity is that black people
do not know what to do for you, those of you sitting here.
The social reality of black insanity is* (that) *most black
people do not realize that they were schizophrenics from
birth. And it was a tough thing to have a mentality that
would allow you to be successful. Nobody is going to put
anything in front of a fan and let it blow to you. You've
got to decide if you are essential or nonessential. If you
are essential to yourself, to your community and to your
family, then you are needed. If you are nonessential,
then you can be done without. And it all comes down—in
this country as well as in the world—to one standard:*
You must be educated. *You don't spell boys* b-o-y-z. *You
don't wear oversized clothing. You have to give people
eye contact when you want something. The social reality
of black insanity is black people have marched with the
time, took everything, accepted it and you have become
the liability. I watched those gestures. They were very
civil and very psychosomatic in the drama that you
created. But you have to understand that education is the
hallmark, the only thing that will allow you to be lucky
like we have been.*

— Applause —

Carl Boyd:

*Let me conclude this round in a way that I think is
appropriate. If the young men would come up... I
neglected to have you tell us your names. From a
psycho-historical perspective, one of the first things
African American males encountered was the taking of
their names. I think that if anyone's name needs to be
recorded in this event, it is the young people to whom we
say we speak.*

The young men took their place on stage. Mr. Boyd handed them
the microphone and they said their names:

Josh Derrams... Chris Segura... Donavan
McClindon... Ryan Byers... Montel Williams...
Danavill Jones... Jesse Fasse... T.J. Rolle...
Jubre Rolle

Carl Boyd:
Thank you so much!

— Applause —

Carlos Nelson asked that the youth enact the "sculpture" one more time so that he and others could take pictures. They did so, and again the response was silence as the audience surveyed the images. Mr. Boyd then thanked the youth, and they exited the stage.

— Applause —

Warren Jabali:
As we step over into the next section I think it would be good for us to reflect that we have been told by the researcher that the Odyssey that he has documented began in slavery and the Civil War and reconstruction and the civil rights struggle, which was called a second reconstruction. And then either I stopped listening or it wasn't made clear to me: Well, what are we doing now? And I think that this next section is designed to come up with something.

The brother here has said that whatever it is, it should be moral and it should be principled. Other people have said that it should be about education. And those things sound pretty good to me, so if we're not talking about how to institute a moral, principled, scientific education program then we won't be talking about what we need to do as a next step. We will simply continue to spin our wheels with information we have gathered individually over the years and share back and forth.

Kansas City has people who are doing some things. I can remember coming back here year after year after year when I was playing and I would always go past the little place on Cleveland. And I would look up and I would see W.E.B. Du Bois Learning Center. And I said, "One of these days I'm going to go up there and see what they're doing, but today I'm too busy." Finally, my wife and I went up the hill and we met Leon. Subsequent to that, they have expanded the idea and the concept (of the Center) *over into Southeast, the building adjacent to the field house. I came back again, and now they're over in the high school. So this is a solid, concrete program that I would hope is among the ideas that we say we want to do something about.*

I was looking at Brother Copeland's material on the Internet. I talked to my brother. His ex-wife is being eaten away by the forces that Mr. Copeland has aligned himself against. And he (Mr. Copeland) *says that he needs help.*

So rather than us coming up with something "pie in the sky," I think we should listen to these brothers so that the researcher will have something to add to the story and it won't have to end with the civil right struggle.

— Applause —

(See Endnote 3.)

Part III: The Odyssey of Black Men in America -- Next Steps

Carl Boyd:
This is critical. You can recall during the movement— whether or not it was Dr. King who coined the phrase, he certainly repeated it—that we are too often victimized by the paralysis of analysis. We are enamored with our ability to bring out the statistics and to discuss those things that are wrong but paralyzed because we like to hear it spoken so often and sometime even eloquently. What we want to do now is talk about things that are concrete and that make sense. We want to record what you are saying, and we ask that you be as succinct as possible. We are looking for next steps, solutions, recommendations, things that make sense from that perspective.

Reverend Willie Baker:

I heard the young man over there mention something about mentoring. Mentoring to me is paramount. In every story in here, I heard somebody say that "somebody took me under their wing and took me down to Jeff City, took me to the park to play basketball, took me to church, took me to the store, took me, took me, took me." So if you don't know where they are, then go find them. That's my suggestion. If you don't have anyone in your family, then you have an extended family; and that means go get them, i.e., the youth that need mentoring. Mentoring to me is key. And it's easy. I can relate to you and your business needs but I can help you, as well

Carl Boyd:

Thank you very much. Recommendation #1: Find at least one youth and mentor.

Leon Dixon:

What I'm getting ready to say is true all over the world. It has nothing to do with race, religion, any of that. It's true all over the world. And that is: Our young people have been endowed by their creator with an inordinate amount of energy. And that energy is not going anywhere. The function of society is to come up with programs, institutions, and so forth that channel that energy in a positive direction. Because if society does not do that then you leave it up to these kids to come up with what they're going to do with that energy. And that's what we're seeing in our communities now.

One other thing, the difference between boys and girls: Girls bond twice in life and break one; boys bond three times in life and break two. When children are born, they all bond with their mothers and the women folk up until around puberty. At that point, the girls stay with the women but men have to take the boys away to turn them into men. That's the first break... boys have to make that break (with their mothers) *but girls don't. Note: it's okay to be a daddy's girl but not a mama's boy. The third bond for boys, the second for girls, occurs around the age of twenty-one. The role of parents and adults is to*

*study the kids, analyze the kids for their talents, abilities,
and interests, and then put them where those talents and
interests can be developed and nurtured. I had a friend
who was in music. I have a background in math. And I
said to my friend: If my son likes music and your son
likes math, then we have to switch sons. That's the third
bond... the mentor.*

*Now, to talk about what we can do right here and now,
especially since we're dealing with athletics: In our
community, athletics plays a tremendous role. When you
study African liberation movements, when they take over
their territory the first thing they do is evaluate their
natural resources because that's how they build their
economy. If we look at ourselves as a nation within a
nation, what are our natural resources? It has been
argued that it's athletics and entertainment. That's what
comes out of our community. But we don't control it.
Like the book,* Forty Million Dollar Slave... *the conveyor
belt they put our children on that they end up
controlling. Thinking about that: How can we use
athletics and the interest in athletics* (on the part of our
youth) *to benefit our community?*

*Notice, if you're in high school or college, you have to
be eligible in order to play. If not, they kick you off the
team. My suggestion is that we start with the little kids,
eight-, nine- and ten-year-olds, give them a test. If they
fall below levels then we won't put them off the team but
we will tell them that if you want to continue to play,
here's some places you can go to get some tools.
Because the young people—seven, eight, nine, ten—they
look up to these coaches and the athletes we talk about
in our communities. If we change the environment to the
point where we're encouraging these youngsters to
tighten up their academics, I think we can go a long way
in helping our kids.*

*One friend of mine coached Little League baseball in the
Shelby organization. I asked him, "Of all the boys you
worked with in the Shelby organization, how many got
into trouble with the law?" Answer: "Zero." "How*

many of them graduated from high school?" Answer:
"All of them. One went pro but I don't know how many
got college scholarships." We have to look at what
athletics can do for our kids. If we work with our kids
when they are seven, eight or nine, they'll do whatever
we tell them to do. The brain goes through a change
around eight years old. They say that up to eight, you
learn how to read; after eight, you read to learn. Up to
the age of eight, they'll do pretty much what we ask them
to.

As fond as I am of Jabali, I would encourage us to look
at Jabali's friends who didn't go pro but who finished
college anyway and had decent lives. There are more of
them than went pro. And we need to convey this message
to our kids so they can use their athletic ability to get the
most out of it. Most are not going pro. Very few are like
Jabali.

Carl Boyd:
Unfortunately, we are up against a time limit. I need
some guidance on how we can follow up on our topic
properly. (Someone suggests that Leon Dixon should be
the contact.) *All right, yes, contact Leon Dixon. I'm not*
cutting off discussion entirely but our time is nearly up.

Archie Williams:
I'm thinking that this is such an important event that we
need to see about using the Center to continue the
discussion into this evening.

Carl Boyd:
There is the documentary to be shown later this evening
at the downtown library. We need to keep that in mind.
For now, please make sure that we have your contact
information. We can continue this for another few
minutes and then we'll have to cut it off.

Ron McMillan:
What I want to do is start networking with young people
who want to change their predicament. I want ten, ten
people I can work with, ten people who want to get into

the new economy...not looking for jobs but creating
jobs...working with each other, making ourselves
marketable. The new technology, which is wireless, and
soilless food...we have to be attuned to the future.
Manning up means being ready for the new way money
is going to be delivered. Let's get some networks
together. I want ten people if you'll join me. We all need
to actively commit.

Mr. Tolbert:
I want to follow up on what Leon Dixon said. So much of
what I'm about these days I got from Leon Dixon. Many
people have said today that we used to have community,
we used to have people down the street who would
chastise you when you misbehaved, we used to have this,
we used to have that. Some have said we don't have a
black community any more. I think the thing we ought to
do is start re-creating black community institutions. I'm
advocating a change of philosophy and a change of
strategy for the Black community of North America.
Ever since the Martin Luther King speech, Washington,
DC, 1963, I think the majority of black Americans have
been following a strategy and a philosophy of melting
pot integration. I went along with that until Obama, in
his run for president, got to Pennsylvania and Hillary's
campaign played the race card on him. I thought we
were beyond that in America. And there it was. And
every black commentator I've listened to since says that
the unreasoning, unfair criticism of Obama is probably
because he is black. That says to me that we as black
people need to reevaluate our strategy. We need to start
rebuilding black community institutions, starting with
the family.

(Unfortunately, it is at this point that the videotape ends. My apologies to
Mr. Tolbert. His presentation was followed by applause.)

    In the few minutes that remained, attendees were reminded to
send their ideas and suggestions for follow-up to Mr. Dixon. Mr. Boyd
was thanked, as were others instrumental in making the event happen.
The Watkins Center's staff and board of directors were thanked, and in
response, Archie Williams, Board Chairman, offered the Watkins Center
as a meeting place for future sessions so the discussion could continue.

With that, the gathering adjourned. No one was in a hurry to leave. As people milled about, cameras and equipment were packed up and carted to cars, the room returned to some semblance of its original condition. *"Break down,"* said Michael, *"is the best part of any event."*

DECEMBER 28, 2010: "45 Years Across the Bridge: The Battles of Selma"

At 8:00 p.m., Michael welcomed a large audience to the Helzberg Auditorium in Kansas City's downtown public library. It was a crowd made up of many of Michael's long-time friends and also of a number of individuals who had attended the Odyssey. Michael told two stories: first, how this particular showing of his documentary had come about, and second, how the documentary itself had come about.

He mentioned the event that had just ended, "The Odyssey of Black Men in America," and how, when he was invited to that event, he wondered if there might be some way of showing his documentary. He thanked the individuals who had helped make that possible and he mentioned that present in the audience was a person who had provided inspiration for the day's events. He asked Warren to stand.

He then told the story of the documentary. Michael said that he and his wife (and co-producer), Melissa, were driving through the South in early 2009 and noticed that they were only a short distance from historic Selma, Alabama. He indicated that when they arrived in Selma and saw the Edmund Pettus Bridge, the memories of "Bloody Sunday" came flooding back. It was then that they decided to explore what had happened since then. So began the making of their documentary.

When the showing of the documentary was over, it was met immediately with applause. People visited informally and then slowly exited, filing past the table on which Michael had made available DVDs containing footage not included in the documentary.

EVALUATING "THE ODYSSEY OF BLACK MEN IN AMERICA: A KANSAS CITY PERSPECTIVE"

How are we to evaluate an event like the "Odyssey"? Did the story—the story that is the odyssey—actually get told? Was there enough "theater" in the telling to make it memorable and worthy of those who attended? And did anything come of the telling (and of the event)—any follow-up—or was it simply an afternoon that went no further?

First, did the story get told, the story of black men in America? I believe it did, a small part of it. As each man spoke, the narrative that runs across a lifetime unfolded. From the richness of childhood (in modest or economically depressed circumstances), to integrated or segregated high schools, colleges, military service; to family, community, the larger events of the day *(Dr. Tuttle's "history, culture and age");* the difficulties and successes that men in their sixties and seventies call to mind when asked to do so. And the truth that emerged was not a surprise: the story of black men in America is not one story but many stories, each being told—at our event and elsewhere—out of an intuitive sense that the telling must go on until what is common to all the stories is extracted from American life and the stories are of individual lives and not of race.

The story of black men in America—to a degree, at least—got told, and with it advice on what is needed in and for the black community. But there was another story that needed to be told, as well, a story impossible to separate from the larger story and integral to it. It is the story of the young man with prodigious gifts who sets out to share his gifts with the world, only to discover that the world was out of balance and must be put right. It is the story of the would-be hero.

For many of us of a certain age in Kansas City, we were lucky. We knew Warren's story (see Endnote 4). Here, certainly, was the young man with prodigious gifts, the young man who discovered the imbalances present in the world and who was rightfully indignant, rightfully outraged. We were lucky. We had a "stand-in"—someone from the neighborhood, the community, the city we grew up in—and we could watch even as we were called on to address the injustices that we discovered on our journeys. The specifics of each journey vary—as Joseph Campbell taught us—but the storyline is the same.

So, did *that* story get told, the story of the would-be hero? My answer is yes. If not in the words that were spoken, then in the unspoken thread that brought us together and that gave the benefit of the doubt to our event. I served as the coordinator for our gathering, but I would not have gotten anywhere were it not for the fact that I could say that Warren was involved and that what we were doing was a follow-up to the court-naming initiative. Ninety men showed up on a weekday afternoon during the Christmas/Kwanzaa holidays to participate. In the auditorium where we gathered was (I believe) an unspoken respect for the journey that each man must take, the journey or "Odyssey" by which the self is made and by which the world is changed, depending on the self one chooses to make (depending, that is, on what each man does with his opportunities). In essential respects, this was the story—moving and profound—told by each man as he spoke at our event (the story told by all men whenever they speak).

Was there sufficient theater in the telling? It depends on your tastes. There was the art of storytelling exhibited by any number of men; witness the laughter and applause. There was the artful weaving of one moment to the next by our moderator—a performance, in my judgment, without a misstep. There was the "sculpture" enacted twice and then the ritual or initiation-like stating by each youth of his name before a gathering of elders. And then there was the singing of "My Girl." All of this inside a room lined with Robert Carson portraits of Count Basie, Miles Davis, Big Joe Turner, Charlie "Yardbird" Parker, and others. There was, I believe, theater in the room. But was it sufficient? For some it seemed to be, certainly for those who wanted to continue the discussion although our time to adjourn had come and passed.

Did anything come of the telling, any follow-up to speak of? I hope Mr. Dixon received follow-up assistance of one kind or another. An initiative like the W.E.B. Du Bois Learning Center is always in need of ongoing assistance and support. And certainly, regarding Mr. Dixon's lifelong effort to create and sustain the Center, not enough can be said.

It is the case that Michael—with assistance from individuals met through the Odyssey—was able to schedule another showing of his documentary. In less than a year, he showed "45 Years Across the Bridge: The Battles of Selma" to an audience of 400 at the Plaza branch of the Kansas City Library. Attending the showing and the discussion that followed (moderated by Mr. Boyd) were a number of individuals who had attended the Odyssey as well as leaders from throughout the community, including Congressman Emanuel Cleaver (former mayor of Kansas City). Also attending was Reverend W. Douglas Tanner, Executive Director of the Faith and Politics Institute in Washington, DC. Reverend Tanner flew in from North Carolina for the showing with the purpose of examining whether or not Michael and Melissa's documentary might be used in other Congressional Districts as a catalyst for dialogue and change.

Still, on the issue of "outcomes" and "follow-up" I am of a slightly different mindset then perhaps I once was. Certainly, one test of any event is the difference it makes. And if a difference can be made, one event making possible the next, each in the right direction, then we are on to something. On the other hand, it is difficult to know what leads to what, difficult to know what "good" comes from what we do. The effects are hard to trace. They flow into and merge with the effects of other events, large and small, becoming a part of the culture that shapes us and shapes the consciousness of a time.

When we were planning our event, Warren indicated that he was interested in getting together with old friends and "kickin' it." If that is all that was done at our event, then that is enough. How are we to fill our time—at least some of it—if not by creating ways of coming together and kickin' it, coming together to enjoy the funniest and wisest part of those we have known for years and those we have just met? By so doing, are we not shaping the culture that shapes us, making sure we do not become strangers, deepening and enlarging the community of which we are a part? If our event—even in a small way—permitted this to occur (and I am not saying it did, only that it seemed so to me), then that is enough, with additional outcomes serving as icing on the cake.

DE-BRIEFING ON THE DRIVE HOME

On the three-hour drive home, I talked to Bill about the *Odyssey*. We discussed various aspects of the event, the stories that were told, the paper he contributed, the esteem with which Warren was held, the sculpture, the extraordinary job done by our moderator. But most of all we talked about the history present in the room. It was Kansas City's history, but it went deeper than that. There was D'Morris Smith, whose father—as Leon Dixon reminded everyone—scouted Jackie Robinson. There was the history of Kansas City's Interscholastic League, but there also was Warren's recounting of the time in college when he dunked from the free throw line—before Dr. J did it in the ABA dunk contest— dunked from the free throw line because he was afraid of the jumping ability and long arms of the players chasing him. And there was Mr. Maurice Copeland, whose family history reached back to John Anthony Copeland, one of the five black men who rode with John Brown in Brown's raid on Harper's Ferry. I had not been familiar with John Anthony Copeland's story, or with the story of Lewis Sheridan Leary, Copeland's friend who recruited him to join John Brown's armed party. But in the course of our de-briefing, Bill filled me in.

John Anthony Copeland was born a free black in 1843 in

Raleigh, North Carolina. He attended Oberlin College and became involved in abolitionist and antislavery activities. He was one of thirty-seven men involved in the incident known as the Oberlin-Wellington Rescue in which John Price, a runaway slave who had been captured and held by authorities under the 1850 Fugitive Slave Act, was freed and helped to escape to Canada.

A year following the Oberlin-Wellington Rescue, Copeland joined John Brown for the raid on Harper's Ferry. He was captured by a regiment of marines (a regiment led by Robert E. Lee), tried and later hung alongside John Brown (the above according to Wikipedia). (See Endnote 5.)

Copeland's friend, Lewis Sheridan Leary, married Mary Patterson in Fayetteville, Arkansas in 1858. Both Leary and Patterson (like Copeland) were dedicated abolitionists and served as conductors on the Underground Railroad. One year after their marriage, according to *The Life of Langston Hughes* by Arnold Rampersad, Lewis Leary "rode away (accompanied by John Anthony Copeland) without telling Mary where he was going.... On the night of October 16 he (and Copeland) was in John Brown's party of twenty-one men when they attacked the federal arsenal at Harper's Ferry. The next day Leary was shot as he tried to cross the Shenandoah." According to Rampersad, Leary "endured two days of bitter pain before he died. A friend brought his blood-stained, bullet-riddled shawl home to Mary..." It became one of her most valued possessions.

Ten years after Leary's death, Mary married Charles Howard Langston, also a staunch abolitionist. In 1902, the poet Langston Hughes was born to Mary and Charles's daughter, Carolina, and her husband, James Hughes. From early childhood, Langston lived with his grandmother. He slept covered by the shawl and later was told the story behind it, told also about his abolitionist heritage. According to Rampersad, the young poet "nursed a sense that he was obliged within his lifetime, in some way, to match (the deeds of his abolitionist forbearers). Because of these men and, above all, his grandmother, no one could convince the boy that he was intrinsically inferior."

Langston Hughes eventually inherited the shawl, and years later when his Harlem apartment flooded—long after he had become one of America's most beloved poets—the shawl was the only item he recovered.

REFLECTIONS ON "KICKIN' IT"

What does it mean to "kick it"? At the very least it means "to have a good time."

But to have a good time—*a really good time*—requires that we drop our hardened habits of thinking and doing, the habits that obstruct the free and spontaneous flow of energy. What is more important than that? Everyday life is held in place by these habits, by "holding patterns" that lock perception in place. To escape these holding patterns even briefly is renewing.

Old friends help us do that. They help us stand outside ourselves where we can observe with some detachment the story of our lives, which is also the story of our time. Old friends help us experience our humanity. They remind us that "laughter" and "liberation" have a lot in common.

As I see it, this is the wisdom that Warren expressed when he said he wanted to get together with old friends and kick it. I'm not saying that our event accomplished this end at any level or to any degree, only that this was one of the impulses behind our event even though we never thought to say it. (See Endnote 6.)

CONCLUSION

A few weeks after our event, Warren unexpectedly had open-heart surgery. Though his condition was obviously serious, all went well and Warren made a steady recovery. A few weeks into his recovery I called to see how he was doing.

We talked about his operation, about what had made it necessary, and about the changes—though minor—that it was making in his lifestyle. I mentioned that I finally had met Reggie Marshall, the individual who also had written a tribute to Warren—a beautiful tribute—posted on the "Remember the ABA" website (see Part I). I repeated what Reggie had said to me: that he is in Miami on occasion and would look forward to meeting Warren in what he hoped would be the not-too-distant future.

I then mentioned that I was in the process of writing up the *Odyssey* and that when I was done, we should give some thought to the next event, something different perhaps but something that would give us a Part IV—a final part, perhaps—to our book.

Warren's response: "You mean you're proposing that we just keep kickin' it until we can't kick it no more?" "Well, yes," I said, "I guess I am." "I'm good with that," he said.

ENDNOTES TO PART IV

1. Following "the game that changed college basketball," Coach Haskins "received bags of hate mail, many of them postmarked from Kentucky, and there were death threats directed toward both the coach and his players. If that wasn't bad enough, Rupp, according to Haskins...was out there trashing Texas Western after the game, calling them 'a bunch of crooks' and telling a Kentucky newspaper that Haskins had recruited Lattin, who transferred to Texas Western from Tennessee State, 'out of the Tennessee state prison.' The next year, *Sports Illustrated* came to town and wrote that Haskins was exploiting his black players, that they weren't real students and that the city was unfriendly to minorities, and that none of the players' wives could get jobs. None of Haskins' players was married. Haskins wanted to sue, but the school felt it was better to let it blow over." (From an article by Dick Weiss, *Daily News* Sports writer, entitled "Crowning Glory: In '66, Texas Western's 5 Black Starters Beat All-White Kentucky to Earn National Championship," dated Sunday, January 8, 2006.)

2. What a beautiful player Lucius Allen was...so quick to his right or his left...and then the rise into a picture perfect jump shot! And such range! And if not the jump shot, then the pinpoint pass or the darting move to the basket, always, always with beautiful form. Who would not have loved to play like Lucius Allen?

   It is one thing for me to say that Warren was the greatest player ever to come out of the Kansas City area, quite another for Lucius Allen to say it.

   In an article in the *Kansas City Star* dated June 23, 2011, and entitled, "The Stuff of Dreams," the writer, Blair Kerkhoff, discusses the players from the Kansas City area who went on to play professional basketball. Allen tops the list for points scored as a professional and is arguably the most well-known player from the Kansas City area given that he played with Oscar Robertson and Kareem Abdul Jabar on championship teams. But as the headline states (on page B4 where the article continues): "Allen says Jabali is the best to come from KC."

   > As productive and successful as he was, Allen doesn't
   > believe he's the best player to emerge from an area high
   > school. He doesn't even think he was the best in the
   > metro area while he was playing.

"Warren Jabali," Allen said. "He was Warren Armstrong then. One-on-one, I didn't have a chance against him."

"...he intimidated me," Allen said. "He was a physical specimen."

Would the writer of this article have known to mention Jabali's name had it not been for Allen's comment? In discussing this article with Leon Harden, I was reminded of the debate that raged in certain quarters during the mid- to late '60s: *Who is better, Allen or Armstrong (Jabali)?* Those who saw them both had their opinions and many felt they knew the answer; and now, Allen—so known for the style and grace of his game—has put the issue to rest.

3. We were enormously fortunate to have in the room the people we had. At the same time, there were many who were missed, who we hoped would have been able to attend: Bill Boykin, Kennie Denmon, Dr. Herman Watson, Warren's long-time friend and teammate Al Smith, all with scheduling conflicts. Also missed was the Reverend Nelson "Fuzzy" Thompson, who, like the others, would have added much to the discussion but was unable to attend because of health concerns. And we missed Len Trower; Len had been involved in planning the event since the beginning. However, snowstorms in the Northeast prevented his attendance.

Even so, within a few days of the event I received the following essay from Len summarizing what he would have contributed had he been able to attend.

A few words on the topic of males... What I have to say has to be taken in context; in this case, the national context of the economy, what could be considered recent history, the political climate, and the emerging national mood. The context also includes my recent reading of Nathan Glazer, the late Chalmers Johnson, Chris Hedges, and Morris Berman.

It would be an understatement to say things aren't uplifting. I recently received a call from James Mtume, the NYC radio talk show host and former musician/songwriter/singer, about 5 or 6 homicides in Newark, New Jersey within 48 hours of one another where young Black males, 13 to 16, were viciously gunned down for no apparent reason. Some were shot 4 and 5 times. There was no robbery, no drugs, no jealousy over girls, and no gang-related ill will. This was just killing for killing's sake because so many young Blacks have given up hope. Mtume (pronounced em-TOO-may) is calling for a mass march on Newark's City Hall with the intent of shutting down municipal operations because, despite the presence of a Black mayor, municipal operations haven't worked for Newark's majority of Black residents. For that matter, for African Americans in general, neither has the election of a Black President.

I recall ex-First Lady Barbara Bush's stated commitment—at the beginning of her husband's last term in office—where she expressed the need to emphasize the plight of boys in America because *they have been neglected and completely overlooked for so long.* The implication of her commitment is that, for a period longer than most people are consciously aware of, the focus in this country, however inadequate, has been on girls. Personally, I cannot recall what efforts were made by Mrs. Bush on behalf of boys, but I believe it's safe to say that her efforts probably were not focused on African American boys. And if in the eyes of Mrs. Bush the neglect has been so obvious on white boys, imagine what it has been when it comes to Black boys, who remain this country's most feared and despised element. Unlike Hispanic boys, who are vilified because they are seen as the illegal underpinnings of a failing economy, or Middle Eastern boys, who are looked at askance because they might be of a despised religion, Black boys are seen as overarching threats to civilization.

It is no accident that females in this country for the past 3 decades have made incredible leaps over males in higher education and employment. Defined groups don't accomplish such advancements without broad social and political approval. Likewise, defined groups who fall behind don't do so without broad social and political indifference.

Mtume raised a very true and disturbing point in our phone conversation the other night when he said that the most disturbing development has occurred among African Americans, the middle class of which now "sees Black boys through white eyes." Simply put, I believe he meant that there is something inherent in the cultural values in this country that is racist, excessively individualistic and is so obsessed with material security that many people are rendered incapable of seeing the pain and indifference experienced by others. The point could be made that there is so little distinction between class and racial perceptions that quite possibly they may have merged; that to see oneself in the mainstream is to embrace and view life through a racist prism. For example, as has been the case in previous economic downturns, the nation now recognizes and acknowledges millions of its citizens who are hurting because of unemployment, under-employment and mortgages under water, but does so principally because most of these troubled citizens are white and are assumed to have played the game fairly and done all the right things. But if and when (which isn't likely in the near future) the economy returns to its "normal and acceptable unemployment rate" of 6% or less, the people who will comprise this normal and acceptable statistic will be forgotten because they will disproportionately be African American males. Many Black males will not be counted at all unless, of course, they are among the disproportionate numbers of incarcerated Black males whose numbers are needed to economically and politically bolster rural white communities where most prisons exist. Homelessness will regain national attention because it will carry the face of a Black or white mother with children; but when the economic dust settles and homelessness has the face of "a brother" on the corner begging for your loose change, he will likely be cursed, told to go find a job, or ignored as some inanimate fixture. There will be no plethora of social programs for him; no special series of newspaper articles about the plight of the poor.

In the context of the global economy, many scholars believe that the United States is in irreversible decline, a decline that will be gradual but still painful, and will take between 15 to 25 years to settle at a depressing "new normal." Some folks argue that in such a situation the African American male will continue to survive because for so long, unlike everyone else, he has become accustomed to making something out of nothing, even if that something is illegal.

No one can predict the future, but I believe that it's safe to say that the African American male will continue to be socially neglected, and that it will be up to African American males—a key segment of them—to save themselves. In a culture obsessed with individualism (where even the long-term white unemployed are increasingly being typecast as lazy), there simply isn't the cultural framework, both historically and at present, to generate the kind and degree of non-racist compassion to effectively address our problems.

Addendum to Endnote 3. Early in the planning of the *Odyssey,* I asked individuals to send quotes that I might write on large tablet pages and place around the room for people to peruse. I also asked for music that should play before and after the session and during breaks. Len offered the following:

> Reaching for a Black thinker would be far too easy. So I looked around and found a book I read when I was 18, during my 1st semester at Wichita State, by UN Secretary Dag Hammarskjold entitled "Markings." Here are two quotes:
>
> *"Never, 'for the sake of peace and quiet,' deny your own experience or convictions."*
>
> *"The only kind of dignity which is genuine is that which is not diminished by the indifference of others."*
>
> Recommended music: Miles Davis's "Kind of Blue" and Pharaoh Sanders's "The Creator Has a Master Plan."

4. The August 15–22, 2011, edition of *The Nation* was devoted to "sports and politics." In that edition, a "distinguished group of writers, thinkers and advocates" were invited "to pay tribute to their favorite sports heroes" and in the process to explore "the areas in which sports culture intersects with the pursuit of social and economic justice."

    Warren's story was not told in that edition, but certainly his story (or journey) cannot be told without taking into consideration what the editors of *The Nation* hoped to explore.

    > "Howard Cosell called it rule number one of the jockocracy—the idea that sports and politics don't mix. Playing the game, and playing it well, is all that matters.

And yet the closer you look, the more it becomes
apparent that it's not sports and politics that 'don't mix.'
It's sports and a certain kind of politics—the politics of
protest and resistance. Athletes who speak out on issues
of social justice invariably pay a price. It's a problem that
powerful commercial interests control the language of
sports, not just because it shuts out alternative
perspectives but because sports culture shapes other
cultural attitudes, norms and power arrangements. Politics
runs rampant throughout the sports world, a broad arena
in which struggles for racial justice, gender equality and
economic fairness are played out." —The Editors.

5. Six days before John Anthony Copeland was executed, he wrote a
letter to his brother from jail:

"And now, brother, for having lent my aid to a general
no less brave [than George Washington], and engaged in
a cause no less honorable and glorious, I am to suffer
death. Washington entered the field to fight for the
freedom of the American people—not for the white man
alone, but for both black and white. Nor were they white
men alone who fought for the freedom of this country.
The blood of black men flowed as freely as the blood of
white men. Yes, the very first blood that was spilt was
that of a negro... But this you know as well as I do...the
claims which we, as colored men, have on the American
people." (Wikipedia)

6. I would like to take this line of thought one step further. I believe that
there is a direction to history and that this direction is moral in nature.
Moral because in this wired-up, interconnected, mutually dependent
world, we just can't get away with it like we used to. We can't win at
the expense of others without experiencing some degree of loss
ourselves. Increasingly, winning (not in the sports arena but in the
arena of life) depends on others winning as well.

I'm well aware of the counter argument, i.e.: *Wake up! There are
plenty of groups at this very moment 'winning' at the expense of
others, experiencing no discernible loss and not bothering to look
back. Even if what you are saying has some truth in it, it's a long-run
truth and we live in the short run, here and now, and there's not*

enough of what you are describing in the here and now to make a difference for us.

I've always felt that the counter argument had the power to end the discussion right then and there. Still, I maintain that what I am saying is more true now than ever before, to the point that it is not a mere abstraction but a felt reality by an ever-increasing number of people. There are setbacks galore—and maybe we are in the midst of one now—and the outcome is not inevitable. But historical time does seem to be converging with everyday time and bringing with it a need for—a search for—arrangements that permit us to swim and not sink together.

The view I am expressing here—that history is moving in a specific direction, that we win together or perhaps not at all—has been elaborated in recent years by Robert Wright in his book, *Nonzero: The Logic of Human Destiny.* Near the end of his book, he writes:

> "My belief that some workable infrastructure for concord will very likely emerge does nothing to drain the drama from the present, for one plausible route to long-run success is near-term catastrophe. However close inevitable stable world governance may be in the long run, here and now we are playing for the highest stakes that have ever been played for, and winning will depend in no small part on continued moral growth. Which is to say: winning will depend on not wanting other peoples to lose." p. 332.

I take this theoretical excursion only to say that "kickin' it," as we have defined it, seems to me in service to the development of "new and just arrangements," indeed, even to "moral growth" as much as anything we can do on a personal level—the kicking or loosening of the hardened habits that obstruct creative thought and limit possibility.

Part V

Kickin' It

*"You mean you're proposing that we
just keep kickin' it until we can't kick it
no more?"*
"Well, yes," I said, *"I guess I am."*
"I'm good with that," he said.

One year later, Warren and I were planning to get together again. We
wanted to carry forward in some fashion what we had done with the
Odyssey event, though what form it should take was undecided.

Finally, Warren suggested that we simply make the rounds,
visiting the people and haunts of his youth. Perhaps the themes of the
previous year's *Odyssey* would be touched on, but more than anything he
wanted to "kick it" with old friends.

I would videotape the meetings and perhaps it would result in
material worth including in our project, whatever it was to be (book,
video).

(At this point, I must extend my apology to Mr. Will McCarther.
He was the first person we visited because he was, in Warren's view, the
person who had perhaps gone the farthest, from very humble beginnings
to his professional life as an educator and hospital administrator. The
video recorder failed to work (something I discovered much later when I
sat down to transcribe the conversations that follow), so I was unable to
transcribe his interaction with Warren. However, Mr. McCarther did
participate in the *Odyssey* and his insights and reflections, less extensive
than what he shared in conversation with Warren, can be seen in Part
IV.)

—

One of our first stops was Gates Bar-B-Q in Kansas City, Kansas, where
we met with William (Bill) Robinson and Ernie Moore. Warren knew
Bill Robinson, but I don't believe he had ever seen him play.

Bill played for the University of Nevada. As a freshman, he was
first team All-Far Western Conference, leading the conference in both
scoring (22.5 pts per game) and rebounding (15.5 per game). At 6'4", he
played center against the likes of Iowa's Don Nelson, Purdue's Terry
Disenger, and Creighton's Paul Silas. Against Rick Barry's Miami, he
scored 28 points and 28, again, against Ollie Johnson's Temple. He got
as high as third on the small college national scoring list at 28 points a

game. Prior to an injury to his right knee that effectively ended Bill's playing career, *Coach and Athlete* magazine stated, "Bill Robinson could make any major college team in the country and play first string on 98% of them."

Warren was close with Ernie Moore and a great admirer of his game. According to the Wichita State Athletics—Go Shockers website, Moore, a four-year starter, played on some of the finest teams in WSU history. During Ernie's tenure,

> The Shockers won 78 games, including a 23-6 mark in Moore's senior season of 1963–64. Moore quarterbacked that squad to its first Missouri Valley Conference championship, averaging 17.4 points per game. That output was second on the team only to Dave Stallworth's 26.5-point average.
>
> Moore averaged in double figures each of his four seasons, finishing his career with 1,055 points, joining only seven other Shockers at that time in the 1,000-Point Club. Moore's top-scoring game was 30 points in a victory over Tulsa in 1961.

Despite Moore's scoring ability, according to the website, he was feared by opponents for his extreme quickness and strength, which made him a defensive force in the backcourt. Ernie Moore was inducted into the Wichita State Athletic Hall of Fame in 1997. On that day, the *Wichita Eagle* carried an article that began as follows:

> Dave Stallworth came to Wichita in 1960 and became the most amazing player in Shocker basketball history. But Stallworth's first year on campus was when he learned what amazing was.
>
> Amazing was named Ernie Moore.
>
> "He was a sophomore and I was a freshman," Stallworth said. "I'm out there with this guy, and he was just taking people to school.
>
> "I learned so much of the game from Ernie, it wasn't even funny."

Stallworth calls Moore the greatest guard to come
through the Roundhouse. He had quickness that came in
handy when harassing defenders, a court sense that made
him a valuable assist man and was a 45-percent shooter
for his career.

Bob Lutz, a reporter for the *Wichita Eagle,* ranked the 100
greatest Shockers. Here are the first fifteen Shockers on his list,
published in 2016:

1. Dave Stallworth
2. Xavier McDaniel
3. Antoine Carr
4. Cleo Littleton
5. Warren Armstrong Jabali
6. Fred VanVleet
7. Cliff Levingston
8. Ron Baker
9. Cleanthony Early
10. Cheese Johnson
11. Jamie Thompson
12. Robert Elmore
13. Kelly Pete (Mohamed Sharif)
14. Aubrey Sherrod
15. Ernie Moore

Warren: I used to sit on the railroad ties at the Dunbar court and watch
lots of games. It was like I was telling you earlier about how I liked to
watch Julius Erving play. I used to like to play against his teams just so I
could watch him play.

So I would watch Ernie play and the word I have consistently
used to describe his play is "artistic." His game was artistic. Listening to
him describe his game as "figuring it out as he was going along" fits,
because that's how it appeared.

*(Prior to meeting with Earnie and Bill, Warren and I talked
about the difference between Warren's game and Ernie's.)* I considered
my game to be a power game, a game where you're trying to get from
where you are on the perimeter into and close to the basket in order to
dunk the ball, as that is what I visualized myself doing.

Ernie's game, on the other hand, was played on the perimeter.
He had to do things on the perimeter that would free him up to shoot his

shot. So all the artistic things I'm talking about were directed toward freeing him up to get his shot. And when he got off his shot, he shot it in such a way that it had the arc that hit nothing but the bottom of the net. It wasn't one of those flat shots that hit the rim and then goes in. *It was artistic.*

And the passes that were made... His vision wasn't just on the rim. His vision included everything that was occurring in front of him so he was able to make exceptional passes. He had a complete offensive game. He said he got his game from other people, but certainly, I've seen people try to emulate his game.

Ernie: I knew Warren when he was a baby. I watched him grow up, so I knew what he could do. Warren says I was artistic. He was artistic also. I've seen him get stopped and just throw the ball up against the backboard and then go get it just to get himself out of a predicament. And then dunk it! At 6'2"!

There were two big guards in this area that always gave me trouble. Warren, number one, and Ray Sedecki, number two, because back in those days they had men bodies, what you call men bodies. I was frail, 5'10", maybe 155 pounds. They took you where they wanted you to go.

Now, Warren could shoot outside, but he could also take you inside and punish you. He just had an all-around game that I admired. And I think I gave him some of my material, too. *[Laughing]* I hope I did.

Warren: Without a doubt.

Ernie: Warren and my brother were good friends. I watched Warren grow up. I watched him begin playing basketball. I watched him get good, and I watched him get great. At that time there were two basketball players that I would pay to go see. That would be Warren and Richard Dumas. They were good. *They were good.*

Warren: We would take from each other's game. And there wasn't any doubt that I was sitting there watching Ernie in order to learn how to play because he was playing the game so well. Ernie says he got his ball handling from Johnny Keith. I was watching television and I learned how to hold the ball by watching Elgin Baylor. But you don't get the feel of an offensive maneuver simply by watching television. You go out and see it live, especially as close up as you can see it on a school ground. So I watched the techniques that Ernie used: the arc, the upper arm perpendicular to the floor, the follow-through after the release of the ball—all the things that coaches teach today, Ernie did them naturally. So I incorporated almost all of those things into what I did.

Ernie: I only played with William (Bill Robinson) one year, but at the time I thought William was the best center in the state. He had the jump shot, he had the hook, he had all the moves around the paint that you could ask for. And he had a good temperament. He should have been taking more shots than he took. He was the best center in the state.

Bill: Talking about Ernie... I met Ernie at the Dunbar court. I said to myself: *Man, he knows every crack on this court!* I had a coach, he later became the coach at Nevada, and he watched Ernie and some of the others play and he said that some of the best players in the country came out of Kansas City, Kansas. And Warren, he came out of the crib playing. *[Laughing]* God blesses a whole lot of folks. I couldn't believe the things he could do at 6'2".

Ernie: I know. It ain't fair. It ain't fair.

Bill: You can talk about Jordon and Dr. J, but man, *at 6'2"!*

Ernie: One time I remember being really hurt... It was when the NBA and the ABA merged. Nobody in the NBA picked Warren up, and for one lousy little incident. In the ABA All-Star game, Warren got most valuable player and nobody picked him up!

Warren: I remember what I was going to tell you. I mentioned that I liked to watch Julius Erving play and I liked to watch Ernie play. Ernie used to come up an alley behind the Dunbar court. If he was wearing his Converse, I was happy because that meant he was going to play. Most of the time, though, he came through wearing his suit. He would be going somewhere and I would be disappointed. *[Laughing]*

Ernie: I wasn't going anywhere. *[Laughing]*

D. Thomas: Ernie, Fuzzy Thompson told me that he thought you influenced the development of a lot of players in the Kansas City area. Like Warren, he described your game as artistic. He said that even if you were going to fall, you wanted to fall like Ernie Moore.

Ernie: I don't care who you are, if you're a basketball player, somebody at some point is going to mess all over you. When I was playing, I use to watch the faces of the guys I was playing against and if they dropped their heads after I scored on them, I knew I had them.

D. Thomas: What did the Dunbar court mean to you and to the community?

Ernie: I don't know that it meant anything to the community other than it got the kids out of the house in the evening. But for us, it was just about everything. We didn't have anything else to do. They had railroad ties along one side of the court and sometimes there would be people from one end of that wall to the other watching and waiting to play. If you lost, you were out. You could forget about it.

Warren: Unless you were Ernie.

Ernie: Nah.

Warren: They would hold a place for Ernie.

Ernie: No. Sometimes, but not all the time.

Bill: That's where the competition was. I remember Fred Slaughter showed up one time. He played center for UCLA.

Ernie: Bill Bridges. Maurice King. They came over on occasion.

Bill: I always wanted to play against players better than I was.

Ernie: Me, too. I always wanted the competition.

Bill: The greatest thing I ever had was a library card. I used it to go to the library and get a book on rebounding by Bill Russell. That book told me everything. Rebounding was position. If you got position on somebody, then you could take care of business.

D. Thomas: Did either of you see or hear of anyone coming from the second block on a missed free throw, grabbing the ball in mid-air and dunking it, anyone other than Warren?

Ernie: No. *Never.*

Warren: You never saw it.

Ernie: I didn't see it, but I sure heard about it. And when they told me about it, I wasn't surprised.

Bill: God just blessed him, that's all.

Ernie: Warren could force his will on the game. I couldn't force my will on anyone unless I had somebody my size, like Wally Jones. I could force my will on him. And I did. *[Laughter]*

Warren: You played against Villanova?

Ernie: Yeah, in Madison Square Garden. I had my way with him, but the bottom line is they wound up beating us by two points. Me and Dave (Stallworth) had words in that game because I thought Dave was too passive.

Warren: He was too passive.

Ernie: Wasn't he?

Warren: He definitely was.

Ernie: This man (Stallworth), at 6'7" was probably the best basketball player in the world at that time. If he would have forced his will on people... But he wouldn't do it.

Warren: At 6'7" he could handle the ball and pass it like Ernie.

D. Thomas: Who were the all-time greats from your point of view?

Ernie: From this area?

D. Thomas: From this area and overall.

Ernie: Well, for sure, these three (referring to Warren, Bill, and himself). Richard Dumas. Would you all agree, Richard Dumas?

Warren/Bill: Definitely.

NOTE: Richard "Rich" Dumas (born in 1945) is a

retired American professional basketball player who spent one season in the American Basketball Association (ABA) with the Houston Mavericks during the 1968–69 season. He attended Sumner High School in Kansas City, Kansas (1962) and later Northeastern State University. (Wikipedia)

Ernie: And I'll tell you someone. Do you remember Doc Green? It just goes to show you: Anyone can play this game. You just have to be determined. Doc Green had a heart condition as we were growing up, so he never played basketball. He started playing after I started playing at Sumner. I use to see him up on Dunbar after everyone had gone home working on his game. Now he got his game together to the point that he was relevant at least on the playground. Now, if you put him in an organized situation, I'm sure he would have probably been out of his element.

Warren: He was "school-ground".

Ernie: That's right. Because of his health, he never got involved with organized ball. And he did die of a heart attack eventually. Anybody can learn how to play this game. I worked on my game. I was small, so I had to "think" the game. I would work on my jump shot... it would be dusk-dark, you could only see the corner of the rim and I would practice shooting.

Warren: You had coaching, too. I really didn't have much coaching. Lanny Van Eman said that I had a game from 15 feet in, but nobody was saying, "You need to develop your game from 15 feet on out." And in addition to that, nobody said, "You need to get in shape," because I was never in shape. *[Laughing]*

> NOTE: Lanny Van Eman recruited Warren out of high school. He was a WSU athlete from '58 to '62 and later an assistant coach.

Ernie: You said they told you that your game was from 15 feet in, and that nobody told you to develop a game from 15 feet out. *That's because you had your way from 15 feet on in! [Laughter]* Now, I'm not taking up for the coaches, I'm just saying that if I was the coach and you're killing them from 15 feet on in and you started talking about how you want to shoot 3's, I would say: *Hold it. I'll let you shoot a 3 but not this year!* No, you had your way. *[Laughter]*

D. Thomas: But still, you have your place in the ABA record books for 3-point shots.

Warren: Well, I was talking about Lanny Van Eman's assessment of me as a high school player. And most of the time, I didn't need more in high school. But going into college… See, I wasn't a scorer in college.

Ernie: Yeah, you were. You were a scorer. You weren't a shooter, but you could score on anyone.

D. Thomas: Who were the best players you played against?

Warren: The best I played against in college was Walt Frasier. Walt Frasier made me realize the conditioning aspect of the game. This boy would play just as hard on defense as he did on offense.

Southern Illinois came into Wichita and whipped us by 20 points. We didn't know what hit us. I would guard him and he was 25 feet from the basket. There wasn't a 3-point line in those days. He would put the ball back over his head to shoot and just look at me. So I would back up and say, "Okay, you shoot it!" And he would hit it. *Bam!*

And when I looked at how thoroughly they whipped us, that's what it was, defensive conditioning and offensive efficiency. They mowed us down. But when I say there was an absence of coaching, nobody told me that I was about to go up against one of the best guards in the country.

Ernie: I'll tell you a story. I bet you don't know about this. I was a freshman and we were having a party after the game and I was supposed to get the punch together. So that's what I did. I poured the alcohol in the punch and took a sip… and took a sip… and I got tipsy.

As I said, we had a game that night. The coach smelled the alcohol on me and he said, "You're outta here. You just lost your scholarship." I didn't say nothing because it was my own fault. So I turned around and headed to the locker room and he said, "No. I'm going to make you embarrass yourself. You're playing tonight. Get out there!" He made me play the whole game!

So the game was tied with a minute left. By the way, I was having a phenomenal night. *[Laughter]* The coach told our center to take the last shot but if he couldn't get his shot, he's suppose to kick it out to me. And that's what happened. He got me the ball with about 9 seconds left and I drove the baseline. I put up a floater that went in and we won the game. I didn't even stop, didn't even know if it went in. I just kept running to the locker room and started packing up my stuff to go home. The coach came in and said, "Well, you got your scholarship back." *[Laughter]*

D. Thomas: What did Alex Hannum mean when he said you were the smartest player he ever coached?

Warren: I saw that. I don't know what he meant. I think a lot of that had to do with promoting the ABA. In addition to being a coach, Hannum was a part owner of the Denver Rockets. *[Pause]* He may have meant being able to influence teams…

Ernie: *[interrupting]* You were undersized and you were always putting your influence on the game. Your print was always on the game. For a guy 6'2"… That's what Hannum is talking about. That's hard to do.

Warren: I remember one night… Ralph Simpson was the other guard. Dave Robish, out of Kansas, was the center. Ralph would get the ball on the wing and he would shoot it. His focus was on the rim, that's it. So he would shoot his jump shot every time he got the ball.

So Robish is throwing a tantrum. I say to him, "Look, man, if I'm over there on that wing, do you think I'll throw you the ball?" "Yeah." "And when Ralph is over there, do you think he's going to throw you the ball?" "Nah!" "Well, then, why don't you turn your ass around and get in position for the rebound?"

Ernie: Right. You going to quit playing just because you don't get the ball?

Warren: "If I get it on the wing, I'll throw you the ball." He said, "Okay, man." Cause otherwise you're just creating an antagonism on the team. If he's going to shoot it, what do we need in case he misses? We need a rebound. I noticed that Hannum overheard this. So, it may be that kind of stuff that Hannum was talking about.

Bill: The person I liked was Chamberlain.

Ernie: Me, too. I liked him over Russell. Russell couldn't do anything with Chamberlain. Now Russell played good defense but there wasn't anything he could do with Chamberlain.

Bill: To me, the best player I played against, he wasn't the best but he was the strongest, was Don Nelson. That was a strong, corn-fed dude. There weren't that many guys stronger than I was when I was at my peak, so I was impressed with him.

Ernie: *[Tape ended. Lead-in to this story was not recorded.]* Two white dudes were guarding me; one was 6'2", the other 6'3". And I was killin' em. So they brought in this black dude off the bench to guard me, brought him in cold! I said to him, "Don't let them do you like that. I am hot!" He said, "No, I got you." And before he could get those words out of his mouth I scored. I set a (WSU) field house record that night. *I mean, when you're on and in your rhythm, you know it!*

—

From Gates Bar-B-Q, we drove to the vacant lot where Dunbar Elementary School and the Dunbar court once stood. As indicated previously, the Dunbar court was considered by some to be Kansas City's Rucker Park. It was a cold day and we stayed only a few minutes.

Warren: Here was where the school was, a brick school, you can probably see the outline here on the ground. Then we would come, I would come through those houses up there and walk on this wall. And then jump down, and jump down, and the court would be over here. And down by that telephone pole was a little alley, and Ernie Moore would come walking up through that ally.

D. Thomas: What are your most vivid memories about playing on this court?

Warren: Listening to J.B. Hill do the play-by-play. *[Laughter]* Watching Richard Dumas shoot his jump shots and hook shots; watching Ernie Moore shoot his jump shots. I wasn't dunking much then, so everything I was doing was related to shooting. And they were the best shooters: Richard Dumas, Ernie Moore, Johnny Keith, Herman Watson...

—

As we drove from place to place, Warren and I had an ongoing exchange covering a range of topics.

D. Thomas: What should be and shouldn't be remembered?

Warren: Well, what shouldn't be remembered are those things that are trivial, things like sitting upstairs at a movie theater, the Jim Crow laws. Those things were so trivial in nature they should be forgotten. Things that *shouldn't* be forgotten, though it may seem paradoxical, are the people who fought against those laws.

So, I guess Jim Crow as a concept should be remembered—that laws were established and created to hold people back—but the exact descriptions and details of it should be forgotten but not the people who fought against it.

D. Thomas: How good are you at letting go of the trivial things and remembering what's essential?

Warren: Well, I think I'm pretty good at it. I think, perhaps, one of the things that made me better than the average person was the alcohol addiction that I had at one point and listening to the philosophy of the 12-Step founders. They advise you to recognize the difference between the things that you can change and the things that you can't change. I use to say that all the time to myself: "Grant me the serenity to accept the things I cannot change; the courage to change the things that I can; and the wisdom to know the difference."

And if you listen to that and hear it enough times, it begins to sink in. And you begin to apply it to circumstances and try to learn the difference between those things you can change and those things that you can't. And if you can't change them, then you're supposed to accept them. And in that acceptance you begin to limit the amount of frustration that you might feel about one thing or the other. So it's not me, it's the wisdom and counsel of people that has made it something that I can do.

D. Thomas: And it's also about the ability to apply that wisdom, right?

Warren: Yeah, well, you have to be able to apply it. It gives you a framework. It's one thing to recognize that you need to do something. It's another thing when you've been given a play. Like in basketball, coaches give us plays. So if you execute the play properly, you're likely to end up with a good shot. The serenity prayer gives you a play. If you execute it, then you're going to get a good shot.

D. Thomas: That's something I didn't know: You had an alcohol problem at one point?

Warren: After I stopped playing and moved to St. Thomas in the Virgin Islands. I started having a lot of disagreements with my first wife. By that time, there were four children and I felt trapped in a circumstance I didn't like. I started increasing the amount of alcohol that I would drink because it made me not care about what I was going through. So I became alcohol dependent in that sense.

D. Thomas: So did you enter a 12-Step Program?

Warren: Well, I was court referred. I ended up with two DUIs. So you have to do whatever the sentencing requires. That was one of the stipulations: that I go through a 12-Step program. Not a "program," but go to AA meetings that use the 12-step program. I didn't go into a facility or anything like that.

D. Thomas: Did you end up stopping drinking altogether?

Warren: Yeah.

D. Thomas: So how many years since you've had a drink?

Warren: Probably about twenty.

D. Thomas: Was that a difficult thing for you to do, giving up alcohol?

Warren: No, it wasn't. I went down to the Employee Assistance Program because whenever you have an arrest in Dade County they want to examine every aspect of it. So I went to the Employee Assistance Program and they asked me a lot of questions.

This woman, as far as I was concerned, had a nasty attitude. She said something like if she had her way, she would put me in a detox program for six weeks. So I was sitting there listening to her and my attitude was: She doesn't know anything about me. If I wanted to quit, I would just quit. And so, that's what I did because she pissed me off.

I didn't realize at the time that that was one of their techniques. Whatever it took to stop somebody from drinking, that's what they would do. If insulting you would work, then they would insult you. If insulting you didn't work, then they would try something else. So, she insulted me. Pissed me off. So I said: I'll show you! *[laughing]* I stopped drinking, just like that!

D. Thomas: When you stopped drinking, that meant you didn't have one of the ways you buffered yourself from a situation you didn't like. Did that mean you dealt more directly with the situation you were in?

Warren: Nope. Because by that time I was out of it. I was no longer in that situation. I just had the alcohol addiction. I had the habit.

That's what I tell young people about smoking. They puff on these things in order to be cool, but after a while the nicotine grabs hold of them. You're not smoking to be cool any more; you're smoking because you have a nicotine addiction. It's the same thing: I wasn't drinking any more because of this person and this situation. I was drinking because I had an alcohol addiction.

So I guess it was easier for me because I was only dealing with the physical addiction as opposed to the physical addiction *and* the emotional issue.

D. Thomas: On your sixtieth birthday video, you referred to Mary as the love of your life. After your divorce, did you deliberately set out to find someone who would be that person in your life?

Warren: Well, yeah. By that time I was almost fifty years old and had plenty of experiences. I had wanted some companionship, and I was seeking someone who could fill that role. So that would be: Yeah.

—

The Sportsmen Barbershop is an institution in Kansas City. Ralph Brown, the owner, started it in the early '60s. He named it the Sportsmen Barbershop because of all the professional athletes who came there for their haircuts. Inside the barbershop is a gallery of photographs and posters commemorating the history of sports in Kansas City. We arrived there around 5:00 p.m. and the place was busy, with several customers waiting.

Barber #1: There was someone in here earlier talking about Warren. If he was in here right now, he'd be asking for Warren's autograph.

Barber #2 (Mary): Yeah, they talk about him all the time.

D. Thomas: And what do they say?

Barber #2 (Mary): They talk about what a great person he is.

Barber #1: I'm going to call that fella right now. Tell him he left too soon. *[On the phone: "Yeah, he's in here right now." Barber #1 passes the phone to Warren.]*

Barber #2 (Mary): That's awesome!

D. Thomas: So, what just happened here?

Barber #2 (Mary): The gentleman who comes in here and talks about Warren all the time, that's who Warren is talking to on the phone.

D. Thomas: But Warren doesn't know him, right?

Barber #2 (Mary): No, Warren doesn't know him, but he knows Warren.

D. Thomas: And you say this is making his day?

Barber #2 (Mary): The rest of the year. He's going to be happy the rest of the year!

Ralph Brown: We came out here in 1965. Jabali and most of the fellas were just youngsters then. They would come into the shop all the time.

D. Thomas: What did Jabali mean to the community?

Ralph Brown: Well, that's why they named the field house court after him. He's the one who brought the crowds. He was the first fellow to play above the rim. Doin' that, they came to see him play. Filled the place. I went to the games. In fact, I followed him all the way through college.

D. Thomas: And why is this place called the Sportsmen Barbershop?

Ralph Brown: I named it that. All the athletes used to come in here. The Chiefs came in here.

D. Thomas: And what were the conversations about?

Ralph Brown: Sports, mostly. At that time they were trying to decide who was the best basketball player around here: Claude Hardy, Arthur Strozier, Lucius Allen...

D. Thomas: Who was the greatest, in your view?

Ralph Brown: All-around? Jabali. That's what Coach Wilkinson use to say. Wilk had great players. Maurice King, for example. *(Maurice King was the first black starter in Kansas University basketball history— 1954—and Wilt Chamberlain's teammate. He played in the NBA.)* But none of them played above the rim. That's what made Jabali so great.

—

About this time, Michael Walker came into the shop. I recognized him from the year before, when he had attended the *Odyssey* gathering. I knew that he had played at Central where he was a highly regarded athlete.

The fellow with whom Warren was visiting on the phone had by that time returned to the shop to visit in person with Warren.

Michael Walker: I'm friends with Mary (Barber #2), and I thought I would stop in and say hello. When I saw Warren, I knew who it was immediately. I had met him when they had the court-naming ceremony, but other than that, I had never met him. Never talked to him, but I always wanted to. You know, he was a basketball player and I was a basketball player.

D. Thomas: You played at Central High School?

Michael Walker: Yes. I went to Junior College in California after high school and then played two years for the University of Missouri, '81 to '83. After that, I tried out for a couple of teams overseas but didn't make them, so I came back and basically started working.

D. Thomas: What do you know about Warren?

Michael Walker: All the stories about his athletic gifts... Mostly his jumping ability... But as I got older and I read about him, I realized that it wasn't just his jumping ability. He was an all-around great player. That's something that gets overlooked. You know, you hear how he jumped over this guy or he dunked from this angle or that angle, but the more I learned about him, the more I realized that he was just a great basketball player.

I did know that he took a political stand. I heard about that as I was growing up. But I came to understand it a little bit more as I read about him on the Internet, especially as I started playing at a major college level and I saw what it took to compete. I began to understand where he was coming from. There were issues back when I played, but in his day, the '60s and early '70s, there was a lot more to deal with. So I have a really good understanding of why he took the positions he took. And to continue to be a good player at the same time—that was a heavy burden.

—

The next morning we drove to Jack Bush's home. Jack Bush is a legendary coach in Kansas City. Though long retired, he has remained in touch with many of the players who have come through the city. Coach Bush coached against Warren's teams when Warren was in high school. Leonard Jones, one of Coach Bush's players from Warren's time, joined us.

Coach Bush: You know, I didn't take up golf until I was fifty years old.

Warren: And now you're hooked.

Coach Bush: I got hooked on that game and have been playing it ever since.

D. Thomas: Coach Bush, what did you have to do when coaching against Warren? How would you neutralize him, for example?

Coach Bush: All I can say is that whenever we played Central, it was always a battle. Wilkinson was coaching. We were friends and rivals. At that time, the city league was outstanding. The rivalries were outstanding. There were never any problems. There was a lot of camaraderie.

D. Thomas: What would you say your life has been about?

Coach Bush: Well, I've been involved in sports all my life. And my kids are all involved with sports.

D. Thomas: In addition to your family, has it been coaching and the development of your players that has given you the most satisfaction?

Coach Bush: Very much so. My daughters put together a scrapbook for me. You wouldn't believe what is in it. See, back then, they use to have long articles about Interscholastic League games. Now, all you get is a box score.

D. Thomas: What about Warren's game? How does he fit into the history of basketball in Kansas City?

Coach Bush: Well, I think Warren brought everyone's attention to his jumping ability. This is the thing that made him stand above the other players. Some of the things he did, none of the other players could measure up. His jumping ability, his flexibility was outstanding. He played above the rim, the only player of that era that played above the rim. That was one of the ways he stood above everybody else. Everybody referred to that, along with his other capabilities. Getting a rebound off a free throw from the middle of the line and then dunking the ball. That was highly unusual.

D. Thomas: What team was your best team? I thought the 1964 team was outstanding.

Coach Bush: That's hard for me to say. I've never stopped to think about it.

Warren: I never saw a Manual team after '64. But if there was a team better than that '64 team, I would be surprised because that team was the best team in the city. They were better than my team. I might have been able to help us win when we played them, but man for man, that Manual team was the best team. And that was because of the camaraderie. Those boys, even today, stay in touch with each other. So if you think of the concept of "team" as everybody pulling for one goal and maximizing their talents and abilities, then I would say that the 1964 team was the best team.

Coach Bush: Well, that's a nice analysis. I would have a hard time deciding which one was the best, because every time they won I thought they were the best.

Warren: Well, I think we're dealing with the concept of talent and team. Even if we look at the old Celtics and the Chicago Bulls, the Celtics were the best team: they worked together, they believed in each other, and they shared. Chicago was more *executive;* they would take this part out and put that part in and they would win, but when you looked at them you didn't get any sense of family.

(At this point, the conversation turned to the 1963 State Tournament and to the semi-finals game that Warren's team—Central High School—lost.)

Warren: We lost because of coaching. See, Coach Wilkinson (Central's coach) was not like Coach Bush. Wilkinson aspired to be corporate. He was one of these smart dudes who has all this personality and can relate to people and all that kind of stuff. He was coaching because that was all they would allow him to do—this is my perception. Bush is coaching because that's what he loves to do. He's going to study the game.

Now, I have a lot of respect for Coach Wilkinson. I don't want to come across like I don't. It's just that I do not believe that coaching was his highest aspiration. So, therefore, what he put into it was not everything, like Coach Bush put everything into it.

Now, if you look at our struggle, the black folks' struggle, you have Booker T. Washington who has always had the point of view of "put down your bucket where you are." And then there was the other philosophy of W. E. B. Du Bois: "We have to get equal rights and participate in the system." Well, if you look at these two coaches, you have Wilkinson and you have Bush. I would say that Coach Bush was a Booker T. man and Coach Wilkinson was a W. E. B. Du Bois man. And then if you look at where we are as a people which is... we don't have the power and influence that equals our abilities, then you would say that the Booker T. model is the model that we should have been following.

[Long pause]

Leonard Jones: You know, I would not have traded my experience with Coach Bush for anything in the world. I got things from Coach Bush that I took with me to the Marine Corps, like how to deal with people. I didn't go to college. I went straight to the Marine Corps. I'll give you an example: I was always chasing girls. I would skip practice to hang out with my girlfriend. Coach Bush would find me. He told me the girls are going to be there and to not skip out on my training.

And as far as training or conditioning, he would have us run until tomorrow. Coach had us believing that conditioning is the most important thing. *Prior planning prevents piss poor performance.* He gave me life lessons that I share with my kids today. He told me that when you lose, you've got to lose with character. I had never heard that.

Warren: *[Addressing Coach Bush]* You have observed the city (Kansas City) for a long time, and I was wondering what your impression is. Is the city going to make it? Is it going to die? Is this something that cities do? All the houses down where I used to live are being abandoned. In cities like Cleveland and Detroit, they are tearing buildings down that have been abandoned so that they don't depress property values any further. What are we seeing? Are we seeing the death of the inner city and the birth of all of these places that I couldn't go to when I was young? What are you seeing in Kansas City that has been significant over the years?

Coach Bush: Well, for one thing, we're losing our citizens. They're moving out because of so many problems they've encountered. For example, I go to a lot of high school games at the field house and the coaches act like nuts. They run up and down the court. When I was coaching, if you got off your chair to contest a call, it was a technical foul. I wish they would reinstate that rule. And something else that bothers me even more: It doesn't appear to me that they coach throughout the week in preparation for the game. They don't begin coaching until the game begins. There's no way for the kids to know what they're supposed to do. They're lost out there on the court. Now I don't know if that has anything to do with the larger question you asked, but that's what I see.

Warren: How old are you?

Coach Bush: I'll be 88 in February. I grew up in Kansas City and I came back in '52. But my first job was in the Bootheal: Cruthersville, Missouri. For three years, no indoor toilets, dirt roads. I had never seen cotton. I had never seen what I was exposed to there. Shotgun houses, that's a house you can see straight through from the front door to the back door. I had a basketball team but we didn't have any basketballs. I went out one time to pick cotton. *That was the last time.* People don't realize that when that cotton opens up, there are stickers surrounding the pod. My hands were swollen by the time I came home. That South, they didn't like us down there. *And I never stepped beyond the line.*

Warren: No, if you crossed that line, you wouldn't come back.

Coach Bush: That's right.

Warren: So if you were the Mayor of Kansas City, Missouri, at this time (2011), what would you do?

Coach Bush: Well, one of the first things I would try to do is improve the school district. It seems like it's only gotten worse. Do you realize that when you were in school, we had close to 150,000 students in the Kansas City School District? We're down to less than 20,000. And if you count the students in charter schools, that's only about 10,000 more.

Warren: Do you think that there should be an organized effort on the part of black people in this country to do anything? For example, should we join the NAACP, or the SCLC, or the Urban League? Or should we just pursue our own individual interests, go at it that way? I'm asking because of your age, you've seen a lot of change in your 88 years.

Coach Bush: Well, I think that depends on the individual. But I don't see how we can accomplish what we'd like to accomplish without coming together. We have to join forces because there is no way we can solve a problem if we're all going in different directions.

Leonard Jones: There are a lot of my friends, people in my peer group, who do not vote. I ask them if they are registered and they aren't even registered. And that sends a damaging message to their kids.

Warren: Well let me ask you, Coach. When you were in elementary school, were you just taught reading, writing, arithmetic, the basics, or were you taught what you should do as citizens, as black kids facing... What was your education like? Was it strictly academics, or were there social aspects?

Coach Bush: I think I was denied some things when I was in high school. There were things I should have been exposed to and I should have been encouraged to be a part of. For example, I never thought about physics or chemistry or a foreign language. And to go one step further, we did not have counselors. There was nobody in the high school I could go and talk to about what classes to take. Later on in life, after I knew a little something about it, I realized I would have eaten up physics or chemistry. That's right up my alley. I could have been a fantastic physicist. No tellin'. *[Laughing]*

D. Thomas: Coach Bush, when you were coaching, did you focus on character development or did you focus primarily on basketball-related skills?

Coach Bush: I was interested in the kids, period. Grade-wise, I had cards printed up that the teachers had to sign indicating that the player was doing his schoolwork. Punctuality was paramount. You weren't late to my practices. I had one player who wanted to fight when anything went wrong. I said to him, "Something is wrong. You can't do that. I'm not going to allow you to play anymore until you see a psychiatrist." I talked to the psychiatrist and I talked to the player's mother. I never had any more trouble with him after that. Book-wise and team-wise, I had my players under control.

D. Thomas: How would you like to be remembered? What would you like to be remembered for?

Coach Bush: Well, I would like to be remembered for what I enjoyed doing all my life, and that was working with youngsters. And I thought the State did me a great honor when it inducted me into the State of Missouri Hall of Fame. That was something I really appreciated.

[Long pause]

Warren: Well, at least he didn't say he wanted to be remembered for his golf game. *[Laughter]*

———

Alex Ellison has been a good friend of Warren's for over fifty years. They were high school teammates and have remained close ever since. When Warren played at Wichita State, Alex would on occasion drive Warren's mother to Wichita to see the games, and it was Alex who flew to Florida so that Kansas City would have a presence at Warren's Florida funeral. Both Alex and his wife, Alice, have been deeply involved in community affairs for years. It's highly unlikely that the effort to name the field house court in Warren's honor would have been successful without Alex's guidance and involvement.

Alex: When we went to Africa, to Liberia, we went to Mission stations. The only way they could have lights was to run a generator. We paid extra so we could have lights at night. And then, when you went out to some of the remote areas... We're so used to flipping on the switch. In one village, they had a satellite dish. I thought they had TV, and they did but only one day a week, Saturday. And that was so they could watch football—their football, soccer. We have so many things to be thankful for. No matter how bad it might seem, somebody else is worse off.

Now, there's a long way to go if you're talking about economic opportunity or education. Yeah, we're a long way from that, but on the basic things, if you've got them, you're blessed.

Warren: Pat Buchanan is saying that black people don't have anything to complain about, that we should be grateful that white folks came and got us since we live better than most of the black people in the world.

Alex: We come from kings and queens; that's what I know. He must not know that.

Warren: He was just trying to justify the thievery. He was saying that conquest has been the way of the world, and so you can't really condemn the Europeans for what they have done because that's the way of history. But I would think that an enlightened society... For example, when the United States and Europe developed their interest in Middle East oil... After the people got educated and said they wanted to renegotiate the deal, I think the U.S. and Europe should have re-negotiated the deal. Instead of 75% of the profits going out of the country and 25% staying in, maybe it could be 50–50. And then, after still more education and development, maybe it's 25% going out of the country, 75% staying in. And the same thing would apply with respect to the mining of diamonds and gold. But they (the corporations) didn't do that.

Alex: When we were in South Africa, we saw a lot of strip mining. The land was devastated, left barren. There appeared to be little or no regulation concerning the repair of the land.

Warren: So what's going to happen with the school system?

Alex: *[Alex is a former member of the Kansas City School Board]* The Kansas City School District has lost its accreditation, and this may lead to State takeover. This is what happened with the St. Louis School District. Now, it's interesting to me that both Kansas City and St. Louis were under a court-ordered desegregation plan. The State has spent millions trying to correct the wrong that has occurred over decades, and it has not been successful at securing accreditation for St. Louis. I don't believe there are reasons to think it would be successful in Kansas City.

D. Thomas: Warren, let's get Alex's response to what you were saying earlier. If you were the Secretary of Education, you would do what?

Warren: *[laughing]* I was being facetious earlier saying that if I was the Secretary of Education and had all power to make the changes that I thought were necessary, I would do the following: I would extend the school day and extend the responsibility of the school to include eradicating the prison values that are permeating the black community. You would do that by feeding the kids right after school and then putting them into various programs: enrichment, tutoring, cultural, whatever you want to do until about 6:00. At 6:00, you would feed them a hot meal followed by more tutoring and homework. And then you would have school buses to take them back to their communities with the specific instruction to parents: *Give them a bath. Give them a hug. And if we find them on the street, we will arrest you.*

Alex: Eradicating that prison mentality or mindset—I would have to agree. Extending the school day, well, there are pitfalls in that. What you're talking about could be close to a twelve-hour day. That's a long time with attention spans being what they are. And those kids, whenever you send them home, are going home, many of them, to single-parent households, sometimes no parents at all. If there's nobody home, those kids aren't going home.

Warren: I hear what you're saying, and clearly there would have to be specifics that you would have to work out. But what is the alternative? Right now, in an urban setting, the supervision of children after school is minimal. So the question is: How do we increase the supervision of children after school and thereby break and overcome the prison-mentality culture that is permeating the neighborhoods? And what I'm saying is that the only institution we have that can deal with this issue is the school.

I'm not saying that you put them in front of a book the minute the normal school day is out. You give them some supervised free time, of course, among the other things I mentioned. But you keep them there and at the end of it all, you give them a hot meal.

When our kids come home, they are not under a neighborhood constraint, or a family constraint. Not anymore. The culture has and is changing. The kids are free to do virtually anything they want to do.

Alex: You talk about the culture having changed. Some would say that it has changed by design.

Warren: And I would agree. I think it's quite possible that think tanks, funded by conservative billionaires, have concluded that we really don't need urban public education in order to run the American system. Your corporation needs *this* set of skills, and your corporation needs *that* set of skills, and we can get those skills from private schools, charter schools, and high-functioning public schools. We do not need low-performing inner-city schools in the United States of America, so just let them wither on the bush and die. I can see these think tanks drawing that conclusion very easily.

Alex: I can, too. But it can be done. The schools can be turned around. Lincoln College Preparatory Academy, for example, now ranks high in the nation in achievement, in high school graduation rates, in sending kids off to college, and so on. That's exceptional. There are a lot of factors involved, including how administrators and teachers choose to perform their jobs, but it can be done.

Warren: Yeah. It's not a matter of intelligence. It's a matter of focus.

—

Both Warren and I had driven to Alex's home, and as we left, Warren told me to follow him. Five men had already gathered when we arrived at "Snake's" house. Four were friends of Warren's from high school. One was a younger man who had only heard of Warren. (I regret that I was unable to get the names of two of the older men.)

There was considerable reminiscing about the "good old days" and considerable laughter, an abundance of what Warren would consider "lies" or exaggerations concerning his legendary high school playing days.

A brief review of Warren's high school teams occurs, one of which was composed almost entirely of football players.

Willie Moe: So they weren't athletes, then.

222 • JABALI: A KANSAS CITY LEGEND

Warren: No, they were athletes. An athlete can play football, but an athlete just can't play basketball.

Jerome Holmes: I've got some questions for you.

Warren: More than one?

Jerome Holmes: If I ask the one question, it will cover all the others. Something I always wondered about when you were playing: Why did the hammer fall on you like it did? You know what I'm talking about? It just seemed like some things happened and all of a sudden you were in trouble.

Warren: Oh, you mean in the pros. You're not talking about high school. I thought you were talking about high school. Is there something I don't know about? *[Laughter]* You had me going.

Jerome Holmes: No. In high school you could do no wrong.

Warren: When I left here, you have to understand the kind of person that I was. And if you remember, you all were always showing me where it was at. So I wasn't like out front, gregarious, able to relate to any situation. I'm laid back. You would say, "You want some of this?" "Yeah!" *[Laughter]*

Jerome Holmes: He *was* like that.

Warren: But here I am getting ready to go off into this thing that has all this glitz and glamour. So I'm doing the same thing. I'm standing around checking things out. People think I have an attitude. They take me out to dinner, all these utensils sitting there... My feeling was "I don't like this!" I was uncomfortable 'cause I don't know how to eat at a restaurant. So I've got to go through life with everyone thinking there's something wrong with me 'cause I'm not relating to these circumstances.

So, then, I'm in the college dorm room one night and this dude is playing this LP: *"What you got to understand is that back during slavery, you had two kinds of Negros. You had the house Negro and you had the field Negro."* So I listened to that whole album and the light came on, a switch was turned and I began to look at things from the point of view of a black man. So here I am. I've already got this reserved thing about me. And now, if you're a white man, I'm looking at you like *"Are you the devil?"* *[Laughter]* So they don't know how to take me.

I didn't create any friendships or relationships with any of the white people in Wichita, no in-depth conversations. We [black players] began to read more and study more. And when we would be introduced before a game, we would run out there and if it was a black dude, we would slap hands, arms, move our fists to our chests, and so on; and if it was a white dude, we would shake hands politely. *[Laughter]* So all of this is being noticed. Nobody is saying anything, but it is being noticed.

So then the draft comes along. I was drafted third by the Knicks, and the ABA draft was so confusing, no one knows how it worked. I was drafted by the Oakland Oaks. I'm sure then that those leagues had a person in Wichita who they talked to and he gave his opinions, so on and so forth. I'm playing in the first year. I go through the camp, I went through the pre-season, the season began, and I'm averaging 21 points, nine rebounds. By then, I figured out that I'm halfway decent at this. I can do this.

Back then, Rick Barry was shooting twenty-five times, making ten or twelve shots. But he's also going to the basket, getting fouled and making fifteen free throws. He's a good free throw shooter. So he's making 35 points a game. I figured this out.

So I start driving to the basket. And bam! Bam! I'm getting fouled, but I'm not getting any calls. Alex Hannum says in the newspaper, "The thing I like about Warren Armstrong is that he can go to the basket, take a blow, and still make the bucket." But I was only taking the blow. I wasn't getting the fouls called. That was pissing me off.

If Rick Barry gets touched, he's up in the referee's face, complaining. Never gets any techs. So this dude one night, a white boy, he grabs my arm, steals the ball, and as we're getting ready to go down the court I look at the ref and the ref looks the other way. So I knocked this fella down and stomped on him. "That was your fault, though" *[pointing to Jerome Holmes]. [Laughter]* So, after that, they really didn't know what to do with me. They thought, "Well, now, we can't get rid of him. He's averaging 21 points, nine rebounds, second on the team in assists."

Jerome Holmes: That answers a lot of questions right there.

Warren: But see, if we had had advice as we were going through this thing… somebody would have said, "Look, man, do you know where you live? Do you know what's going on? Rick Barry is able to get your league publicized, get your name in the newspaper. You should be giving him five or six more shots a game. Look here, he's even pumping you up, see what he said about you?" But, no, you don't have anyone giving you advice. All you've got is Jerome Holmes and Malcolm X. What kind of examples are they to set for somebody? So you go through life and you make these decisions and you live with the consequences. I was still good enough to get some notoriety. But had I been a more well-rounded person, a person who had had some experiences with the middle class...

For example, Jim Laffoon sent me a video. You remember Jim Laffoon?

(xxxx): That boy could shoot.

Warren: He sent me a video, a stroll down memory lane. Fifty or sixty places and events around the Kansas City area that he and his friends went to when they were in high school. I only knew one of them. This whole experience that this dude had... I'm in the same town and I don't even know what he's talking about. What I'm saying is that without the exposure...

Had it not been for the newfound knowledge I acquired, I would have just gone through these things quietly and been accused of being surly. They used "enigmatic" instead of surly because they can't figure these things out.

Snake (Rudolph Riley): When Warren came back one time, he told me that he had entered a completely different world—that it wasn't like the world we grew up in.

Warren: But I would say it impacted me more in college than in the pros. In the pros I made the ABA All-Star team, the Most Valuable Player in the ABA All-Star Game, named to the 30 greatest ABA players. Now someone could say, well, maybe you should have made more All-Star teams or ranked higher among the thirty. But the recognition is there.

The blatant stuff was at Wichita State. Wichita State retired Dave Stallworth's jersey, Xavier McDaniel's jersey, while my jersey wasn't retired. They say it was because I didn't make an All American team. That's what they say. But when I left there, I had the rebounding record, the assist record, and was fourth on the all-time scoring list. Today, as we speak, I have the assist record. Now you've got someone who has a record that lasts from 1968 to 2012 and that's not good enough. That's why I say the blatant stuff happened in college. That's when it began, when we hit our chests with our fists.

(yyyy): You know that barbershop up on Swope Parkway, 59th & Swope Parkway, the Sportsman Barbershop? They've got pictures of Warren on the wall in there, this high over the basket *[arms spread apart]*.

Willie Moe: *[Asking for an autograph]* I wasn't around then, but I'm here now and this autograph will be worth something to me.

Jerome Holmes: But did you have fun?

Warren: No, it really wasn't that much fun. It wasn't that much fun in college. The coach we had was not a very good coach. No recruitment. So I had to play virtually by myself. So that was a struggle. And then going into the ABA wasn't that much fun because you were constantly dealing with compensation issues. "How much is he getting paid and I'm getting paid only this amount!"

And referees: One night I got into it with a referee. He looked at me and said. "We don't call the game the way you play it. You play the game the way we call it." I started to hit him: *"What are you talking about?"* So they were controlling the flow of the game. That's how I'm looking at it. I'm not looking at it like it's not personal. I took everything personal. It wasn't personal. If I wouldn't have taken things so personally, I would have had more fun.

I had fun during the playoffs of the first year. We were playing the Indiana Pacers. I was averaging 33 points a game, 13 rebounds. Wayne Hightower, you remember that name? One night in the playoffs I was killing Denver so bad, they put Wayne Hightower on me. I still got 42. He came running at me and jumped to block my shot and I switched to my left hand and made the basket. I laughed at him all the way down the court.

The playoffs are a different game. The playoffs turn into school ground. They let you go. You can play your game. So the playoffs were fun.

Willie Moe: How did it get to be Warren Jabali instead of Warren Armstrong?

Warren: Well, it's like I was saying. After listening to Malcolm, you start thinking about these things that he's talking about. The next phase was when we went to Los Angeles and met Maulana Ron Karenga who developed the US organization. Do you know who Karenga is? Karenga wrote a cultural doctrine. A part of it was that African Americans should name themselves, define themselves, speak for themselves. Karenga is the originator of Kwanzaa where we have the seven principles. So, in that you're supposed to name yourself. Armstrong is the name of white slave-owners in Arkansas or Louisiana. So you take Armstrong out and put Jabali in. That's what happened.

Willie Moe: What does Jabali mean?

Warren: The rock. A large and conspicuous rock. *[Laughter]* That's what the dudes in East Africa said: "JABALI, A LARGE AND CONSPICUOUS ROCK." *Okay, brother, I got it! [Laughter]*

Jerome Homes: *That works! That works! I knew it all along! [Laughter]*

[Pause]

Snake (Rudolph Riley): What I worry about these days are the kids. I don't know what it takes to reach them.

(yyyy): Part of it is what Jabali was saying. I went to college in '71. I experienced that same thing with all these utensils placed in front of me. *Which one is it?* The experience that sticks in my mind was seeing someone write a check to pay for something. I never knew you could do that. If I needed money, I would call up Slick: "Slick, I need fifteen dollars." You're not exposed to things society might even consider simple.

Warren: It's easier if you can play it off and hide from it. *Well, I just won't go in there.* But if the team is going, then that's where you've got to go.

Jerome Holmes: I went to East High School. My senior year, 1962, there were three black players on our team. We went for our basketball banquet and when we got to the restaurant, the owner called the coach over and told him that the three black players had to sit at a separate table or they wouldn't serve us. The coach said that none of us will eat there and we all left. *1962.*

Snake (Rudolph Riley): When we first moved here in '58–'59, there were five black families on this block. The rest were white. The police would stop me at the end of the block and would want to know where I was going. They told me I better have my Social Security card on me. I was a kid. I didn't have my Social Security card on me.

(xxxx): You know what I thought was the worst part of it: When they assassinated Martin Luther King. Down there where that club used to be, down on Indiana Street, some little dude was in there robbing, tearing the place up. I said, "What you all doing? You need to stop it!" He said, "Some cat named King got killed." He didn't even know who King was.

Willie Moe: I thought Martin Luther King was my uncle. I was three years old and everybody was crying. Everyone was so upset I thought he must be my uncle. *[Laughter]*

[Pause]

Warren: Did I answer your questions, man?

Jerome Holmes: You answered them. I always did wonder about that, though, about what happened when you went into the pros. Sometimes people provoke you. And being where we come from, there's always something that can make you go crazy. If it's not one thing, it's another.

(xxxx): *[pointing to Warren]* He's the best player I've ever seen.

———

As we were leaving, Jerome Holmes said to me as an aside and as a long-time friend of Warren's: "It's good you're doing what you're doing. Somebody has needed to do this." I took him to be saying: We all know how exceptional Warren is. There needs to be a record.

Warren and I walked to our cars, laughing as we talked about the afternoon. It had been a great afternoon, a great two days as far as I was concerned. I was grateful to have spent it with him.

We embraced before making our way to our separate cars. It was 4:30 in the afternoon. In late December Kansas City seems always to have a silver-grey sky. When I got to my car I turned around. Warren had turned around as well. He raised his arms. The sun was behind him, muted by a silver background. It was a remarkable image. I regretted that I had put the camera away as this was goodbye.

— *Gallery* —

The pictures that follow are from several sources: high school yearbooks, pictures Warren gave me, pictures his mother gave me, the WSU athletic archive, the "Remember the ABA" website and archive, etc.

There are some pictures I have been unable to trace. I welcome corrections or additions so that in subsequent editions all pictures may be properly credited.

Central High School – Kansas City, MO

Warren Armstrong, Central High School yearbook, 1964.
All-City, All-Metro, All-District, All-State, All-American

Central vs. Southeast, 1964: Warren guarded by Ken Christopher, a 2nd team All-City guard and honorable mention All-District. Behind Warren is Russell Washington, honorable mention All-Metro center, and later, an all-star offensive tackle for the San Diego Chargers. (Photographer unknown)

Central vs. Pem Day: Warren blocking a layup
attempt by Robbie Allen, an honorable mention All-
District guard and grandson of "Phog" Allen. From
the Pem Day High School yearbook, 1964.

Central vs. Lincoln, 1964: Warren (6' 2") rebounding against Vernon Vanoy (6' 8"), *field house filled to the rafters.* Vanoy was an exceptional athlete: University of Kansas basketball and football and later, defensive tackle for three years in the NFL. From the Lincoln High School yearbook, 1964.

Wichita State University

Warren entered Wichita State University in the fall of 1964. He was an All-Missouri Valley Conference selection in 1966, '67, and '68, the three years for which he was eligible for such an honor. (Photographer unknown)

This picture, and the two that follow were provided by Mrs. Armstrong, from her scrapbook of Warren's playing days at WSU. (Photographer unknown.)

Warren led WSU in rebounding for three consecutive years. For years he held the Shocker record for assists in a game (14 vs. Bradley, 1968), season (194 in 1967–'68), and career (429 from 1965–'68).

In 1985, Warren was inducted into the WSU Basketball Hall of Fame. At 6' 2", he ranks in the top 20 all-time at Wichita State in scoring, rebounding and assists.

Caption reads: Wichita's Carl Williams, center, blocked
Lew Alcindor. It was too late as Warren Armstrong
(53) watched ball go in. (From WSU Athletic Archive.)

During his playing career at Wichita State Warren averaged 16.7 points and 10.8 rebounds per game.

This picture—taken when Warren was a sophomore—was featured in the 1966 *WSU Parnassus* (yearbook).

American Basketball Association (ABA)

WARREN ARMSTRONG G OAKLAND OAKS

1968–'69 ABA rookie picture: Oakland Oaks. ABA career: 1968–1975. 1968/'68 Rookie of the Year, MVP in 1969 Oakland Oaks – Indiana Pacers Championship Series, four-time ABA All-Star, MVP of 1972–'73 All-Star Game, named to the 30-man All-Time ABA Team. Averaged 17.1 points per game during professional career. (Photographer unknown)

First year in league: Oakland Oaks vs. Denver Rockets, playoffs. "Bob Bass, coach of the Denver Rockets, heaped tall praise on Armstrong following his 41-point explosion."

"Give one guy credit for that win—Warren Armstrong," said Bass. "He blocked shots, passed, made steals, rebounded, shot inside and out—what else is there to do in the game of basketball?" (News from the Oakland Oaks, April 11, 1969; photo: Remember the ABA)

"There is little question that Armstrong deserves Rookie of the Year. As Bob Netolicky, forward for the Eastern Division Champion Indiana Pacers put it, 'Who else could you vote for? No rookie is even a close second to Armstrong.'" (News from the Oakland Oaks, April 11, 1969; photo: Remember the ABA)

1969–'70: Playing for the Washington Caps, second season in the league, before knee surgery. (Photo: Remember the ABA)

1969–'70: Playing for the Washington Caps, driving against Artis Gilmore and Cincy Powell of the Dallas Chaparrals. "Every game I saw him play was more impressive than the last." (Reggie Marshall) (Photo: Remember the ABA)

1971–'72: Playing for the Floridians. "Jabali, acquired from the Pacers prior to the '71–'72 season, had a great season. Jabali quarterbacked the Floridians to their third playoff appearance in four years." (from RemembertheABA.com; photo: Remember the ABA)

1971–'72: Playing defense against Rick Barry. "Warren was a hell of a player, ahead of his time. You didn't see guys that were as gifted athletically as he was. Thirty, forty points: no problem for Warren." (Interview with Rick Barry; photo: Remember the ABA)

1972–'73 to 1973–'74: Playing for the Denver Rockets. Named first-team All-ABA Guard in '73. (Photographer unknown.)

1972–'73 to 1973–'74: Denver Rockets. Playing defense against Julius Erving. "We had our battles. He could go anywhere on the court he wanted to go. He belongs in the Hall of Fame." (2015 radio interview with Dr. J.; photo: Remember the ABA)

1974–'75, last year in league, playing for the San Diego Conquistadors – could still leap, when needed. Said backcourt partner Bo Lamar: "Every team has a leader. But before we got Jabali, I don't think this team had one... I think he inspires the rest of us and gives us confidence." (Photo: Remember the ABA)

Part VI

The Sumner Connection

"It's one thing to be a great ball player. It's more important, ultimately, to be a great person. And to be somebody to be respected and looked up to for their principles and the things they take a stand for. "

Reverend Nelson "Fuzzy" Thompson

There is a story to be told that is only alluded to in this book. It is the story of Sumner High School. Sumner was an all-black, inner-city high school located in Kansas City, Kansas. For over seventy years, until it closed in 1978, Sumner served youth from some of the City's most impoverished neighborhoods.

Sumner High School was named for Charles Sumner, a Massachusetts senator who served in the United States Senate from 1851 to 1874. A noted abolitionist, Sumner was brutally beaten by South Carolina Representative Preston Brooks following a speech in which Sumner argued for the immediate admission of Kansas as a free state. He spent three years recovering from the beating. (See https://en.wikipedia.org/wiki/Charles_Sumner)

The Sumner High School song:

In the northeast part of old Wyandotte,
Stands a building that's tall and wide,
It received its name from the famous man,
This building is Sumner High.
Sumner was a man despised in the land,
For his kindness towards the blacks,
And for this same cause, without fear or laws,
He, while unarmed, was attacked. ...
We must gain fame to add to our name of Sumner
which we love:
Men will sing its worth throughout the earth,
The name of Sumner, dear old Sumner,
Sing the name of Sumner High.

(Words by T. H. Reynolds – Carrye Whittenhill; see http://www.kckps.org/disthistory/ penbuildings/sumner_03.htm)

Warren remarked on occasion that neither in elementary school nor in high school was he introduced to the names, let alone the stories of key figures in the history of the black struggle. Sumner students, on the other hand, attended a school where such knowledge was implicitly valued. The name itself—"Sumner"—was selected by the black community, and though Charles Sumner was white and not black, he nevertheless was an important early figure in the history and story of civil rights. Sumner students, mostly from poor neighborhoods, were the beneficiaries of a school culture whose hallmarks were racial pride, pride in self, and personal achievement.

Herman Watson, MD (Class of 1962), noted that Sumner was unique in several respects. Its teachers, he recalled, were extraordinary. They came from prestigious colleges and universities and were intent on establishing high educational standards. Students were expected to perform. Sumner's basketball coach, Thomas Rhone, an outstanding Denver University basketball player and later principal of Wyandotte High School, scheduled games with schools throughout the state. According to Watson, "Rhone, along with Sumner's principal, Solomon (Sol) Thompson, and others wanted us to have the experience of staying in a hotel, ordering in a restaurant, things we had never experienced." To a considerable extent, Sumner readied its students for life after high school. It's worth noting that of the ten players on Sumner's 1962 basketball team—the team on which Watson played, as did others mentioned below—three became MDs and a fourth a PhD.

It's also worth noting that John McLendon attended Sumner High School (after having attended Dunbar Elementary). McLendon is a towering figure in the history of basketball. He was the first black head coach in any professional sport and was twice enshrined in the Naismith Memorial Basketball Hall of Fame. Interestingly, McLendon failed to make the Sumner basketball team and served instead as its manager. After attending Kansas City (Kansas) Junior College, McLendon transferred to the University of Kansas, where his advisor and mentor was Dr. James Naismith.

Had Warren stayed in Kansas City, Kansas, he would have gone to Sumner, a fact bemoaned by his Sumner friends. As it was, his game was shaped on the neighborhood courts on which the Sumner players honed their skills, the Grant and Dunbar school grounds. Herman Watson, Monte Owens, Red Starks, J. B. Hill, Johnny Battles, Richard Dumas, the great Ernie Moore—these were the players that Warren observed, played with, and later competed against. His toughness and style of play was formed on the courts that these men, who were two, three, and four years his senior, dominated.

To varying degrees, Warren lost touch with these individuals from his youth, but he made a point of reuniting with them in the last years of his life. These men admired Warren; they thought the world of him but were not awed by him. They had watched him grow up. They had tutored him. And they had never cut him any slack. Warren trusted them and felt at home in their presence.

Except for Ernie Moore, Warren and I weren't able to visit in person with these individuals as we made our rounds in late December. I therefore made an effort to contact them. I wanted to invite them to share any recollections they might have of Warren, or any stories about their own careers that might further illuminate the time they shared with him.

—

Herman Watson: I went to Drake on a basketball scholarship. When I was a freshman, the coach wanted to make sure that I did not lose my eligibility and so enrolled me in ridiculously simple courses: *archery of all things!* But I was from Sumner. My sophomore year I enrolled in advanced courses. I never required an academic tutor. Never. In fact, I was offended when offered one. I will say this, however. Although Sumner prepared us in every way it could, I was shocked to discover that my dorm room bed had two sheets on it. *I had never seen a bed with two sheets on it!*

My roommate (and teammate) at Drake was McCoy McLemore. We became good friends. I had his back and he had mine.

> [In 1964, McCoy McLemore led the Drake Bulldogs to the National Invitation Tournament [NIT] at Madison Square Garden, their first-ever post-season appearance. At 6'7", McLemore led the Bulldogs in both scoring and rebounding. After Drake, McLemore went on to an eight-year career in the NBA and was a member of the '71 Milwaukee Bucks team—led by Lew Alcindor (Kareem Abdul-Jabbar) and Oscar Robertson—that won the NBA championship. Also in '71, he received an award from the Army for entertaining U.S. troops in Vietnam with his singing talents.
> [http://www.godrakebulldogs.com/news/2009/4/29/3733 323.aspx]

My senior year, my coach told me that both the Associated Press and the United Press had named me the top defensive guard in the nation.

I was only 170 pounds, at most. But it was a matter of pride. I wasn't tough like Warren. Warren had an innate toughness. But I could not stand to be disrespected, either on or off the court. I reacted immediately to any kind of personal affront.

It happened a couple of times on the court, situations that were wrong, or that I perceived as wrong, and I went after the person in question. So, when I say that McCoy McLemore had my back, that's true except, perhaps, on one occasion.

We were playing against Louisville, *Wes Unseld's Louisville!* I was driving to the basket, full steam ahead, a clear shot, and Unseld fouled me. It was a hard foul, not mean or dirty but hard, hard enough to send me ten rows into the stands. I could not let that go, and I started toward Unseld. My teammates grabbed me and aimed me toward the bench. In the meantime, McCoy was calling time out. *McCoy was calling time out, not the coach!* "What the hell are you doing, McLemore?" the coach screamed. "I call time out. Players don't call time out!" "I know, Coach, I know, but me and Lacy (the other black starting guard whose real name was Billy Foster) want to get something straight. Rooms (that is what Mac called me as we were roommates while he was at Drake), if you mess with him (meaning Unseld), we ain't with you tonight!" The coach went crazy and cursed us all out.

In retrospect, the whole thing was hilarious. I guess in a sense McCoy did have my back. He was letting me know that I was alone if I started something. That's how strong and imposing Unseld was, and besides, everyone knew he was a nice guy. It helps to remember that we beat Louisville, beat them every time we played them, as I recall. That should be noted.

Now, you asked me about Warren. He was younger than the rest of us. He loved basketball, but a lot of guys loved basketball. Warren was different. Over the years he developed a moral compass, a real sense of social justice. Who was Warren? *He was a strong, confident, deep-thinking, proud black man.*

———

J. B. Hill: *(The following comments were made at Warren's sixtieth birthday celebration, held in Miami.)* We all love Warren in Kansas City, all of us. And to see that you people here in Florida feel the same way about him that we do, it's just a blessing. In disguise. *[Laughter]* It's truly a pleasure.

We went to the All Star game last year. Warren was talking to Oscar Robinson. I mean, that's the "Big O"! The Big O is the Big O!

When the Big O saw Warren, he jumped up and hugged him. He said. *"Ah, Warren!"* He was all happy and excited. *I got excited. [Laughter]* The Big O's happy to see Warren like I am. It was such a pleasure to see him act the same way I act. So man (speaking directly to Warren), it's a pleasure to see other people care about you like we do.

(From my phone interview with J. B.) I'll tell you something else: We were down at the NAIA Basketball Tournament in Kansas City. That was a big deal in those days. Everybody went down to that tournament. There were a few guys around me and Warren was standing off to the side. I don't even remember who those guys were, but they were giving me a hard time, saying I couldn't play. All of a sudden Warren spoke up. He said that I was a good player, that he always respected my game. The guys around me didn't say another word. That shut them up. They knew that Warren was *baad.* So for him to say that about me... Well... Warren was always doing things like that. He was a special brother.

—

Monte Owens: You have to understand how we grew up. We didn't have any understanding of the outside world. We didn't go to the County Club Plaza. All we did was compete. We competed at everything. That's how it was at the Dunbar court. If you lost, you might not get back on the court the rest of the day.

Here's a story about Warren—about the mess I got him into, really. I wrote it down to make sure I got it right.

> In 1962, I was on my way to Kansas City (Kansas)
> Junior College. Warren Armstrong was a ninth-grader,
> the new *phenom* on the Dunbar School playground. This
> was the school ground where the kids in the city came to
> improve their skills and compete for a place on their
> high school teams. However, there was something
> different about Warren. He was only 5'11", but you
> could tell he was going to get bigger and that he had
> talent that was not like anyone his age or older. He had
> big legs, a big body, and large hands to go with his large
> head.
>
> I remember holding court with some of the kids in my
> neighborhood. One of them asked me who was better:
> me or Warren? *I was in junior college and Warren was*

only in the ninth grade! Although I gave the persona that
I was better than just about everyone, I remember not
answering as even then his potential scared me. The tale
of Warren Armstrong was beginning to reverberate
throughout our small community. Because of what he
could do on the court, people could not wait to see him
play. His leaping ability, his toughness, his attitude
(mean), made him a bully, and his intimidation was also
part of his persona. And it all worked.

After moving to Missouri and leaving Kansas, where he
was supposed to be a star at Sumner High School, he
attended Central High School, Sumner's hated rival. He
became Benedict Arnold and the Sumner team of 1963
took it personally. Central played against Sumner
Warren's sophomore and junior years and Sumner
destroyed Central both years (winning by 25 points his
sophomore year, and by 2 points his junior year). Then
came his senior year. By then, Warren was close to 6'3"
and 220 lbs. He was the talk of both cities. He had
achieved All-City Honors as the best player in Missouri,
and other awards, as well. But he did not have bragging
rights. He had not beaten his old team from Kansas and
he wanted revenge.

Then came January 4, 1964, Sumner High School,
Kansas City, Kansas, his old nemesis against whom he
would get his revenge and solidify himself as one of the
greatest basketball players to come out of the Midwest,
period. I did not see the game. My grades had caught up
with me and I was drafted and had to report to the U.S.
Army one day before the game. I considered reporting
one day late but I decided I had better not do that, so I
reported to Fort Leonard Wood. My heart was broken
when I got the newspaper following the game. My worst
fears had come to pass. He had gotten his revenge, and
solidified his place as the best of the best. The only
comparison was the great Lucius Allen out of Wyandotte
High School. The two would forever be linked by
comparisons as to who was the best.

Warren broke the high school scoring record in Kansas by scoring 44 points and beating Sumner badly. Offers from many schools began to come his way: UCLA, KU, Wichita State, and many more. Later, he revealed why he chose Wichita State. It was due, he said, to the fact that he identified with the black players at Wichita: Kelly Pete, Nate Bowman, the All-American Dave Stallworth; and also because, at the time, the Missouri Valley was the #1 conference in basketball.

While in the army I played for the Fort Riley Post Basketball Team. I was elected captain of the team and became the leading scorer, averaging 24 points per game. We often played against elite universities. For example, we traveled to Oklahoma to play Tulsa University. That particular game was one of the worst games of my career. I was 5 for 13 from the field and only scored 10 points. Eldridge Webb, a phenom from New York, was too much for me. They beat us by 12 points. I got a technical foul and was benched in the second half.

After the game, the Tulsa team came into our locker room. One of the Tulsa players asked me where I was from and when I told him Kansas City, he asked if I knew Warren Armstrong. I said: "Oh, yes, I know him. He is one hell of a ball player!" Tulsa's next game was that Friday against Wichita State. I told them how good Warren was and I remember them saying he better not come down to Tulsa trying to take over on their court. They had already heard about him and I certainly fed more into the legend of Warren Armstrong. Maybe he could get some revenge for me, I thought.

That Saturday I got the morning paper to see how the game went. I could not believe what the paper & TV were reporting after the game. There had been the biggest fight between the two teams and I don't believe the game was finished.

Years later, I told Warren about how Tulsa had beaten my team, and how afterwards, all they wanted to talk

about was "Warren Armstrong." I told him that I told
them how great he was, how strong and physical.
Warren looked at me and said, "Monte, so you are the
one that started that mess. You got them guys all fired up
and I know how you like to talk trash. No wonder those
guys were ready to fight just listening to you!" He had a
point. I never thought about how the running of my
mouth along with my interest in having Warren get my
revenge may have gotten Tulsa even more ready for
Wichita! Warren and I fell out laughing, but Warren
really got on me. He said I nearly caused a riot with my
big mouth. He knew how I hated to lose.

Warren moved to Miami, Florida, and it is now 50 years
later. I purchased a condo in Miami and an old friend
who was a neighbor of Warren's in our childhood,
Fernando "Federal Judge" Gaitan, also purchased a
condo. Warren, the judge, and I got together for lunch.
We had so much fun. We talked and laughed and made
fun of our old neighborhood, laughing about how much
we did not have. The sun was shining and it was a
beautiful day. My wife and sister-in-law had also joined
us. Warren even told my sister-in-law about the crush he
had on her and we all laughed. It seems so long ago. We
talked about getting together again, but it never
happened. A year or so later, Warren died in his sleep.

My friend, Warren Armstrong, had gone from a poor,
black, ghetto kid to a person with some militant
blackness to a mild-mannered, soft-spoken, intelligent,
responsible person. I am sure if we had to do it over
again we both would say, "Let's not change a thing,
nothing could replace 'the splendor in the grass.'"

———

Rev. Nelson "Fuzzy" Thompson: [*Fuzzy was a prominent figure in the
Kansas City area. A minister, a radio host, long involved with civil
rights, he is largely responsible for making Kansas City's celebration of
Martin Luther King Day among the largest in the country. Fuzzy was in
the circle of Sumner friends quoted above and also a good friend of
Warren's. He passed away in 2014. What follows are excerpts from the*

interview I conducted with him in 2008 as part of the court-naming initiative.]

Of all the athletes that have come through the Kansas City area, and there have been some great ones, Warren was the most explosive. He had incredible jumping ability. Before his legs got injured, and his back, he could jump as high as anybody I've ever seen in my life. You talk to anybody. They've all got stories about how he could jump.

Warren expressed himself rather than holding it in. That's a quality I admired in him. It took a lot of courage. It took a lot of sacrifice. Because that means you don't get certain things. Nobody rewards you for doing that. Your own people will criticize you. But he took stands and organized demonstrations that cost him his career. If he had kept quiet, gone along with the program, been concerned about himself and his situation, he would have probably played five, six, seven more years in the league, made more money, and all of that. But internally, it eats away at you.

He tore up his knee. And, I believe, all the rest of his career he played on one leg. Now you've got to understand, *he was great!* That just goes to show you how great he was. I remember the game he was playing against the Doctor, Dr. J.—a four-overtime game. And Warren literally took over the game in the fourth overtime and won the game by dunking twice on the Doctor. He was really playing on one leg. But he had such explosiveness, such power, such confidence, that he just went up over the Doctor and dunked it. Now, he's 6'2", the Doctor is 6'7", *and he dunked on him!*

So we asked Dr. J when we were at the All-Star game about that game, when Warren dunked on him in the fourth overtime to win the game. He wouldn't talk about it. He told us point blank that he didn't want to talk about it. He was serious. He wasn't playing at all. He didn't talk about it. That let me know how he felt about it. Because I saw the game... My friend in New York and I called back and forth during the game: *This is unbelievable!*

[Warren] had a certain air about him, especially after he became involved in the black struggle, and became very militant, became very conscious. He read a lot. He studied a lot. He became somewhat philosophical, which he still is.

He is someone I admire. He is someone I appreciate. I most appreciate his commitment to the struggle for freedom and justice for our people, for all people. I admire his courage and his conviction. It's one thing to be a great ball player. It's more important, ultimately, to be a great person. And to be somebody to be respected and looked up to for their principles and the things they take a stand for. And I think Warren is that kind of person, and so I admire him for that even more than I admire him for his outstanding basketball career.

—

Johnny Battles: Herman and I went to visit him not long before he died. Warren drove us all around Miami. He was very philosophical. He reflected on his life, his childhood experiences, the decisions he had made in his career, the guidance he had and didn't have. He talked about the difference between his career and Lucius Allen's career. He shared with us his experience with the kids at the school where he taught, and as he always did, he shared his love of music. It was a remarkable time together. I wouldn't have traded it for anything. He was in bad shape at the time, though. I can tell you that. He couldn't walk a flight of stairs without being winded. That concerned me.

Who was Warren? *Well, he was a real, real, real good dude.* If he ever got away from that, he always came back to it.

Part VII

The Wichita State Connection

Asked if he had seen another sophomore comparable to Armstrong this season, the 1965 Missouri Valley Coach-of-the-Year (Gary Thompson) said: "Inch for inch, I wouldn't trade him for any player in the nation. He is definitely All-America caliber."

1965 - WSU Sports Information Office

I knew Warren's high school career. And I knew a great deal about his ABA career. As indicated earlier, I lived in Denver during his days with the Rockets. What I did not know much about was his college career at Wichita State University.

In my effort to learn about Warren's WSU days, I discovered the ranking by *The Wichita Eagle* newspaper reporters of the 100 greatest WSU players. The reporters were Paul Suellentrop, Kirk Seminoff, and Bob Lutz. Number one on their list was Dave Stallworth. Number five was Warren Armstrong.

I contacted Bob Lutz to set up a phone interview. In his e-mail, Bob wrote: *I would be happy to talk to you about Warren Armstrong, although I was just a kid when he played at Wichita State, still in junior high and high school. But I was a huge fan of his and still regard him as one of the greatest players I've ever personally seen.*

When we visited on the phone, Bob offered the following comments:

Warren was so athletic. He was just an abnormal athletic specimen. He was tough. Competitive. A high basketball IQ. When he first arrived, his outside shooting was a weakness, but he overcame that. I don't think he had any weaknesses as a player: shooting, passing, rebounding. He was a little like LeBron James.

I was in high school when he came to Wichita State, a highly touted recruit, and I would go to the practices. The freshmen would play against the varsity. It was more exciting watching Warren than it was watching the varsity. He was just a mesmerizing player. Next to Dave Stallworth, he is my favorite Shocker... All Time.

Bob Lutz was a sports reporter for *The Wichita Eagle* for forty-three years. He is now a radio host for KFH radio in Wichita, and is, as well, the founder and executive director of League 42, a baseball league for urban youth.

—

In an online discussion of the 100 Greatest Shockers, Paul Suellentrop suggested that Warren Armstrong should be the next Shocker to have his jersey retired. Warren had expressed disappointment that his jersey had not been retired, although he was pleased that he had been inducted into the Shocker Athletic Hall of Fame.

I contacted the Sports Media Department at Wichita State to inquire about the criteria for retiring a player's jersey. I was told that while the criteria are not set in stone, one key criterion is All American status.

Warren was not an All American while at WSU, though he was either second-team or first-team All Missouri Valley Conference during his three years at WSU (freshmen were not allowed to play varsity at that time). He ranks among WSU's all-time leaders in points, assists, and rebounds; and he is on the list of the 50 Greatest Players in the history of the Missouri Valley Conference (MVC). There have been 38 triple-doubles in the entire history of the MVC: Oscar Robertson with 10, Larry Bird with 5, and Warren Armstrong with 4 (tied with one other player). One player has 3 and the rest, fewer.

In 2006, Bob Lutz published an article in *The Wichita Eagle* entitled: "Forgotten Shocker deserves better." In it he writes that as far as he is concerned, Jabali "ranks right there with Cleo Littleton, Dave Stallworth, Antoine Carr, Cliff Levingston and Xavier McDaniel, former players whose jerseys are retired." Jabali's statistical contributions are comparable to theirs, as was his overall value to the team, so why not a retired jersey? Lutz notes that there was tension between Jabali and Coach Thompson, and Warren is on record as having said he lost respect for his coach. And Thompson admitted that he had a difficult time communicating with his star player. Still, Lutz points out: "Despite their differences, Thompson believes Jabali is deserving of having his jersey retired at WSU."

Following Warren's death, Lutz again published an article in *The Wichita Eagle* in which he argued for the retiring of Warren's jersey: *"Nobody at Wichita State has been able to explain why his jersey isn't hanging from the Koch Arena rafters... Ask the old-timers who saw Jabali play...and then get ready to have your head spun. Stallworth raves about Jabali, as do many others. ...There has never been a player like him in Shocker basketball history. Has there ever been a 6-2 college player who could do so much?"*

Lanny Van Eman was an assistant coach at WSU in the mid-'60s. It was Van Eman who recruited Warren to play at WSU. "I've recruited 17, 18 guys who went on to play in the NBA, but I can't think of any who had in his body what Warren had," said Van Eman (this from a July 15, 2012 *Wichita Eagle* article by Kirk Seminoff published following Warren's death). "He was never a prospect. He was an absolute player."

I met Lanny when I went to Wichita in early December of '18 for the unveiling of the statue honoring Dave Stallworth, WSU's most beloved basketball player. We met in front of the statue and as soon as I mentioned my purpose in being there, he was quick to share his thoughts: "(Russell) Westbrook (of the Oklahoma City Thunder) is the only person that I can think of with similar athletic gifts. Warren was so strong in the air, and a great finisher."

In a follow-up phone call in January, Van Eman said that he wasn't sure what else to add to what he had already said. "He was just a special guy," said Van Eman. "They don't show up very often. And sometimes coaches don't know how to work with them when they do show up. This is especially true when the player has a strong personality."

"I've often felt," continued Van Eman, "that coaches should be called managers, especially the higher in the sport you go. That's what they are called on to do—manage personalities. Warren definitely had a strong personality. He knew what he could do and he knew what he didn't want to do. And then, it was the time (the late sixties)."

I related to Lanny the story that Melvin Reed had told me earlier in the day. An African American student had tried out for the WSU cheerleading squad. "She jumped up in the air," said Melvin, "and before she came down she was cut from the tryouts." Warren, Melvin, and another player went to the president's office and waited patiently for an opportunity to speak to the president. "We weren't demanding anything," Melvin recalled, "We just felt she hadn't been given a fair opportunity to make the squad. There had never been a black cheerleader at WSU."

The president listened, and, as it turns out, within a short period of time she was on the squad. According to Melvin, Warren was at the forefront of this effort. "That doesn't surprise me," responded Lanny.

—

I made an effort to track down WSU's first black cheerleader. I wanted to find out if she knew of Warren's involvement in her story. "That time meant a lot to me," said Joan (Huff) Minor, reflecting on her time at WSU. "For whatever reason, I always wanted to be a cheerleader. It was a dream of mine.

"Since I changed high schools," she continued, "I wasn't able to realize my dream in high school. So when I got to WSU I looked into the cheerleader 'try out' schedule. As it turns out, my freshman year, I was the only black student who tried out for the squad. I didn't make the cut and, to be honest, I did feel that race was a factor. Still, I moved on with my plan of trying out for the squad my sophomore year.

"By the time my sophomore year rolled around there was a wellspring of support for a black cheerleader at WSU. Three blacks in fact did try out, but I was the only one selected as a finalist. From ten finalists they would choose six cheerleaders and two alternates.

"As I remember it, the gymnasium was packed—blacks on one side of the gym, whites on the other side. You could feel the tension. There was an eerie silence as the six individuals selected for the squad were named. I was certain I had made the squad. I felt strongly that I had done enough to be one of the six. My name was not called. I remember the silence as people filed out of the gym, after the two alternates were named. My name was not among those either. I also remember going home and crying my eyes out.

"The next day I awoke to phone calls from reporters: *How do you feel about being the first black cheerleader at WSU?* There was a headline in the newspaper: 'Negro is added as cheerleader.' Something had happened. All ten finalists were now included on the squad. I never knew exactly what happened. But what stays with me, what sustained me at the time, was the feeling of *community,* the support I received that night in the gym.

"Warren never mentioned anything to me. I do know that throughout the season, those athletes looked out for me. The trip we made to UCLA, for example: We (the cheerleaders) had never seen anything like Pauley Pavilion. I remember that Warren and Carl Williams made sure I was okay and that I met Lew Alcindor."

Joan left Stanford University in 2000 after a career there as a Human Resources manager. Today, Joan Minor is a jazz vocalist living in Paris. She performs internationally (New York, Berlin, Athens, Paris) and has served as a "cultural ambassadress for jazz," traveling on behalf of the U.S. State Department to Zambia, Tanzania, Niger, Madagascar, Comoros, and Gabon.

"I remember Warren as a beautiful and talented gentleman," she said. "I never knew of his specific involvement in my story and I was sad to hear of his passing."

—

According to Oakland Basketball, Inc., "...Armstrong's peak marks (at WSU) were 33 points against Arizona State, 24 rebounds against NYU in the 1966 NIT, and 12 assists twice, against Bradley in 1966 and against Mississippi State last season (1968)."

—

Ron Mendell was a teammate of Warren's at WSU and a great admirer of his abilities. (I should add that Warren considered Ron among his favorite college teammates: "Of my favorite players," wrote Warren, "were the two guards, Greg Carney and Ron Mendell. Both were tough little men who did not back down from any challenges.") In visiting with Ron, I learned (as he points out in the article that follows) that he played at Rockhurst College in the summertime. I played at Rockhurst in the summertime as well. Those were wonderful summer nights. High school and college players formed pick-up teams and sometimes the caliber of play was very high. It was especially high when Warren played. Lucius Allen also played on occasion, as did many superb players whose names I never knew.

In his book *Hoop Roots*, John Edgar Wideman talks about how the game of basketball was formed. "On a rectangle of asphalt . . . some of the best players in the world competed in some of the best basketball in the world. More than simply congregating and competing, these (young men) were inventing . . . the game." That's how it felt at Rockhurst College. I'm sure that's how it felt at the Dunbar court when Warren was just learning the game, or at the Rucker Park courts in New York, or on a thousand other courts around the country. There was self-expression, teamwork, and for some, like Warren, there was the high wire. Wideman wrote, "When it's played the way it's supposed to be played, basketball happens in the air, flying, floating, elevated above the floor, levitating the way . . . people of this earth imagine themselves in their dreams."

What made those summer nights at Rockhurst so memorable and those playground courts so much fun was the theater of it all. You were inside an art form with others from the neighborhood. Together you were making each other better—raising each other up, as Wideman would say—and in the process enjoying one of pick-up basketball's hallmark pleasures: "Beneath the contest lies the friendship: beneath the serious lies the playful..." (Alan Watts)

When Warren died, Ron wrote a tribute to Warren that was picked up and published by eight newspapers around the country. The following appeared in the *Wichita Eagle* on July 22, 2012:

He was a truly legendary Shocker
by Ron Mendell

When word arrived last Friday afternoon that Wichita State basketball legend Warren (Armstrong) Jabali had died in his sleep at his home in Miami, my first thought was: Superman is dead?

Warren and I were teammates for three years. Physically, he was the most imposing athlete I've ever known. He had the look of a finely-chiseled fullback or heavyweight fighter, yet aerodynamically, his 6-foot-2, 200-pound body defied gravity. Legend has it, but not confirmed, that he once touched the top of the backboard in practice. There are simply few words to describe the strength and athleticism he brought to the game.

In the 1960s, Wichita State was a place making a lot of noise with its basketball program, but it was an urban setting in a tumultuous time, where it was hard being a young black man. By his sophomore year, it was clear that Warren's passion for the game was matched, if not surpassed, by his quest for changing society. He found an outlet in the Black Power Movement.

Much of the rest of his career at Wichita State and in the pros was significant in terms of accomplishment, yet he took considerable pride in taking a militant stance on civil rights. It was not surprising that he later changed his last name to Jabali ("the rock" in Swahili) as a further sign of his commitment.

He was truly a complicated guy: wildly intelligent, terribly stubborn and incredibly talented. He was an enigma, even to his college coaches, who were frequently puzzled by him and that extended to others in the Shocker family. I would like, however, to remember Warren as my friend and basketball teammate.

We met originally on my recruiting visit to Wichita in the spring of 1965. I was a wide-eyed kid from small-town Kansas. Warren was upbeat about the Shockers. He was still a teenager and you could not imagine a more relaxed or engaging person. In the dorm he showed me the dozens of recruiting letters he had received in high school that were still proudly saved in a shoebox. The serenity of that meeting would not last.

Over several summers after I signed at WSU, we played pickup games at Kansas City's Rockhurst College—not far from my hometown of Ottawa, and maybe four miles from where his legend began at Central High. Usually, I picked him up at his house on South Benton. He was one of 11 children and I'm sure it was not easy for him growing up. The experience helped me realize the enormous economic gap between black and white neighborhoods.

We had good times and eventful road trips at Wichita State: a date with the Wizard of Westwood and Lew Alcindor in 1967; three years in marquee games at the old Chicago Stadium, and Missouri Valley Conference outings in such difficult venues as Peoria, Cincinnati and Louisville. We were in Chicago on New Year's Eve several times—not a bad place for college guys to ring in the new.

Fortunately, we averted disaster in 1966 on a basketball tour through South America. An engine failure on a flight between Rio de Janeiro and Sao Paulo forced us to make an emergency landing—Warren was not an easy flier and did not want to re-board when Varig Airlines sent another plane to pick us up. This came on the heels of a numbing experience in Mendoza, Argentina (near the Andes), where for the lack of a gym, we played outdoors in the wintertime and wore topcoats to stay warm on the bench.

Warren played and excelled at every position. He was the Shockers' assist leader for decades and grabbed 20 or more rebounds three times (keep in mind he was 6-foot-2). His enormous hands enabled him to move the ball around like a juggler, and he could snatch a rebound with one hand and fire a full-court pass almost in one single motion.

After basketball, Warren never lost his fire as an activist, and he seemed to find his true calling in the Miami area school system. He taught elementary school for years and was considered a beloved teacher and community leader. At one point he was commissioner of the Overton Midnight Basketball League—an excellent fit for his mission to keep young people properly directed.

Dave Thomas played against Warren in high school and tracked his career. Some years back he posted a tribute to Jabali on the Internet. He claims that Warren would have been better served, or remembered, had he played for a higher-profile program, such as Kansas or UCLA. I disagree. If he's not as well-known today as other stars, it's more related to a loss of collective memory and to the era in which he played. Wichita State was a basketball power at the time and the Missouri Valley arguably the best conference in the country, better for several decades than the football-happy Big Eight. Although the Valley had a weekly game on its own network, sports on television then was a far cry from what it is today—ESPN was well down the road.

Warren also received little exposure from the ABA, which had no national television contract before the merger with the NBA. It was Warren, after all, who turned down the Knicks and a chance to play "When the Garden Was Eden" a description (and book) of the period by New York sportswriter Harvey Araton.

Warren will be buried on his native soil of Kansas City.

He was the original LeBron James. He did amazing things in a different time on a smaller scale. I'm sure he cared about his legacy in the end, but doubt that he worried about the choices he made and the audiences that might have been.

A Wichita sports announcer started calling him "Batman" during his sophomore season, but to me he was simply and always "Superman." We could debate the future, but Wichita State and most basketball fans nationwide will not see the likes of him again.

Part VIII

The ABA Connection

"Warren is the strongest 6-2 player I've ever seen," said Hannum. "He's unique among basketball types. He's so strong that I can play him at forward, and I wouldn't hesitate to do so in NBA competition. He's a good outside shooter, an exceptional middle distance shooter, and his great jumping ability and excellent body control make him an exceptional driver.

Then too, and this is very important, he has a feel for getting the ball to the open man and gives up the ball for very many important points."

News from the Oakland Oaks, April 11, 1969

"When I met Warren, Doug [Moe] and I came to Oakland, and we used to play Henry Logan and Warren two-on-two. Warren was 6'3", strong, one of the most gifted guys I've ever played with. And I didn't think he liked white guys very much, but he respected us on the court. Even though he might not have felt comfortable around you off the court, on the court you were his teammate. And he was an incredible, unbelievable competitor. Had enormous hands, could shoot it outside, could dunk in a crowd. Guards couldn't guard him—he was simply too strong. Big guys couldn't guard because he's so good off the dribble. He was as tough as anybody."

Larry Brown, quoted in *Basketball: A Love Story,* Jackie MacMullan, Rafe Bartholomew, and Dan Klores

Following his graduation from Wichita State, Warren received professional contract offers from both the New York Knicks of the National Basketball Association (NBA) and the Oakland Oaks of the American Basketball Association (ABA). He signed with Oakland. Asked about his decision to sign with the Oaks, he stated: "I weighed both offers, talked with both clubs and decided that I would have a better future with Oakland. Actually, the Knicks offered me more money, but I was very impressed with Coach Hannum, the prospect of playing alongside Rick Barry, and the Oaks organization." (Oakland Basketball, Inc.)

———

In their book, *We Changed the Game,* Bob Netolicky (a former ABA player), Richard Tinkham (co-founder of the ABA), and Robin Miller (journalist) argue that out of the ABA came the modern NBA: the three-point shot, the dunk contest, the wide-open full-court game, the improvisation. The NBA, eventually, and to its advantage, opened itself to these innovations.

The ABA was a league that seemed to be of its time: 1967–1976, a time of considerable change. See Arthur Hundhausen's website, "Remember the ABA," for insight into the league and insight, as well, into the time. There is a loyalty that basketball fans feel to the ABA. It represented and reflected the creativity that many felt was in the air, the openness to a greater degree of improvisation and flair than had been present in the NBA.

Warren joined the league in 1968. In the course of his seven years in the league, he was Rookie of the Year, four times an All-Star, and Most Valuable Player in the 1973 ABA All-Star Game. And he was involved in controversy. There was the Jim Jarvis incident.

Warren has already discussed this incident in Part VI of this book. It took place during Warren's rookie year. He knocked Jarvis down and "stomped" on him. By all reports it was brutal and would hang like a shadow over Warren's career.

In response to the tribute I wrote and published on the Remember the ABA website (Part I), I received the following email from a person who witnessed the event:

> I just read your tribute to Warren Jabali. It was VERY interesting and touching. I know he was an incredibly gifted athlete. I was ball boy for the L.A. Stars for the 1968–69 and 1969–70 seasons. I saw him play several times for the Oakland Oaks, both as a natural guard and, incredibly, as a starting forward who, if I recall correctly, even jumped center on at least one occasion.
>
> I was in the Sports Arena the night of the Jim Jarvis incident. I was sitting underneath the basket to which the play was coming when it occurred. In my mind, I can see Jarvis falling to the floor, face down, in the backcourt, and Jabali slowing down, purposely, as he ran past, and stomping on Jarvis' head for no apparent

reason. I have no idea what interaction, if any precipitated Jabali's conduct, which was stunning in its apparent maliciousness.

Jabali was kicked out of the game. I was given a key to let Jabali into the visitors' locker room. I remember little about that other than finding his demeanor remarkably stoic and calm given what had just occurred.

The only thing I remember about the incident occurred when I accompanied the team on its next trip to Oakland. We arrived Friday night. On Saturday afternoon, before that night's game, the team gathered in the hotel to watch film of the Jabali/Jarvis game and to hear Coach Sharman's comments. For whatever reason, motivational or otherwise, Coach Sharman played that incident over and over.

Jim Jarvis was quite a nice fellow. I believe he left the league after that season. I doubt that his departure was due at all to the incident. I hope both he and Jabali have found peace and contentment with their lives.

Thanks for the article.
B. P.

———

In Warren's autobiography (partially completed and included in Mary Beasley's book), Warren writes: "He was harassing me and hacking me and trying to steal the ball. One time he did get the ball, but he had almost taken half of my arm with it. I turned around and looked at the ref and the ref just turned his head. So I turned back around and impulsively swung and knocked Jim Jarvis down and went over and stomped him. That was an example that I offer no defense for; I mean that is something that I shouldn't have done."

In Terry Pluto's book on the ABA, *Loose Balls,* in a chapter entitled "The Meanest Men in the ABA," Warren is characterized as a thug. "(To categorize what I did) as a result of the thug life—it wasn't a result of the thug life," Warren writes in response. "I wasn't a thug. It was a result of political thoughts. The thing that had me thinking the way that I was thinking was not being a thug and robbing or stealing or anything like that. It was that these people who were in control of the league were messing me around. Why is it that I don't get a foul called when there is a foul? ...What went on with Jim Jarvis was, 'How do you handle anger when you are not able to articulate it?' That was my problem then."

———

Cincinnatus "Cincy" Powell played eight years in the ABA. He was a member of the Dallas Chaparrals, the Kentucky Colonels, the Utah Stars, and the Virginia Squires, and he was twice an all-star.

When I asked Cincy for his recollections concerning Warren's playing days, he offered the following story:

> "For a brief time we were on the same roster: The Kentucky Colonels. Mike Storen was general manager for the Pacers. He became general manager for Kentucky in '70. His plan was to build a team that could compete with Utah and with the Pacers, the two powerhouse teams at the time. He brought in free agents, Jabali and I among them.
>
> "Gene Rhodes was the coach. He was well known around the league for using the n-word. He talked to his players that way. Jabali wouldn't accept that.
>
> "In a preseason game, I had a fast break and went in for a layup. The guy guarding me stayed at the other end waiting for a long pass. There was no way I could get back and guard him. Rhodes challenged me on that. The same thing happened to Jabali. Rhodes should never have spoken to us as he did. Jabali walked right past him and headed for the locker room. This was the middle of the game. "Where are you going?" "Nobody can speak to me like that." I walked out with him.
>
> "The next day we were called to Storen's office. It wasn't long before Rhodes was fired."

"Jabali played hard," continued Cincy. "He never did anything dirty. He was physical and some people didn't like that. He drove to the basket with a vengeance; nobody was going to stop him. And he was a natural leader on whatever team he was on. He would take the risk, the last shot. We would follow him. I really respected him. He was an honorable guy. He was a unique individual—charisma is a word you can use."

"His anger was about the injustice that he couldn't do anything about. He talked about it. He wasn't in a violent mode. He simply demanded respect. He was one of the most respected players on and off the court—respected by players in both the NBA and the ABA. He spoke his mind. He wasn't arrogant. He had a quiet toughness. He wanted things to be fair—fairness is what he valued."

—

Mike Storen, as indicated above, was the general manager of the Kentucky Colonels (and later served as commissioner of the ABA). "I don't remember the specific incident that Cincy mentioned," said Mike when we talked, "but it is true that I fired the coach, even though we had a winning record. The reason was that I didn't believe he could relate to the African-American players. I had a certain philosophy concerning the building of a great team: talented people, a system into which everyone can fit, being straightforward, no hidden agendas, articulating that to everyone involved. And I had rules that everyone had to follow.

"When I traded for Cincy and Warren, I chatted with them about what people thought of them—their reputations—and I detailed their opportunity to be a part of a great team.

"I knew that with Warren I had a great player, a tremendous talent, someone who had great respect as a player but also someone with a strong personality. People felt uneasy when dealing with him. I told him I wasn't in a position to address the philosophical issues of the day. I knew that there was honest respect for his playing ability (I doubt you would find anyone who disagrees with that) and that I could get talent in exchange for him if I did trade him. When I told him that he made the team uneasy and that I had traded him, he said he understood completely. I had a very good, straightforward relationship with him."

—

Eugene "Goo" Kennedy played four seasons in the ABA (Dallas Chaparrals, San Antonio Spurs, Spirits of St. Louis, and Utah Stars) and one in the NBA (Houston Rockets). I had visited with him when we were involved in the court-naming initiative (Part II) and he was quick to offer a letter in support of our effort.

When I called to ask for any additional thoughts he might have concerning Warren's career, he was again quick to accommodate my request.

"I saw him dribble down past the rim and dunk backwards. I can see it now. He was unbelievable. I think about those times all the time."

He then added, "Warren was a leader. People say he was racist, he wasn't racist. To me, he was an ambassador. Everyone listened when he spoke. I idolized him, looked up to him. And none of it went to his head. *He was chosen.* That's the only way I know to say it. If he came downstairs and took a seat, pretty soon everyone would be sitting around him. He was a natural-born leader."

—

Bob Netolicky, like Warren, was a four-time ABA All-Star. For most of his career he played with the Indiana Pacers, but for a brief time he was with the Dallas Chaparrals and the San Antonio Spurs as well. He was named one of the thirty greatest players in ABA history.

"Some coaches and some players didn't get along with (Warren) but I always thought that was a bunch of crap. I got along with him great. And he was a great player. Even with his knee injury he was fantastic. When he was here (Indiana) with Freddie Lewis, I thought we had the best guard team in the history of the ABA."

In addition to publishing his book (*We Changed the Game* with Richard Tinkham and Robin Miller), Bob has been deeply involved in the effort to secure pension funding from the NBA for former ABA players.

—

Rick Barry needs no introduction to basketball fans. A member of the Hall of Fame, he was named one of the fifty greatest players of all time. I explained my purpose in contacting him in an email, not knowing if the email would reach him or if he would be interested in responding. Within minutes of sending the email, I received a call. "Yes," he said, "Warren was a hell of a player, ahead of his time. You didn't see guys that were as gifted athletically as he was. I felt the same way about Henry Logan, another teammate of mine. Thirty, forty points: no problem for Warren. I was jealous of his ability to dunk the ball!"

Rick then turned philosophical: "Life happens to us...we're not the same person today hopefully that we were back when. He had his biases, his prejudices. But Warren's story is the story of a man who became a terrific human being. I stayed in touch with him on occasion. I knew of his work in south Florida. It's a good thing to memorialize such a special person."

—

Warren's time in the ABA was controversial. He played hard and he was physical, and he used his physicality to his advantage. But as I indicated in Part I, for him to be characterized—as he is in Terry Pluto's book, *Loose Balls*—as a thug seems way off to me. I never saw anything in his two years as a Rocket that would justify such a label. I watched every home game and never saw him play in a way that could be described as dirty or mean. As for Dave Twardzik's comment (quoted in *Loose Balls*) that "the whole league hated Jabali," that, too, seems over the top. Cincy Powell agrees. "There were cliques in the ABA," he said. "If you didn't play a certain way, they didn't like you. Twardzik's comment is perhaps true for a segment of the league but not the whole league. There were a lot of guys who were physical, who were tough—not just Jabali. And there were fights (for which there was often very little consequence other than expulsion from the game in which the fight occurred)."

I did not see Warren's early years in the ABA. A pre-season exhibition game in his second year (Washington vs. Denver), two games as a Floridian against Denver, every home game for two years as a Rocket: That is my sample. If anything, I thought he was underappreciated by those who wrote about the league. The emphasis seemed to be on his physicality, the Jarvis incident, the way many players felt intimidated when playing against him; what he brought to the game as a player was too often ignored, in my estimation.

For example, in ESPN's *Basketball: A Love Story*, Terry Pluto is quoted as saying that the reason the Oakland Oaks won the 1969 ABA championship was because it had Rick Barry, Doug Moe, and Larry Brown. That statement is terribly misleading. Rick Barry was lost mid-season to an injury. He played only thirty-five games that season and did not play in the championship series. Doug Moe and Larry Brown, good as they were, were not the reason Oakland won. It was Warren Armstrong who filled the void left by Barry's absence, averaging 28 points throughout the playoffs and 33.2 points and 12.9 rebounds in the championship series. If any one player was the reason Oakland won, it was Jabali—named, accordingly, most valuable player in the championship series. So far as I know, only two players in the history of basketball have been in their rookie seasons both rookie of the year and most valuable player in the championship series: Magic Johnson and Warren Jabali.

—

This book is about the man I knew during the last twenty years of his life. But it is also about the player I respected, appreciated and followed since he was a junior in high school. For me, he will always be the standard by which I evaluate other players. When he was healthy, there wasn't anything on the court he couldn't do. Equal to what he called his "power game" was, from my point of view, his intelligence, his court awareness, and his imagination. He surprised you with his passing and with his creative offensive and defensive playmaking. Some of those plays have been recounted in this book, recounted because they remain indelible in the memories of those who witnessed them. Warren had a thoroughly distinctive mix of power, art, and presence. Despite the controversy that surrounds his pro career, I hope that sections of this book serve to restore his standing as one of the truly great players of his or any other generation.

Afterword

The week Warren died, he called me. I later learned from his wife that he had been in the hospital a couple of days before. In fact, on his way home from the hospital he could tell that something was wrong and he drove back to the hospital and spent another night.

He called me and the first thing he said was: "Fatty, I love you, man." That's what he said. I didn't know anything about his condition. "I love you, too, Warren." I thought we were just talkin', but he knew what was about to happen.

> —Fatty Taylor
> LaSalle University
> Washington Capitols
> (ABA) '69–'70

My phone was full of messages. They were from Warren's friends, now my friends as well, saying that Warren had died.

It had been six months since Warren and I were together. I called Mary the next day. She was distraught. Through tears, she told me that they had been shopping, had purchased two chairs that were to be delivered the next day. As she was going to bed, the phone rang. It was Len Trower-Mfuasi, perhaps Warren's closest friend. Len told me that he and Warren talked as they had always talked, and that Warren indicated that he and Mary would be visiting Philadelphia in the coming weeks, as planned.

The next morning, Mary thought that Warren was sleeping later than usual. When she looked in on him she discovered that he had passed away during the night.

—

When prominent black athletes are mentioned for their commitment to the African American community, Warren's name is not among them. I do not know why. From my perspective, he deserves to be on the list. He was a professional athlete who publicly embraced a black-centric consciousness and in so doing, risked and perhaps cut short his career.

Muhammad Ali—the most prominent black athlete concerned with racial injustice—never lost his commitment to the African American community. He did, however, enlarge his circle of concern. As Ta-Nehisi Coates wrote, *"Remember...consciousness can never ultimately be racial; it must be cosmic."* Muhammad Ali became increasingly reflective, *soulful.* I believe the same can be said of Warren. He devoted his life to the African American community. He made a difference in the lives of African American youth and in the African American communities of which he was a part—a fact that I hope this book makes clear. But in the process, he became ever more soulful in outlook and manner.

By soulful I do not mean something metaphysical. I mean, rather, possessing the capacity to look past surface differences to perceive a common humanity and to be guided by a commitment to that common humanity.

I may be out of my depth here but I believe that, by definition, a soulful person is a person who has gained a measure of interior peace, a calmness that makes him or her less vulnerable to the dramas of the moment. Warren had that as a player. Eventually, I believe, he had it as a man. In an e-mail he sent to me, he wrote, *I feel that by now we who went through the experiences should be able to delve into them without reproach and recrimination.*

I'm not sure where it comes from, this soulfulness, but I do not believe it comes with age or that it is, in any sense, a birthright. I believe, rather, that it is hard-earned. For James Baldwin, if I understand his view correctly, soulfulness represents one of the fundamental counters to racism, the courage to remain sane, conscious, and free in the face of immediate pain and entrenched injustice. Soulfulness, then, is a moral achievement. In my judgment, it was Warren's achievement.

—

There were two funerals. One was in Miami where Warren had lived since his playing days ended, and the other in his beloved Kansas City where he had hoped to live the remainder of his life.

Several eulogies were given, including the one that follows.

Eulogy for Warren Armstrong Jabali

Warren Armstrong Jabali was the first movie star I ever saw. I was a sophomore in high school sitting in the bleachers and he was on the court. From that moment on, I never saw him play—in high school or the pros—but what it didn't seem to me that the camera was on him. Thank goodness so many individuals came together (45 years after Warren played there) to make sure that the court at the Interscholastic League Field House—*the court that he made immortal*—bears his name. I can only hope, as my wife, Paula, suggested, that during the coming season they will find a few moments to dim the lights in his honor.

The last time I was with Warren was this past December. We spent two full days together visiting his old friends, his old haunts, the house in Kansas City, Kansas, where he grew up, the field that was once the Dunbar Courts, the Sportman's Barbershop. We talked about his life and about life in general. Every minute I considered a privilege.

As he drove, I asked questions. "Warren, what about that story Al Smith tells concerning who would be the starting point guard for the Denver Rockets?" Al had been the sixth man with the Rockets. When Larry Brown was traded to Carolina, Al thought he would be moving to the starting lineup. Then the Rockets acquired Warren. For two weeks in training camp, Al battled Warren for the starting position. Then Warren said to him, "We need to talk." According to Al, Warren said, "Look, here's how it's going to be. I'm going to start and you're going to come off the bench. That's the way this needs to work."

When I asked Warren about this story, he said, "Yeah, Al tells that story but I don't ever remember doing that." "Don't you think you would have done that?" "No, I don't," he said. "It seems out of character."

When I told Al what Warren said, he could not stop laughing. "Warren was very direct," Al said. "He intimidated a lot of people who didn't want to hear the truth as Warren saw it. But he was right and that's the way it was. Warren started and I came off the bench."

"Warren, why did Alex Hannum call you the smartest player he ever coached?" Almost irritated with the question, Warren replied, "I don't know why he said that."

Then, after a moment, he told the following story: "We had a big man on the Rockets who was always complaining about the fact that Ralph Simpson, the other guard on the team, would never throw him the ball. Simpson would shoot instead. Finally, I said to him: 'Look, when I've got the ball and you're open, I'll throw it to you. You know that, right? But when Simpson has the ball, he's going to shoot it. You know that, too, right? Well, then, why don't you get your big rear end over to the other side of the basket where you can rebound in case he misses!'"

He then added, "I noticed at the time that Alex Hannum overheard me say that. It might have been that kind of thing that led Alex Hannum to say what he said."

One of the places we stopped during our two days together was Coach Jack Bush's house. Among the things Jack Bush talked about that day was his ongoing struggle with the game of golf. Try as he might, golf is one game he could not master.

I asked Coach Bush what he hoped his legacy would be. He said that he hoped it would have to do with his effort to shape the lives of young men. It was a thoughtful answer and left the room quiet for a moment. Then Warren, whose timing was always so good, said, "That's a relief. For a moment I thought he was going to say that he wanted his golf game to be his legacy!"

While on our drive, Warren went to considerable length to explain to me the difference between his game and the game of another Kansas City legend, Ernie Moore. His (Warren's) game, he said, was about power. Ernie, on the other hand, was an artist. When we met up with Ernie Moore, Warren again explained the differences between their games. Ernie listened attentively. "(You) were artistic, also," he said.

Several years ago, I posted a tribute to Warren on the Internet. In response, I heard from people from all around the world. In one case, an attorney for a former ABA player contacted me. The former player had a secret. Throughout his time in the ABA, he could neither read nor write. And it was Warren, he said, who had his back. For this the former player was extremely grateful. He was now literate and wanted to write a note of thanks to Warren in his own hand.

What is the story we are paying tribute to today? It is Warren's story, yes, but what is that story? The hero, we are told, has a thousand faces, a thousand different names.

Here—in Warren—was the young man with extraordinary gifts who set out to share those gifts with the world only to discover that the world is out of balance and must be put right. And so, he engaged in the struggle to put things right. Along the way, though it took time, he found the love of his life. He had children and grandchildren who he adored. And always, there was the effort to put things right.

"What are you interested in?" I asked. "I mean, you have Mary and your family, but after that, what are you interested in?" "Only one thing," he said, "the struggle of Black folks." "The struggle of Black folks," I repeated. "Yes," he said, "the standing of African American people in the human community."

Warren engaged in the struggle to put things right. And he did change things, many things. Already there is talk of naming the grade school where he taught for thirty years in his honor. But also, in the process of changing things, he, too, was changed.

In Mary Beasley's beautiful book, *Shattered Lens,* she devotes much of the last two chapters to the love she found with Warren—in particular, to when they were courting.

This is Warren speaking to Mary:

"I've traveled around the world. I've met many people and I've done almost everything I've wanted to do. I now want you to be fulfilled. I am very content..."

And then he added, "I want to learn to get along perfectly with one other human being. That's my spiritual goal. I want to love and be loved intensely and unconditionally."

I sometimes have had people say to me, "You make too much of him. You overstate the case." No. It is just the reverse. They failed to see what was right in front of them. I am so very grateful that I grew up in this city during the time of the great Warren Jabali. His kind is remarkably, amazingly, sadly rare. We mourn our loss when such individuals depart, but we treasure their impact on us. They mark the path. They call us to a higher standard. And they put wind in our sails. The hero has a thousand faces, yes, and one of those faces is the face of Warren Edward Armstrong. The hero is known by a thousand names, and one of those names is *Jabali.*

David Thomas
July 28, 2012

Closing Thoughts

In early December of 2018, I traveled to Wichita for the unveiling of the Dave Stallworth statue. While I appreciated the role Dave Stallworth played in the history of WSU basketball, my principle reason for going there was to meet with Len Trower-Mfuasi. Through Len I hoped to meet others who were at WSU during Warren's time there and to learn what I could about Warren's college years.

I was able to do just that. In addition to meeting several of Warren's close college friends (Melvin Reed, Kennie Lee, Mansa Moussa Abdul Allahmin and others), I was also able to meet Lanny Van Eman, Bob Lutz, and Ron Mendell. It was a wonderful day: the ceremony for the unveiling of the statue, spending time with the individuals mentioned above, the WSU-Baylor game that evening, capped off by a late night in the hotel bar with Moussa and Len.

Our conversation in the bar was full of old stories about Warren, about the fact that here, in the middle of Kansas, these black athletes came to study, play their respective sports, and, as much as anything, influence one another's worldview. At one point late in the evening the conversation took a serious turn. Moussa turned to me and said: "Superman befriended you. Superman can't do that with just anyone. Superman can't show his vulnerabilities."

"What we're saying, Dave," added Len, "is that Jabali opened himself to you. He didn't know you would be putting your experiences with him into a book. That didn't matter to him. He simply decided to let you in. So in this book of yours, we don't care about what other people thought about Jabali. We want to know what you thought."

I was taken aback, but at the same time I respected that two of Warren's oldest friends were holding me to account.

This book is what I thought of Warren. It is my attempt to take a full-life perspective and set the record straight. From the first time I saw him play, I felt Warren was on a stage larger than the dimensions of a basketball court.

Those who disliked Warren, who hated the way he played, who felt themselves mistreated by him, have long since put down this book. Those who knew him as I did will recognize the truth of what I am saying.

Warren was an artist, a highly principled man committed to putting things right. He struggled at times. His was a challenging path.

Still, if there were a movie of his life I can't think of a single actor who could play his part.

—

Two years after Warren's death, I sent a proposal to ESPN. I had met Steve Marantz, a producer for ESPN's *E:60*. Steve was in Omaha to give a talk on his book, *The Rhythm Boys of Omaha Central: High School Basketball at the '68 Racial Divide*. It's a wonderful book that tells the story of an exceptional player, a promising season ahead for an all-black starting lineup, and the racial turmoil that overtook the city and derailed Central's hopes for a state championship.

Following Steve's talk, I spoke with him briefly about Warren, indicating that I thought Warren's story might be a worthy subject for *E:60*. Steve invited me to send him more information. His response, after reviewing what I had sent him, was that Warren's story was more suited to a *30-for-30* documentary. He told me what to submit and to whom I should submit it, if I wished to pursue the *30-for-30* possibility.

30-for-30 elected to pass on my proposal, indicating that it had "recently aired a film dealing with the '70s ABA era and [didn't] want to hit on such a similar time period and topic at this time."

To make sure that I hadn't crafted a proposal that doomed it from the start, I sent a copy to Steve along with *30-for-30*'s rejection note. If he had time, I wanted to know if he saw problems with the proposal. He wrote back, "Sorry it didn't work out. Your proposal is fine. Could be its time has passed—or hasn't arrived."

I include my *30-for-30* proposal here as a way of recapping ground covered in this book.

The Life and Times of Warren Armstrong Jabali:
A 30-for-30 Proposal

Alex Hannum, coach of championship teams in both the NBA and ABA, called Warren Jabali: *The smartest player I ever coached.*

Al Bianchi, coach in both the NBA and ABA, said of Jabali: *He may have been the toughest competitor I ever was around in a lifetime of basketball.*

Rick Barry, teammate during Jabali's rookie year in the ABA:

> He's unbelievable. As a guard, he's in a class by himself. I've never seen a player his size with so much strength. As great as Oscar Robertson is, well, he couldn't come close to matching Armstrong in jumping and rebounding. Nobody can. He can out-jump and out-score the Warriors' Al Attles. He's stronger than I am; stronger than Robertson. He's so powerful that even at 6'2", he can come in and rebound with 6'7" forwards. And you should see him drive to the basket. No doubt he's one of the best guards I've ever played with or against. Just wait till he gets more experience—nobody will be able to stop him.

In a recent interview on WHYY in Philadelphia, Julius Erving commented:

> He (Jabali) will be in the Hall of Fame. And he should be. He was like Oscar Robertson. There wasn't any place on the court he couldn't go. We had many battles on the court.

Only two players have ever been named both Rookie of the Year and Most Valuable Player in the Championship Series in the same season. They are Magic Johnson and Warren Jabali.

Who was Warren Armstrong Jabali, this four-time ABA All Star about whom so little is known generally? In *Loose Balls,* an ABA history by Terry Pluto, Jabali is remembered as a thug and little else. Years later, Jabali rejected the characterization:

I wasn't a thug. (My behavior) was a result of political thoughts.

You have to understand the term *militancy*. When whites got together and demanded freedom and rights they called it self-determination. When blacks get together they call it radicalism, or militancy. All we're doing is asking for equality. (1973)

Born in Kansas City, Kansas, on August 30, 1946, Jabali was the oldest of eleven children. When he was fourteen, his family moved to Kansas City, Missouri, where he attended Central High School. As a sophomore, Jabali was named to the All-City team; as a junior, he was All-State; and as a senior, an All-American. He was endowed with enormous gifts. At 6'2", 200 pound, he possessed a remarkable blend of both power and grace, along with an extremely high basketball IQ. Said a reporter from the *Kansas City Star* covering the 1963 Missouri State basketball tournament, a tournament that included Jo Jo White:

With apologies to the ones I didn't see, the best all-
around players I saw were Warren Armstrong of Kansas
City Central in Class L, ...only a junior, Armstrong
faces a great future if he consistently exercises all his
tremendous talents.

Following high school, Jabali accepted a scholarship to Wichita State University (WSU), where he set rebounding and assist records and was, for a while, their fourth all-time scorer. He was a three-time All-Missouri Valley Conference selection, ranking in the top 20 all-time at Wichita State in scoring, rebounding, and assists. At 6'2", he led Wichita State in rebounding for three consecutive years.

When Jabali was recruited by WSU, he was also recruited by both the University of Kansas and UCLA. This was during UCLA's run of championships in the mid '60s. Lucius Allen, from Kansas City, Kansas, would go to UCLA the year following Jabali's departure for WSU, as would Lew Alcindor (later Kareem Abdul-Jabbar). Jabali opted for WSU because he felt comfortable there; in his words, he didn't think he had the social skills required in a larger university.

At WSU a fellow student (who would become a lifelong friend) introduced Jabali to the writings of Mauana Karenga and the US Organization. Karenga created the holiday known as Kwanzaa, the first pan-African holiday. Both Kwanzaa and the US Organization promoted unity, pride and self-determination in the African American community.

Jabali took to heart the theme of black self-determination. By the time he graduated from WSU, he was acutely sensitive to matters of racial inequality and committed to the cause of African American people.

Following his graduation from WSU, Jabali was drafted by the Oakland Oaks of the American Basketball Association. That year, the Oaks won the ABA championship. Jabali averaged 33 points and 12 rebounds in the championship series and 28 points for the entire playoffs. He was named Most Valuable Player in the championship series and later, he was voted Rookie of the Year in the ABA.

It was during his first years in the ABA that three events occurred that would affect Jabali's reputation as well as his style of play. The first occurred in his rookie season. Jabali was ejected from a game in which he physically attacked the player guarding him. The player's name was Jim Jarvis.

Here is Jabali's account of the event.

> What went on with Jim Jarvis was, "How do you handle anger when you are not able to articulate it?" That was my problem then. I was watching what was going on in the ABA. Rick Barry shot anywhere from 10–15 free throws a game and then he would make 10–12 baskets and, voila, he's got 35 points a game. The reason why he was getting all of these 35-point games is because he was shooting 15 free throws and making 12 or 13 or all 15 of them some nights because he shot really well. So, I began to realize that I was getting beat up and I needed to shoot some free throws. It got to the point that Alex Hannum made a comment that was published somewhere in which he said that what he liked about Warren Armstrong was that Warren Armstrong was able to go to the basket, take a blow and still make the basket. But there wasn't a foul being called. I was just taking the blow. The thing about guys like Jim Jarvis is that they had to scrap and hustle and do everything that they could in order to stay in the league because they really couldn't play. He was harassing me and hacking me and trying to steal the ball. One time he did get the ball, but he had almost taken half of my arm with it. I turned around and looked at the ref and the ref just turned his head. So I turned back around and impulsively swung and knocked Jim Jarvis down and

went over and stomped him. That was an example that I offer no defense for; I mean, that is something that I shouldn't have done.

The second event was an injury to his knee that occurred in his second year in the league. Al Bianchi, Jabali's coach at the time, recalled the event in a recent interview:

> He was one of the toughest, most competitive players I ever coached. Here's an example of how tough he was: Toward the end of his year in Washington (Washington Capitols), Warren tore up his knee. When the doctor examined his knee, he said he had never seen anything like it. It's a testament to how tough Warren was that he came back and played five more years in the league. Very few players would have been able to do that.

With damage to his knee, Jabali emphasized floor generalship over his previous role as a scorer. He could still soar on occasion, but that was no longer his game. From *Sportscope,* 1973:

> Ask anyone in the league. Jabali, pound for pound, is the best back-court tactician in the ABA. His teammates say he has an uncanny ability to sense player positions on the court and is constantly making "impossible" passes to the open man.

The third event was the changing of his name. In 1971, Warren Armstrong became Warren Jabali. This was the same year that Lew Alcindor became Kareem Abdul Jabbar. The difference between the two name changes: Kareem's name announced his adoption of the Muslim faith; Jabali's name change was a political and cultural act announcing his commitment to black self-determination. In Swahili, Jabali means "rock."

Jabali played seven seasons in the ABA. He was in four All Star games and was first-team All-ABA in 1972–73. It was in that year that he was voted most valuable player in an ABA All-Star game, a game that included Julius Erving, George McGinnis, and Artis Gilmore. That game is known as Jabali's Jamboree.

When the ABA disbanded, rights to Jabali's contract were held by the New York Knicks then coached by Red Holtzman. According to Jabali, Holtzman said that he had heard that Jabali had a problem with authority. Jabali replied that he did not have a problem with authority. His problem, he added, was with unjust authority. Jabali was not picked up by the Knicks, and his career ended.

To make a living following his basketball career, Jabali coached for a while in Africa and the Caribbean and then took a job as a physical education teacher in an elementary school in Broward County, Florida. For several years he ran the Miami Midnight Basketball Program, a program that emphasized educational performance as well as the opportunity to play basketball. His day job, however, was as a physical education teacher in the heart of the African American community. He taught, mentored and coached young boys and girls, including many who lacked a strong male role model.

During this time Jabali continued to work in the community on behalf of political, social and educational issues of concern to African Americans. And he wrote on occasion. Enclosed are two of his essays, one in response to a *Kansas City Star* article about "Kansas City's greatest basketball player" and the other in response to a report alleging that Rick Barry had said that Jabali would not pass him the ball because Jabali was a racist.

In Jabali's unfinished memoir, he writes:

> I have and had a "black conscious" point of view when few other African American athletes did and that point of view colored and guided my life. It is this black conscious point of view that deserves an airing because African American people have never shared sufficiently and appropriately with generations that follow them…this has caused a lack of vision… The inertia gained from the valiant efforts of so many comes to a standstill and eventually results in slippage backward.

Jabali's career in the ABA was controversial. He was an enigmatic figure to many, but his story is archetypal. He was a remarkable player—remarkable not only for his exceptional play but because his life seemed to reflect what was happening in the larger culture. He embodied a changing consciousness. He was not alone, of course. Many, many others in other arenas of life were doing the same thing. But here he was, a professional athlete in the ABA who also served as a stand-in for many who watched and wondered how things would turn out for him and for America's communities, as well. There are many stories from the ABA that deserve to be remembered. Jabali's story is one of them. As much as any player, his life mirrors an important (ongoing) moment in this country's social and cultural history.

Jabali's pursuit of knowledge and, in particular, his pursuit of an understanding of what is required in order for African Americans to find a just and honored place in the human community was lifelong. What may have started out as shock and outrage in response to racial inequality evolved into a deeper philosophical analysis and into strategic thinking about how to address the issues involved. Jabali did not live the thug's life. He lived the hero's life. By serving a cause he believed in, he found that in order to serve it fully he must address his own integration and development as a person. And this he did: a struggle all its own. As a consequence, he was not only respected for what he stood for but beloved for whom he became.

Finally, when I say that Jabali was respected and beloved, I mean to say "by many, certainly not by all." His place within the ABA is controversial. He had his detractors. It's hard to imagine how it could have been otherwise. The issues with which he and society at large were attempting to come to terms were both controversial and complicated, and remain so. *30 for 30* could shine a light on those issues and on that time (and on the ABA itself), illuminating through Jabali's story the way in which sport mirrors the changing consciousness of a time and on occasion furthers a dialogue critical to change.

When players talk about "toughness," they don't mean the ability to physically overpower opponents. There is a physical aspect to the term, certainly, but there is a mental, even spiritual, aspect, as well: The capacity to stay in the game, to not give an inch, unyielding. All great players have toughness.

In a recent interview, Fatty Taylor, a former ABA and NBA player, told the following story:

> Alex Hannum, then coach of the NBA San Diego
> Rockets, was walking through the San Diego locker room
> as his players were hotly debating who was the toughest
> player in the NBA.
>
> Finally, Hannum interrupted the debate: "You guys don't
> know what you're talking about. The toughest player in
> basketball (referring to Jabali) is in that other league."
>
> (Told to Fatty Taylor by Bernie
> Williams, a member of the San
> Diego Rockets)

30-for-30 could tell the Jabali story as few other venues could. It is a story that deserves to be known, a story full of heart, heartbreaking at times, and in the end, for many, inspiring.

There are many former ABA players and coaches still living. Their insights and recollections can round out the story. Hopefully, *30 for 30* producers can unearth video footage of Jabali's career. He was a spectacular player. In addition, Mary Beasley, Jabali's wife, recently published a book on Jabali's life and on their life together. Entitled *Thanks To You: Memories of Warren Edward Armstrong Jabali,* it contains Jabali's partially completed memoir.

In an event held in Kansas City in 2010 entitled "The Odyssey of Black Men in America: A Kansas City Perspective," a hundred men showed up to discuss their own odyssey as black men in the second half of the twentieth century. This event would not have occurred, let alone drawn so many, were it not for Jabali's involvement.

When Jabali died, two funerals were held: one in Florida where he lived and worked, the other in Kansas City where he grew up. The funeral in Kansas City was attended by nearly a thousand people, the majority of whom were men.

JABALI: A Kansas City Legend may be ordered through area bookstores.

To contact David Thomas: dtec@cox.net

Also by David Thomas, PhD:

Human Development and the Theater of Everyday Life
Ethics for Self, Workplace, & Society
Langdon Street Press, 2018

Order at: ethicsofhumandevelopment.com

CPSIA information can be obtained
at www.ICGtesting.com
Printed in the USA
FSHW020458300619
59568FS